W9-CCB-520

WHALES DOLPHINS AND PORPOISES

READER'S DIGEST

WHALES DOLPHINS AND PORPOISES

The Reader's Digest Association, Inc.
Pleasantville, New York/Montreal

Contents

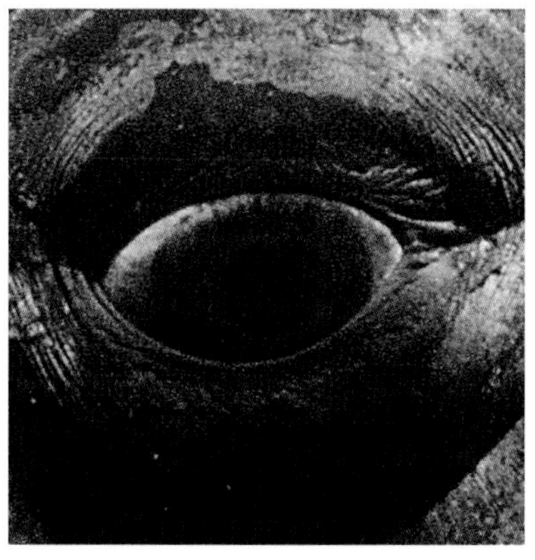

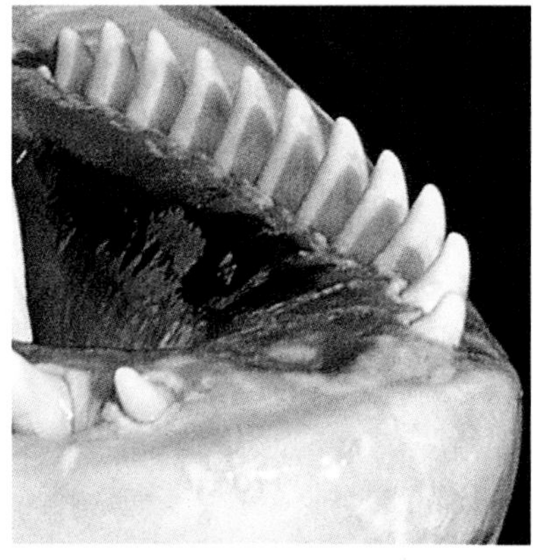

Whale Biology and Ecology 80

Whale Behavior 102

Whales and People 126

A Reader's Digest Book

Conceived and produced by Weldon Owen Pty Limited

A member of the Weldon Owen Group of Companies

The credits and acknowledgments that appear on page 160 are hereby made a part of this copyright page.

Printed in China

Weldon Owen Pty Ltd
PUBLISHER: Sheena Coupe
ASSOCIATE PUBLISHER: Lynn Humphries
PROJECT EDITOR: Fiona Doig
EDITORIAL ASSISTANTS: Vesna Radojcic, Edan Corkill
ART DIRECTOR: Sue Rawkins
DESIGNER: Karen Clarke
PICTURE RESEARCHER: Annette Crueger
ILLUSTRATION RESEARCH: Graham Ross
ILLUSTRATORS: Martin Camm, Chris Forsey, Ray Grinaway, Robert Hynes, David Kirshner, Frank Knight
INDEXER: Garry Cousins
PRODUCTION MANAGER: Caroline Webber

AUTHORS: Peter Gill, Linda Gibson (Chapter 4)

Library of Congress
Cataloging in Publication Data
Whales, dolphins and porpoises
p. cm. – (Reader's digest explores)
Includes index.
ISBN 0-89577-976-5
1. Whales. 2. Dolphins. 3. Porpoises.
I. Reader's Digest Association. II. Series.
QL737.C4W4419 1997
599.5–dc21 97-3331

Understanding Whales

Whales inhabit all of the earth's oceans, as well as many of its estuaries, gulfs, inland seas, and large rivers. Some have adapted to the warm, muddy, fresh water of equatorial rivers; others, to the icy seas of polar regions. Whales are found in shallow coastal bays as well as in the open ocean.

The Living Whales

LEFT: *Earth is the ocean planet, with water covering more than 70 percent of its surface. Beneath the surface of the water is a world unfamiliar to most of us, inhabited by an astonishing array of living organisms. Within this alien realm live the cetaceans—the marine mammals we know as whales, dolphins, and porpoises.*

In the past, when people thought of whales, they often conjured images of giant fishes dominating the open oceans. We now know that whales are not fishes at all—and nor are they all giants. Like humans, whales are mammals. Like humans, too, they often live in large communities that exhibit a great deal of complexity in their social organization.

Whales, dolphins, and porpoises are collectively known as cetaceans. Scientists have classified them as belonging to the Order Cetacea, one of the subdivisions of the Class Mammalia. The word "cetacean" is derived from the Latin *celus* and the Greek *kelos*, both of which mean a large sea creature. Like other mammals, whales are warm-blooded and give birth to live young, which they suckle. Unlike other mammals, most whales have lost all hair, as an adaptation to their aquatic environment.

Cetaceans are unique among water-dwelling mammals in that they spend all their time in the water and do not haul themselves onto land or ice to rest or breed as seals and otters do. They are found throughout the oceans and seas of the world, from the poles to the equator, and even in some freshwater rivers.

Whales and Humans

While human origins have been traced back only 4.5 million years, the earliest known whale ancestor existed more than 50 million years ago. These ancient creatures have always had an extraordinary hold on the human imagination, both as objects of mystery and as a source of food and other essential products. Whales feature prominently in the folklore of many human societies and in art and literature. Despite this, our knowledge of these often elusive animals is far from complete. Until the past two decades, most of what we knew about them was based on observations of animals that had been hunted and killed.

For thousands of years, people have hunted whales, and, especially during the 19th and 20th centuries, have exploited them heavily for commercial gain. Severe problems that are affecting whales include pollution, climate change, habitat degradation from a range of human activities, and deliberate or accidental killing in fishing nets. Some species of smaller cetaceans now number only a few hundred individuals, and are close to extinction, while many more species face an uncertain future.

RIGHT: *Tourists pet a curious gray whale in Laguna San Ignacio, Mexico. As people become eager to discover whales in their natural habitat, the number of tour operators offering contact with whales increases.*

ABOVE: In the Pacific Ocean near Hawaii, a humpback whale calf keeps close to its mother. The lives of whales are ruled by conditions that are quite alien to us, and young calves are vulnerable to many threats. The watery world in which they live is a three-dimensional, low-gravity, low-visibility medium where hearing and touch are the primary senses.

Variation Among Whales

The roughly 80 species of whale, including dolphins and porpoises, exhibit an astonishing diversity of sizes, shapes, color patterns, and habits, and occupy a wide range of habitats. The relative lack of gravity in their watery medium has allowed some whale species to become enormous—the blue whale is the largest animal that has ever lived on the earth—yet many dolphins and porpoises are no larger than humans.

Several species, such as orcas, are relatively easy to recognize; others differ from one another only in subtle ways and are hard to identify at sea, even for the experienced observer. Some species are so rare or elusive that they are seldom sighted.

Our knowledge of some species' appearance is incomplete because it is based only on observations of killed or stranded animals. Most species of whale and dolphin have very subtle markings and colorations, which fade very soon after the animal has left the water.

In general, males and females are not easily distinguishable, although baleen females are larger than the males. Among toothed whales, the reverse is often the case. External differences in some species are evident only in the genital region. In a few species, however, there are obvious differences. The male narwhal's tusk is a stunning example.

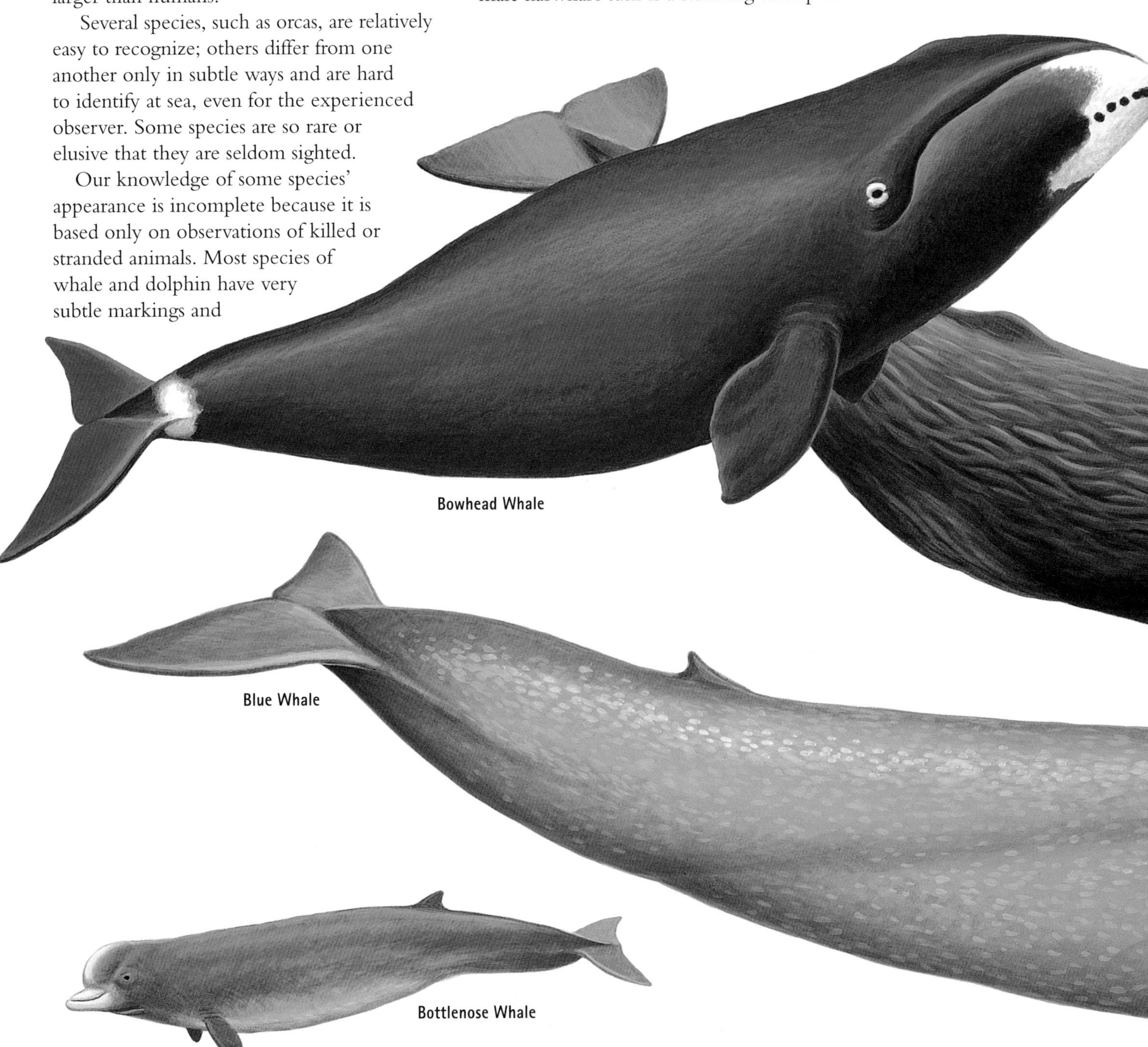

Bottlenose Dolphin

Bowhead Whale

Blue Whale

Bottlenose Whale

Narwhal

Gray Whale

Beluga

Humpback Whale

Sperm Whale

Killer Whale

There is dramatic variation in size, shape, and color patterns among different species of whale. Drawn to scale, the human diver is dwarfed by comparison to most of the whales depicted here.

Whale Evolution

LEFT: Whales evolved from the same distant ancestors, the mesonychids, as did land animals such as these antelopes. The loss of legs was perhaps the most significant evolutionary change that whales underwent as they adapted to an aquatic environment

The fossil record shows that cetaceans were already present—and apparently well evolved—at least 50 million years ago. They appear to have arisen from a family of primitive, hoofed land mammals known as the mesonychids. The closest living relatives of the mesonychids—and of cetaceans—are the artiodactyls, the forerunners of today's ungulates, the even-toed grazing mammals, such as antelopes, horses, sheep, and cattle.

The earliest cetaceans belonged to the extinct suborder Archaeoceti, which showed evidence of an amphibious way of life. It was from this suborder that the Mysteceti, or baleen whales; and the Odontoceti, or toothed whales, evolved—the two present-day suborders of the Order Cetacea.

A Brief History of Whales

Up to 65 million years ago, dinosaurs ruled the waters as well as the land. Their sudden demise opened up new ecological opportunities for other animals, and in this vacuum some mammals took to the sea. The transition from terrestrial to aquatic life was gradual, via intermediate, amphibious forms, such as *Ambulocetus*. Known from a fossil discovered in Pakistan in 1993, this was an archaeocete living about 50 million years ago that had sturdy hind legs with webbed feet. During this early stage of cetacean evolution, the climate was warm and stable, even in the polar regions.

By about 38 million years ago, baleen and toothed whales had evolved, diverging from those archaeocetes that may have fed in warm, shallow coastal waters. From 25 million years ago, the ancestors of both baleen and toothed whales became more diverse. By this time, the archaeocetes had become extinct, possibly as a result of the rise of the toothed whales, which competed for the same food but had the advantage of echolocation (see page 116).

Among the earliest toothed whales were two families: the squalodonts, or shark-toothed dolphins, and the kentriodonts, the probable ancestors of living dolphins. Both families existed between about 25 and 5 million years ago. Around 24 million years ago, sperm and beaked whales appeared.

Also around this time, one of the earliest baleen whale ancestors, *Mammalodon*, appeared. It was followed by the cetotheres, a family that had developed lobes of baleen (see pages 18 and 26) for filter feeding. These were probably similar to present-day rorquals.

About 15 million years ago, a general climatic cooling occurred that led to an increase in polar sea ice. This triggered various oceanic changes around both poles that, in turn, initiated ecological changes, and these eventually produced the rich feeding waters that exist in the polar regions today.

ABOVE: Mammalodon, *a streamlined ancestor of baleen whales, probably filter fed through lobed teeth, just as crabeater seals in the Antarctic do today.*

While their ancestors were small, the larger size of most modern baleen whales evolved in tandem with these changes. Their ability to store blubber helped with heat conservation in the cooler climate, and enabled long-distance migration. By 7 million years ago, all of the presently existing groups of cetaceans had more or less evolved into the forms that we recognize today.

Time Line Tree
This diagram shows one interpretation of the evolution of cetaceans since their ancestors made the transition to living in an aquatic environment 55 million years ago. Some of the more important ancestral forms are shown. Several evolutionary lines became extinct.

Evolutionary Trends

Cetacean fossils are abundant on all continents, and they are very diverse in form. By studying them, we can follow a number of evolutionary changes that occurred and led to the modern cetacean body form. To allow for efficient movement in water, it gradually became more streamlined, shed hair, and lost the hind limbs. As well, the skull bones overlapped, and the neck became shorter and stiffer. The ear adapted to enable hearing underwater, and the nostrils migrated to the top of the head to become blowholes. A thick, insulating layer of blubber developed, and changes that aided propulsion occurred in the tail, bone structure, and muscles. Fins and flukes became modified to reduce drag and to facilitate steering control. One of the most significant developments was the divergence of the feeding apparatus, which led to the present division between baleen whales, which gulp large quantities of schooling prey, and toothed whales, which developed echolocation and teeth to catch single prey.

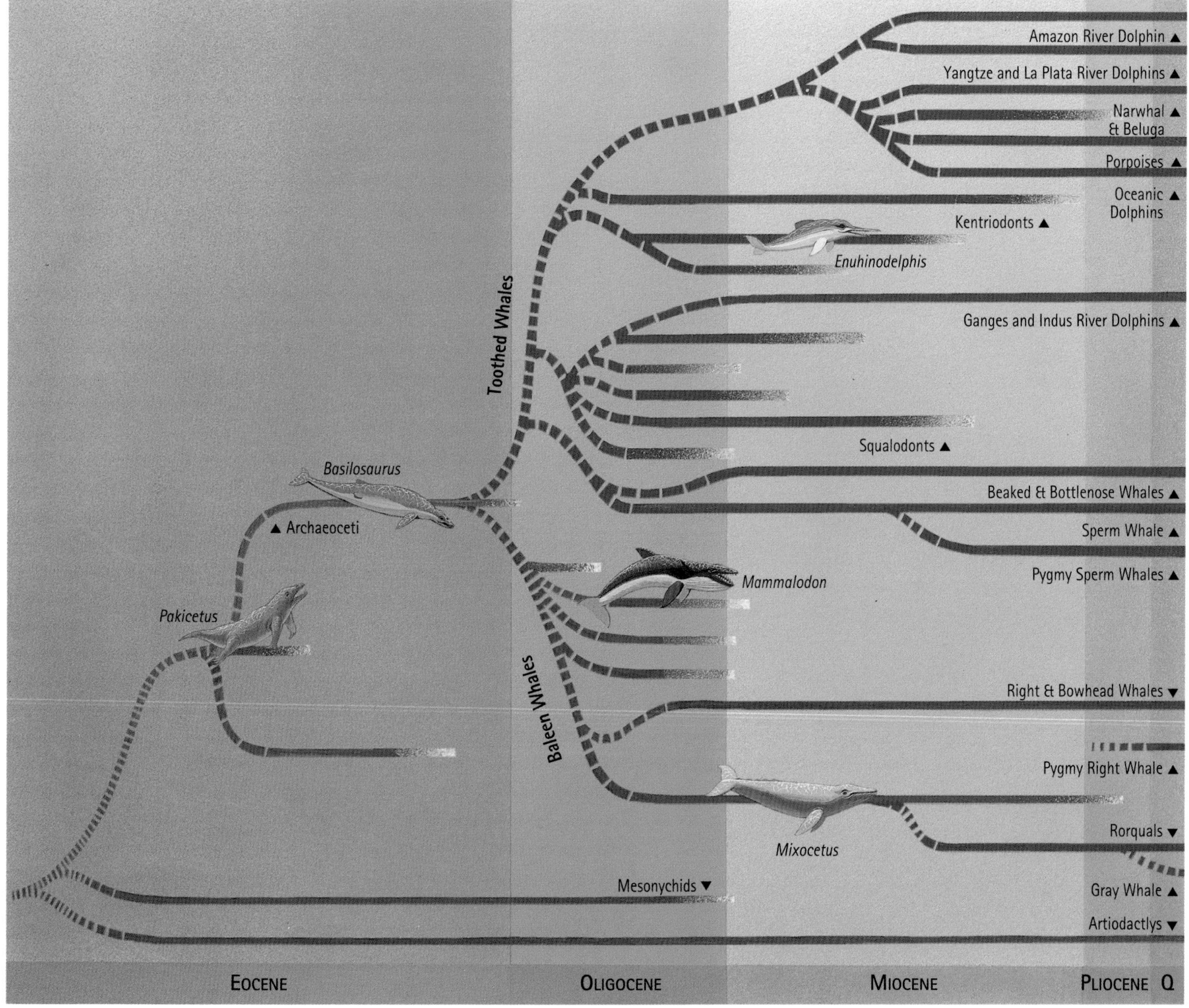

Whale, Dolphin, or Porpoise?

When scientists classify a number of living things into a group, they look for characteristics to show both that they are related to each other and significantly different from members of other groups. For example, anatomical and biological structure are important considerations in classification, but what about more arbitrary criteria, such as size? Although all cetaceans are sufficiently similar, in broad terms, to be classified as whales, we generally reserve the term "whales" for only the largest of them—those at least 10 feet (3 m) long. We tend to use "dolphins" for cetaceans that are smaller than this, and "porpoises" for animals that are slightly smaller again. This system works well enough for baleen whales, which all grow to more than 20 feet (6 m), but it can break down when we apply it to toothed whales.

Sizing up Whales

We get some idea of how confusing these terms can be when we consider that among the oceanic dolphins and their relatives (Delphinidae), some animals are referred to as whales, and others as dolphins, and the names sometimes bear no relation to size. The melon-headed whale, for example, grows to only 9 feet (2.75 m)—sometimes it is called the electra dolphin—while the bottlenose dolphin can measure up to 12 feet (3.7 m). A number of other whales, such as the pygmy killer whale, are also smaller than some dolphins, and some porpoises outgrow several species of dolphin. The spectacled porpoise, for example, at 7 foot 3 inch (2.3 m), is larger than both the 6 foot 3 inch (2 m) tucuxi and the 5 foot 6 inch (1.67 m) Hector's dolphin. Perhaps the one saving grace in this classification muddle is that no porpoise is larger than any whale.

Difficulties with Dolphins

Again, trouble with the term dolphin arises with the tropical fish *mahimahi,* which are not mammals, but are widely known as dolphins. Many accounts of mariners harpooning or hooking "dolphins" refer to these fish—most sailors are protective of true dolphins.

Yet another problem arises with the term dolphin in that it applies to two distinctly separate groups of animals: the oceanic dolphins and the river dolphins. In fact, the oceanic dolphins are far more closely related to porpoises than they are to river dolphins.

In some countries, such as Australia and the USA, many people make no distinction between dolphins and porpoises, calling all small cetaceans "porpoises." Scientists, however, are more exact in their usage.

BELOW: The huge size difference between southern right whales and bottlenose dolphins illustrates popular perceptions of the terms "whale" and "dolphin." Yet some animals known as whales are smaller than these dolphins.

Above: Beautifully colored tropical mahimahi *fish are called "dolphins," but they are true fish, and not even distantly related to the marine mammals known as dolphins.*

Above: Like most dolphins, these Pacific spotted dolphins use this energy-efficient form of travel known as "porpoising," further adding to the confusion that exists between the terms "dolphin" and "porpoise."

Left: Orcas, pilot whales, and false killer whales are indisputably whales but belong to the family that includes all dolphins. Dolphins are all small, toothed whales.

For them, the only true porpoises are the six members of the family Phocoenidae, which includes Dall's porpoise and the harbor porpoise. These porpoises have certain anatomical features that distinguish them from true dolphins. Their teeth are flattened and spadelike, whereas those of dolphins are conical and peglike; and while many dolphins have a bulbous "melon," and a pronounced "beak," a porpoise's forehead always tapers smoothly to a blunt snout. However, the differences between dolphins and porpoises are relatively minor; they are certainly much less marked, for example, than those between any dolphin and a pygmy sperm whale. In fact, the lack of differences reflects the relatively short span of evolutionary time since the ancestors of these two groups diverged.

Whales by Many Other Names

It is not uncommon for one species to have two or more common names in English, and to be known as well by many other names in different parts of the world. The fin whale, for example, is also called the finner or the razorback in English and has special local names in Japan, Norway, Greenland, Russia, France, and Spain.

To overcome this difficulty, scientists have devised an international, and universally recognized, system of classification, according to which each known living thing has its own special name. This system is known as binomial nomenclature, which means that each species has two words that describe it, and it alone. The scientific name for the fin whale, for example, is *Balaenoptera physalus*. The first word, *Balaenoptera*, is its genus, which it shares with such relatives as the blue, sei, and minke whales; *physalus* is its species name, which sets the fin whale apart from all others.

However, there is often ongoing debate about the classification of particular species. As new evidence emerges about an animal's behavior, genetic make-up, and evolutionary history, it may be reclassified and given a new scientific name, or split into two or more new species. This is why it is difficult to state exactly how many species of cetaceans exist.

Identification Dilemmas

Even when a particular whale is well studied and clearly identified, it may still be very difficult to recognize when it is seen in the open ocean. Whitecaps, swell, fog, and poor light can all hamper identification, especially when a whale is moving quickly or behaving unobtrusively. When whales are seen in their natural habitat, they are often glimpsed only briefly. Even a seasoned observer on board a boat might be excused for failing to tell apart species as different as minke, pygmy right, and southern bottlenose whales; they are all of comparable size, and their dorsal fins look roughly similar. Identification becomes more difficult if they are not sighted at close range.

A range of other clues can help in making a correct identification. These include the location and the time of year of the sighting; the frequency of the whale's blow; the whale's surfacing behavior; the size of the group; and any color patterns that are observed.

There is also a more generalized skill that World War II air crews employed to identify aircraft they encountered. It was known as "jizz," and is a corrupted acronym for "general impression of shape and size." With enough experience, tentative identifications of whales can be made even from fleeting impressions.

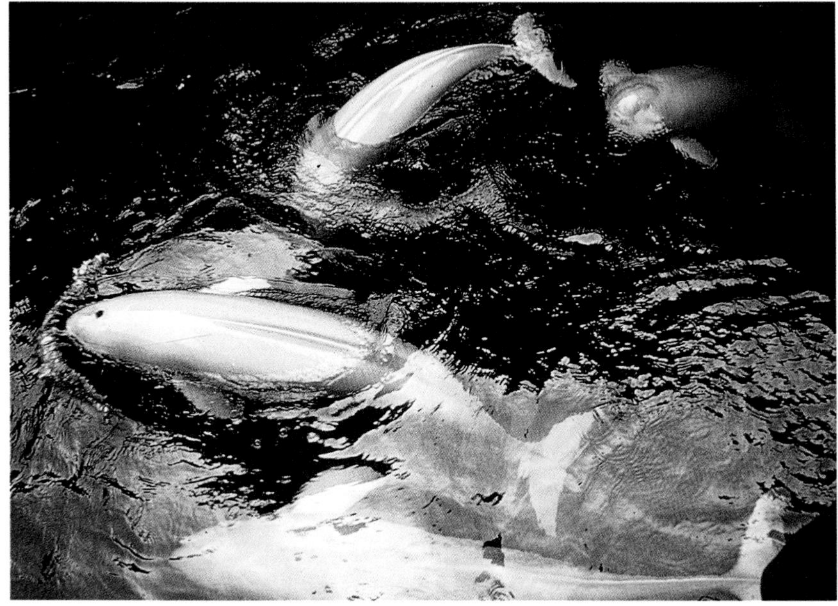

ABOVE: As a group, porpoises are the smallest cetaceans, being slightly smaller than dolphins. They share so many similarities with one another that the terms "dolphin" and "porpoise" are frequently, although often incorrectly, used interchangeably.

RIGHT: *Whales can be extremely difficult to tell apart at sea. Often only a small part of a whale is visible. This minke whale (pictured) could easily be mistaken for another species of similar size or features.*

BELOW: *Many species have a diversity of local names. This fin whale would be called* nagasu kujira *in Japan;* qeporqannaq *in Greenland;* kiit *in Russia;* finhval *in Norway;* vraie baleine *in France, and* rorcual comun *or* ballena boba *in Spain.*

Appearance and Anatomy

The appearance and anatomical features of cetaceans are adaptations to the aquatic environment in which they live. Whereas in most mammals appendages such as ears and male genitals are external, in whales these have become internalized to make for a streamlined form that is essential for easy movement through water. The layer of blubber under a whale's skin is both an energy store and very effective insulation, preventing heat loss from the body. Even relatively small whales, such as narwhals, belugas, and orcas, are so well insulated by their blubber that they can remain comfortable in very cold water.

External Features

As their name suggests, toothed whales have teeth for grasping prey. Embryonic baleen whales also have teeth, but in adults these are replaced by baleen, which allows them to filter feed. Baleen whales have large—sometimes enormous—mouths and big tongues. Nostrils in other mammals have evolved as blowholes in whales. These are on the top of the head, and so are the first part of the body to break the water's surface. Toothed whales have a single blowhole; baleen whales have two, which are protected by a raised "splashguard," or coaming. When whales are not inhaling, muscular plugs seal their blowholes. Cetaceans' eyes are small in relation to their body size; situated at the sides of the head, they offer optimum all-round vision.

Most whales have a dorsal fin, which acts like a stabilizer as they swim. The pectoral fins, modified forelimbs, are flattened like paddles, and have no "elbows," but, like human hands, they have five "fingers" of bone. They are used for steering and control of movement. The horizontal tail flukes, which move vertically, rather than laterally as in fish, propel a whale forward. The fins and flukes also play an important role in the regulation of body temperature.

Internal Features

There are some significant internal differences between cetaceans and other mammals. Rather than a single carotid artery, cetaceans have a series of tiny vessels—known as a *retia mirabilia*—along the spine that carry blood to the brain. A cetacean's respiratory passage is separate from its digestive tract, and a short trachea leads from the blowhole to the lungs. And cetaceans, unlike other mammals, have no appendix or gall bladder.

Cetacean skeletons, too, are unlike those of land mammals. The bones of the skull overlap, making it long and narrow, and in most species the neck vertebrae are fused and inflexible to steady the head. Because a whale's weight is supported by water, its skeleton tends to be

LEFT: The skeleton of a baleen whale clearly shows how different its skull and jaw structure is to the toothed whale illustrated below. Such anatomical differences have evolved to suit the very distinct feeding habits of the two groups.

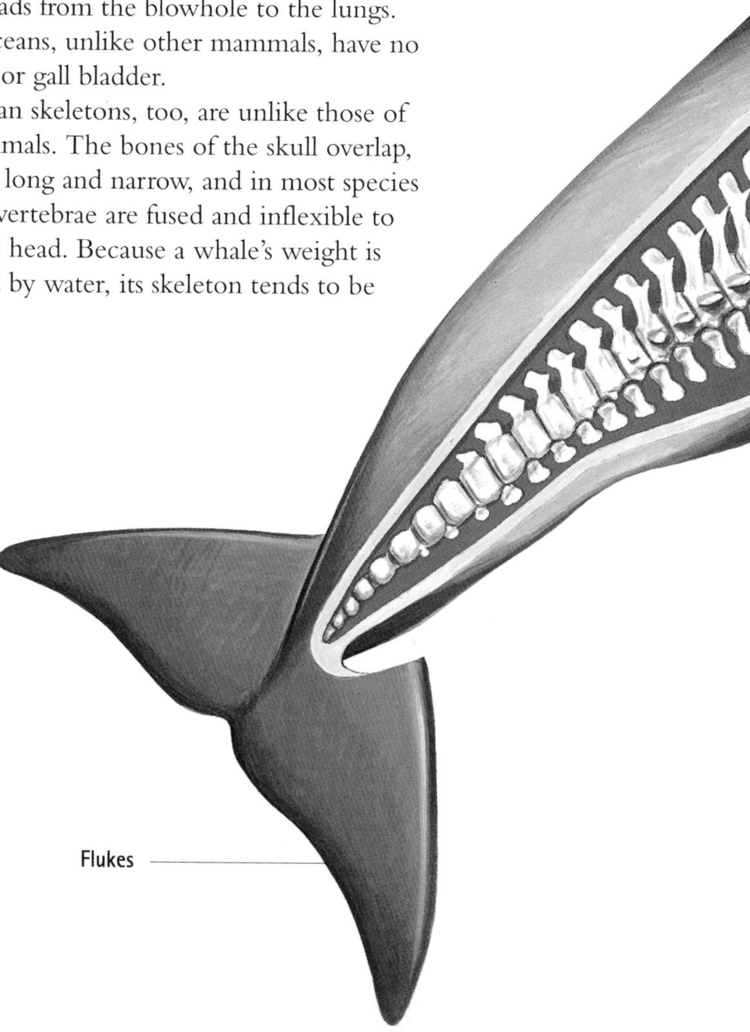

lighter than those of land animals of similar size. If an elephant's skeleton, for example, were as light as that of a whale of similar size, it would not be able to stand, let alone move, on land. An elephant's size is limited by its need to stay upright and move easily. A whale's size is far less subject to such restraints. Except for a remnant pelvic bone in some species, which is separated from the rest of the skeleton, cetaceans have no skeletal hindlimbs. The backbone stretches to the end of the body, and anchors the muscles that power the flukes.

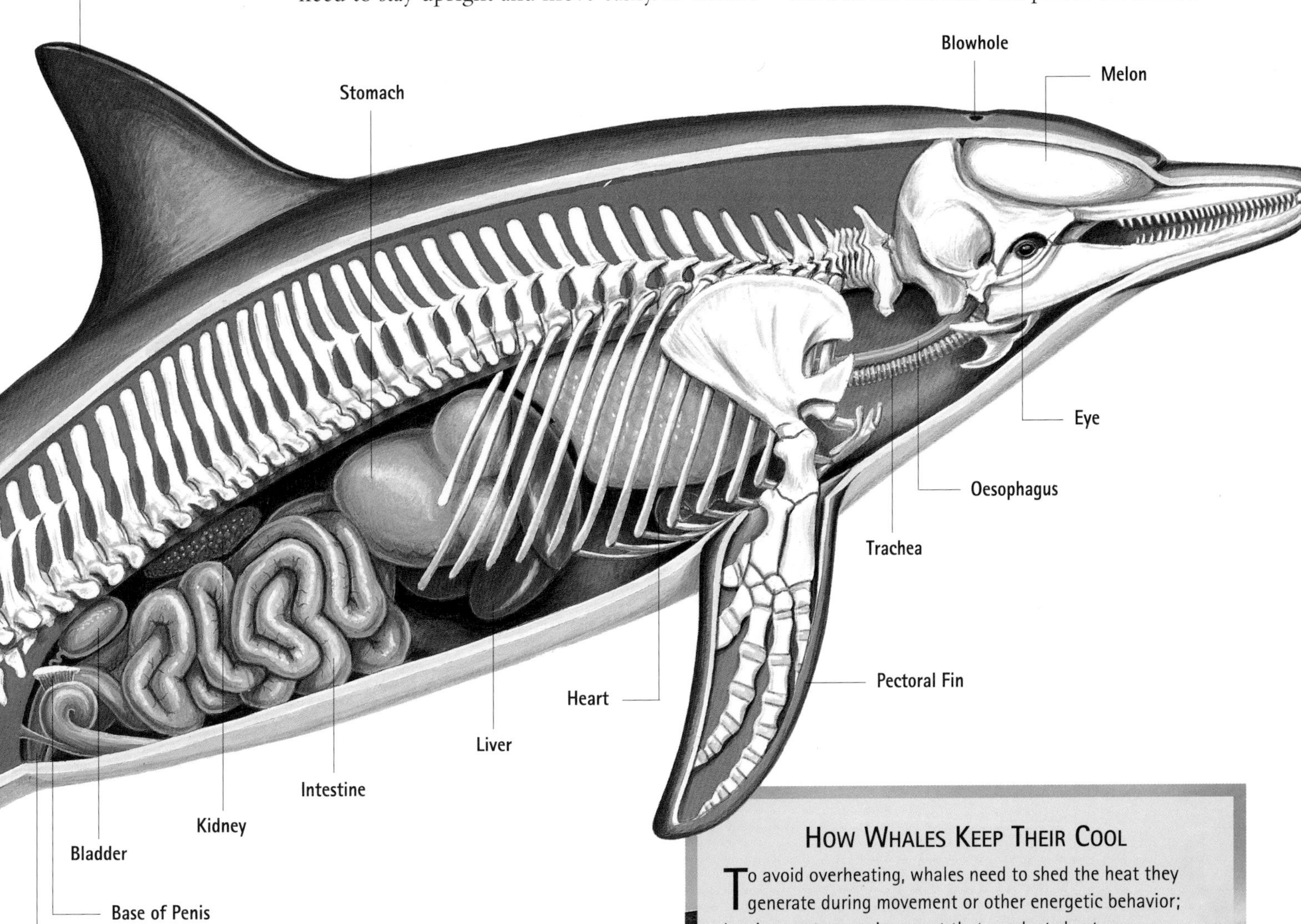

Cross-section of a Toothed Whale
By peeling away the layers, we can see that all whales, such as this male common dolphin, share many anatomical features with other mammals. These include vital organs, such as the heart, liver, kidneys, bladder, and stomach. The large, vertical spines on the vertebrae, called processes, help to anchor the large muscles that power the flukes. These make the backbone much more substantial than those of land mammals. There are also major differences between toothed and baleen whales: mainly the presence of teeth or baleen; and the melon, an adaptation found only in toothed whales.

How Whales Keep Their Cool

To avoid overheating, whales need to shed the heat they generate during movement or other energetic behavior; but in a watery environment that conducts heat very efficiently, they must retain enough heat to maintain a stable core temperature. They do this with the aid of what are known as countercurrent heat-exchange systems. Networks of vessels carry blood from the cool outer shell to the warm body core. These are interlaced with vessels going in the opposite direction. If an animal overheats, warm blood is flushed to the fins, flukes, and skin from where it dissipates into the water, while cooler blood flows to the body core. If a whale becomes too cool, small capillaries open and heat is transferred from the outward-flowing warm blood to the cooler blood flowing inward.

Adaptations to the Environment

LEFT: This sperm whale cow and calf are in their tropical breeding grounds off the Galapagos Islands. Sperm whales can dive to great depths and are able to locate their prey in complete darkness and under crushing pressure. Males also do this in icy polar waters.

In an underwater environment, animals live in a medium that is fundamentally different from that inhabited by land animals. Water is much denser than air and, as any swimmer knows, it offers much greater resistance to movement. It conducts heat about 25 times as efficiently as air, and in cold water body heat is lost very quickly. During a migratory journey, whales can experience water temperatures that range from 28°F to 82°F (-2°C to 28°C).

Water pressure changes with depth far more rapidly than air pressure changes with altitude: it increases by one atmosphere (a unit of pressure) for every 30 feet (9 m) of depth. Deep-diving animals have adapted to cope with this. The oxygen in water is in a dissolved form and marine animals without gills, or a similar breathing apparatus, must surface to breathe in air. Because of its density, water conducts sound much farther than air does and about four times as fast. Light, however, does not penetrate more than a few hundred feet below the surface, and the ocean depths are a zone of permanent darkness. Suspended particles in shallow water render water murky, making vision of limited value to marine animals.

Physical Adaptations

Cetaceans have evolved in ways that allow them to cope with their aquatic surroundings. Their streamlined shape enables them to move with minimal turbulence. Their blubber reduces heat loss. Breathing at the surface has been incorporated into their normal swimming action. Deep-diving species have evolved oxygen-storage mechanisms in the blood and muscles that enable them to hold their breath for long periods and avoid "the bends."

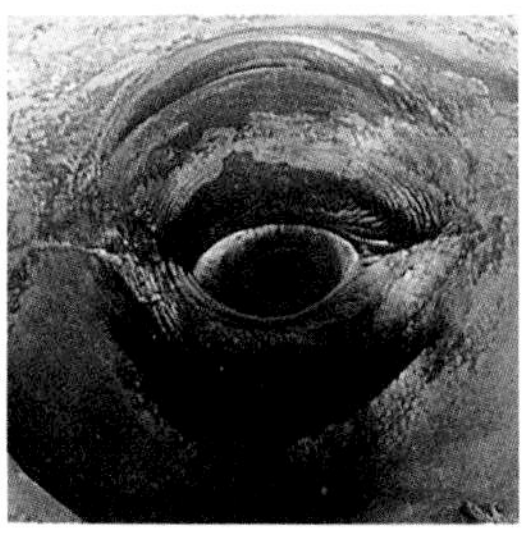

ABOVE: Although hearing is their primary sense, many cetaceans have excellent eyesight, both in and out of the water. In most species, close-range sight plays at least some role in social interactions with other whales, in avoiding predators, and in hunting prey.

BELOW: A female right whale breaches when harassed by another whale. She uses her entire body to respond aggressively to the other whale, perhaps because it threatened her nearby calf (not pictured). Eventually the other whale left.

BEHAVIORAL ADAPTATIONS

Whales have evolved their extraordinary physical adaptations in response to an environment that is hostile to most other mammals. Their behaviors have evolved in conjunction with these physical changes.

In many cases, physical adaptations with a "primary" purpose have also come to have "secondary" uses. For example, although the tail flukes evolved as a means of efficient propulsion, they also serve as a means of communication, as weapons of defense, and as instruments for stunning prey. Pectoral fins, which provide stability and steering control are also used to make gentle physical contact with other whales, and in some species, such as the humpback whale, they are slapped loudly on the water surface to communicate.

Habitat and Distribution

Cetaceans occupy an astonishing range of aquatic habitats, from the shallow, muddy waters of the world's greatest rivers to clear tropical lagoons and ice-strewn polar waters. Some species frequent only the surface layers; others dive to the bottom in all but the deepest oceans. Some remain in relatively restricted areas; others roam the world's oceans. So what determines the distribution of cetaceans?

ABOVE: Spotted dolphins, seen here playing among seaweed, are often found over shallow banks, but they also inhabit the deep tropical seas, where countless numbers of them have drowned after becoming entangled in tuna nets.

The Food Factor

The present distribution of species is the result of many millions of years of climatic change, continental drift, and the evolution of the whales themselves. They have adapted to a wide range of environments, and different types of food.

Availability of prey is probably the most easily identifiable factor, but this, too, depends on such variables as water temperature, salinity, depth, and seafloor topography, as well as seasonal occurrences, such as the flooding of rivers, the formation of sea ice, and wind-driven currents. In apparently featureless deep ocean, differences in temperature or salinity can create invisible boundaries between water masses and can separate even closely related species from each other.

A species' preferred habitat is determined largely by the way it feeds, and the distribution of prey is usually patchy. Baleen whales, which gulp large quantities of prey, favor shoals of small fish or crustaceans, which are more abundant in colder, nutrient-rich waters in summer. Hence, most species of baleen whale, in both hemispheres, feed in polar or subpolar waters. Deep-diving squid-eaters, such as sperm and beaked whales, prefer the edges of continental shelves, where upwelling occurs in deep water. Members of a single species can inhabit a range of habitats: bottlenose dolphins, for example, are particularly wide-ranging; they may feed in locations as diverse as seagrass beds in sheltered bays, or in deep water far from land.

LEFT: A minke whale surfaces through broken sea ice in Antarctic waters. Once it was thought they all migrated north, but some minkes are known to remain throughout winter under the pack ice.

Breeding Needs

The availability of food is only one of the factors that determine choice of habitat. Breeding habits are also important. The migratory patterns of some species, which travel between feeding and breeding grounds, sometimes great distances apart, mean that these whales alternate between two sharply contrasting habitats. Each winter, for example, most baleen whales leave their abundantly stocked summer feeding grounds to mate and calve in nutritionally poor tropical and temperate waters. Humpbacks feed in deep polar regions, but mate in warm, shallow water, where the bottom is flat and there are protective coral reefs; gray whales, too, move regularly between Arctic and tropical waters. Among toothed whales, sperm whales are the best known migrators; they feed in cold polar waters in summer and move to warmer waters in fall and winter.

ABOVE: Although humpback calves are born in warm tropical waters, they soon migrate to their feeding grounds in frigid polar or subpolar seas.

RIGHT: Some dolphins inhabit fresh water—and even "land" environments. In the tropical wet season, Amazon River dolphins can often be seen chasing fish through flooded South American rain forests.

Baleen Whales

Baleen whales include the largest animals that have lived on earth, yet they feed on some of the oceans' tiniest creatures. Most baleen whales are great travelers, making seasonal migrations from feeding grounds near the poles to tropical breeding areas. Some cover a distance almost equal to half earth's circumference each year.

Physical Features of Baleen Whales

Above: Gray whales may become heavily encrusted with barnacles and whale lice. The same is true for the slow-moving humpback whales, while the faster rorquals seem to have fewer infestations.

The most prominent feature distinguishing baleen whales from their toothed cousins is their baleen, the horny plates hanging from their upper jaws. This baleen forms sievelike mats used for filter feeding on schools of small prey. Although baleen was called "whalebone" by early whalers, it is not bone, but a fibrous material similar to our fingernails.

Baleen whales are generally large animals. The smallest, the pygmy right whale, grows to more than 20 feet (6 m), while the blue whale reaches more than 100 feet (30 m) and weighs up to 180 tons (198.4 tonnes). Females are larger than males, perhaps to cope with the long fast required while bearing and feeding calves during their annual migrations.

Some baleen whales are believed to be more than 100 years old, so we may think of them as having lifespans roughly equivalent to those of humans. We can determine the age of dead baleen whales by examining cross-sections of the waxy plugs found in their ear canals—these form growth rings like those of trees.

Dorsal fin size and shape are often a clue to species identification. The largest family of baleen whales, the rorquals, all have a true dorsal fin, as does the pygmy right whale. However, in the gray whale a series of bumps replaces the dorsal fin, while right whales lack the dorsal fin altogether.

Some baleen whales have unusual features on their skin. Humpbacks have a series of bumps, or tubercles, on the upper side of the snout. In young humpbacks, each tubercle may sprout a single hair—a rare example of hair in cetaceans. Right whales have callosities—white, wartlike protrusions of hardened skin—around their heads. These are usually homes for barnacles and "whale lice," small crustaceans that feed on dead skin.

RIGHT: Right whales have exceptionally long baleen plates. The color, length, number, and coarseness of the baleen vary according to species and such features are used to identify stranded baleen whales.

BELOW: Baleen whales have paired blowholes in a symmetrical skull and a "splashguard," or coaming, just in front of their blowholes (inset). The splashguard is lacking in the toothed whales, but is very prominent in baleen whales, such as the blue whale shown here.

How Baleen Whales Feed

It is a curious fact that baleen whales, the largest animals in the sea, feed on some of the smallest. The zooplankton they eat are small oceanic animals, not to be confused with phytoplankton, the tiny plants on which the zooplankton feed. Zooplankton usually occur in schools or swarms, enabling the whales' baleen to capture large quantities of prey at one time. All whales are carnivores, but baleen whales are the marine ecological equivalent of land-grazing animals, such as bison or wildebeest.

ABOVE: Krill is a Norwegian word for "whalefood." These shrimplike crustaceans grow to about 2½ inches (6.4 cm). Antarctic krill, Euphausia superba, *occur in vast numbers in the nutrient-rich Antarctic waters, the summer home of the world's greatest concentrations of whales, particularly rorquals.*

Distribution of Food

Phytoplankton are found near the surface, where they use sunlight for photosynthesis. Their distribution is determined by local oceanographic conditions that cause upwelling of nutrients on which the phytoplankton depend. In polar regions, phytoplankton—and zooplankton—are often heavily concentrated in sea ice. Many whales follow the receding ice edge during the spring melt to feed. Although zooplankton can occur in "megaswarms" many miles across, swarms are more often small, occurring in scattered patches. Making up the zooplankton are shrimplike krill, and other crustaceans, such as amphipods, copepods, and free-swimming larvae of certain crabs. Besides zooplankton, baleen whales may also eat schooling surface fish, such as mackerel, capelin, herring, or pilchards, or such bottom fish as cod or sand lance. In addition, there are records of baleen whales eating squid. Some species restrict themselves to one or two types of food, while others, such as sei whales, may consume a variety of crustaceans, fish, and squid.

Feeding Strategies

Humpback whales in Antarctic waters are often seen in pairs. Pairs may be the most efficient compromise to allow both cooperation between the whales (which will increase the individual's chances of feeding) and a fair share of what is essentially a scarce resource. In the Gulf of Maine, feeding pairs are usually females. Males tend to feed alone.

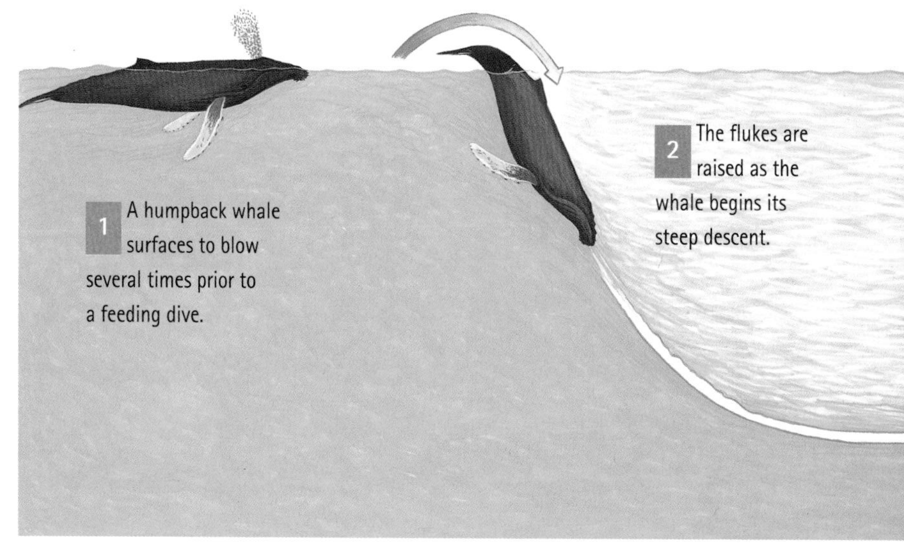

The Feeding Dive

Baleen whales feed where zooplankton are concentrated, anywhere from the surface to 300 feet (90 m) deep. They may dive vertically, and surface near where they dived, or they may travel while they feed as shown here. Feeding dives are usually of short duration with dive length related to the depth at which food is found.

LEFT: A pair of humpback whales feeds in Antarctic waters. The size of a group of feeding baleen whales depends on the size of the zooplankton swarm on which they are feeding. The distribution of zooplankton swarms is generally very patchy, so whales usually feed in small groups.

BALEEN WHALE FEEDING TECHNIQUES

Baleen whales eat up to three to four percent of their body weight each day, yet no one knows exactly how they locate their prey. Perhaps they listen for the minute rustling and clicking made by a swarm of krill, or they may simply recognize locations and conditions in which such swarms are likely to occur. It is possible that they are able to "taste" their prey in the water, or even use a crude form of echolocation, although this is still unproved. However, once they have located their desired prey, they employ one of three basic feeding methods: skimming, gulping, or bottom feeding.

SKIM FEEDING

Skim feeding is a method used by right whales, including the bowhead, and by the sei whale, the only rorqual to do so regularly. Right whales have enormously long baleen to filter large volumes of water—in bowheads, the plates, suspended from strongly arched upper jaws, may exceed 12 feet (3.7 m). With its mouth open, the whale swims slowly along near the water surface through a slick of zooplankton, most often copepods. Water flows into the mouth and is strained out through the baleen in a continuous flow. This contrasts with gulp feeding.

GULP FEEDING

The rorquals have a unique adaptation for feeding. Running lengthways on the underside of the head are many parallel grooves, or pleats, which enable the throat to expand when the whale engulfs a mouthful of water mixed with prey. These throat pleats dramatically increase the volume of food a whale can swallow. After expanding with each

BUBBLENETTING

Humpbacks in Alaska and Antarctica show an elaborate form of gulp feeding, called bubblenetting. The whale slowly rises from below a school of prey, expelling a circle of bubbles from its blowhole. These form a "net," causing prey to panic and converge. Whales then rise through the concentrated prey, mouths open wide.

ABOVE: *The number and length of throat pleats in rorquals vary between species. Humpbacks (pictured) have no more than 36, while fin whales may have up to 100.*

mouthful, the muscular throat pleats contract and the tongue moves forward, forcing water from the mouth out through the filtering baleen. Once the whale has squeezed out the water, it swallows the food, possibly with the aid of its mobile, muscular tongue. Rorquals usually gulp crustaceans, such as krill, or schooling fish.

A fully grown blue whale may take in up to 50 tons (45.3 tonnes) of water and zooplankton in one mouthful, and can consume as much as six tons of krill each day. When its throat is fully distended, it resembles a gigantic tadpole.

Gulp feeding can occur anywhere in the top 300 feet (90 m) or so of the water. Whales often concentrate prey to make it easier to capture—by herding a swarm against the water's surface, the shore, or possibly even other objects such as icebergs. Lunging through the surface, they engulf prey as they go, or they roll on their sides just below the surface and make rapid turns through the prey. Schooling fish are alert, active animals, and feeding rorquals often need to move fast in order to capture them.

Bottom Feeding

Bottom feeding is the common feeding method of the gray whale. Aerial observations show that a gray whale will leave a plume of disturbed mud behind it as it forages along the bottom, where it seeks out mud-dwelling amphipods, shellfish, crabs, and worms. Usually one or the other side of the jaw is more worn, suggesting that they prefer to roll over onto one side to feed. Humpbacks have also been observed bottom feeding, flushing out sand lance, a burrowing fish.

RIGHT: *Scouring the shallows, a gray whale leaves a visible trail of mud. It will either feed as it burrows through the silt or simply disturb the mud in order to flush out tiny animals, returning later to swallow them.*

Right and Gray Whales

The Right Whales

Four species are collectively known as right whales: the northern right whale, southern right whale, bowhead, and pygmy right whale. The term *right whale* was given by whalers, who considered the bowhead and the northern and southern right whales the "right" whales to kill. They were fat with oil, and had long, valuable baleen. They were also slow swimmers, floated when harpooned to death, and were easy to find because they bred in coastal waters. Southern and northern right whales became known as "black" right whales; and the bowhead as the "Greenland" right whale. They were among the first species to be heavily exploited by whalers, and all three came close to extinction. Because of its diminutive size, the pygmy right whale has never been commercially hunted.

All four species have some features in common: an arched rostrum (the long, narrow part of the head above the mouth); a bowed lower jaw, to accommodate very long, elastic baleen with fine fringes for eating small prey; very high lower lips to cover this baleen; certain skeletal characteristics; and a slow swimming speed. However, the pygmy right whale differs significantly from the other three —enough to be classified in a family of its own. It is relatively small, growing to scarcely 20 feet (6 m) and weighing only 3 to 4 tons (2.7 to 3.6 tonnes). The other right whales are large, stocky animals that can reach nearly 65 feet (20 m) long and weigh more than 60 tons (54.4 tonnes). The pygmy right whale has a small but prominent dorsal fin; the larger right whales have none at all. There are small differences between the two "black" right whales, most noticeably the greater number of callosities on the southern species; bowheads lack callosities altogether.

Right whales all differ in their distribution. Bowheads live only in Arctic waters, the northern and southern rights remain in their respective hemispheres, and the pygmy right is found only in temperate waters of the Southern Hemisphere. All four species appear to feed mainly on copepods.

ABOVE: The characteristic short, yellow baleen of a gray whale has curled as it dried out. The bristles are coarse, suggesting that gray whales eat larger prey than right whales, which have long, dark, fine baleen.

LEFT: Bowheads are among the most ice-adapted of baleen whales. They move into the sea ice as it melts back in spring, somehow knowing how to find breathing holes ahead. Bowheads have longer, higher-grade baleen than other right whales, and consequently were more keenly hunted by whalers.

The Gray Whale

The single species of gray whale is in a family of its own. Although naturally gray all over, its body is usually blotched with patches of whale lice and barnacles. Growing up to 50 feet (15 m) long, and weighing 30 tons (27.2 tonnes), it is intermediate in form and size between the portly "black" right whales and the more graceful rorquals. Its baleen is short and coarse, suggesting that its food is relatively large, and it has one or two pairs of throat grooves, which may aid in feeding. It has no dorsal fin. Like all baleen whales, the gray whale is migratory, moving between the cool feeding grounds off Alaska and the warm lagoons of Baja California in Mexico.

Gray whales now live only in the North Pacific Ocean; the North Atlantic population was exterminated by whalers by the early 18th century. Whalers nicknamed them "devilfish" because of their aggressive response to harpooning—like sperm whales, they often attacked whaleboats. By the 1930s, gray whales were almost extinct. They have since made a very successful recovery, and now number more than 20,000, although they are still hunted in eastern Siberia.

The gray whale's ancestry is unclear; the oldest known fossils are only 100,000 years old.

ABOVE: This gray whale is in its breeding waters near the Mexican coast. The migration of gray whales is among the longest and most predictable of all whales. Their annual winter passage, close in along the Californian coast, is a major attraction for whale-watchers.

LEFT: Both northern and southern right whales breed in shallow coastal waters, and females return every three years to familiar calving areas. After birth, calves become accustomed to sandy inshore ocean bottoms and wave-swept rocky foreshores, and then accompany their mothers offshore to deepsea feeding areas. Whales may return in subsequent breeding seasons to the areas where they were born.

The Rorqual Family

LEFT: All balaenopterids have a central ridge on top of the head, in front of the blowhole. Bryde's whale is easily identified, because it is the only whale to have three of these ridges; all others have one.

The rorquals, with six species, make up the most diverse family of baleen whales. Five of them—the blue, fin, sei, Bryde's, and minke—make up the genus *Balaenoptera.* The humpback has a genus of its own, and is in many ways different from the other rorquals.

The word *rorqual* derives from an old Norse word meaning "groove-throat." All six rorquals have a large number of throat pleats—some of them as many as 90—which allow the gullet to expand and the whales to gulp down large quantities of water and prey through jaws that can open to almost 90°. Rorquals have dorsal fins, short baleen plates, and heads that are flat on top, rather than arched or curved like those of other baleen whales.

Most of the balaenopterids are large animals that grow more than 46 feet (14 m) long. At the extremes are the 100 foot (30 m) blue whale and the 30 foot (9 m) minke, with the blue whale weighing 18 times as much as the minke. Body markings vary, from the dappled slate-blue of the blue whale, to the subtle swirling chevrons of the fin whale.

Apart from Bryde's whale, which spends the year in warm seas, most of the rorquals are great migrants, traveling between polar and tropical waters. Earlier this century, rorquals were the mainstay of the commercial whaling industry, particularly in the Antarctic. They were vulnerable to whaling then because of their large populations and tendency to assemble in huge groups in feeding and breeding areas.

The Humpback

Stockier in shape and a much slower swimmer than the other rorquals, the humpback, which grows 50 feet (15 m) long and can weigh up to 40 tons (36.3 tonnes), is a particularly easy target for whalers. Its most remarkable feature is its extraordinary pectoral fins, which are about one-third as long as its body—in other rorquals these measure only one-seventh of the body length. Despite its slowness, the humpback is an acrobatic whale; no doubt its long pectoral fins make it highly maneuverable under water. It is noted for its song, longer and more complex than that of other whales.

RIGHT: Large, slender, and gracefully streamlined, the fin whale can swim more swiftly than most other cetaceans. Until the advent of fast steam-powered vessels, its speed protected it from whalers. Fin whales were butchered wholesale in the 1950s and 1960s, but they are now protected worldwide.

ABOVE: Herman Melville, the author of Moby Dick, *described the humpback as "the most gamesome and light-hearted of all the whales." Humpbacks are certainly the most active of the rorquals, and they frequently engage in breaching and other kinds of energetic behavior.*

Toothed Whales

From the bulky sperm whales to the delicate porpoises, toothed whales inhabit a variety of habitats, ranging from harbors, shorelines, and coastal rivers to the deep sea. The most familiar group, the dolphins, belong to the family that claims the greatest number of species. They are noted for the variety of their vivid skin patterns.

Physical Features of Toothed Whales

The most obvious differences between toothed and baleen whales are in their heads and mouths. Toothed whales, for instance, have only one blowhole instead of a pair. But the main feature that sets toothed whales apart is that, instead of baleen, they have true teeth. However, the number and form of these teeth vary greatly between species. Some oceanic dolphins have up to 260 cone-shaped teeth, evenly distributed between their upper and lower jaws. At the other end of the spectrum, the male narwhal has only two teeth, both in its upper jaw, and one of these grows outward to form a spiral tusk.

Size and Body Form

In size, toothed whales range from the tiny 5 foot (1.5 m) vaquita, of the Gulf of California, to the 60 foot (18 m) sperm whale, one of the giants of the oceans. While most toothed whales are smaller than baleen whales, a few, including sperm whales, several beaked whales, and orcas, grow as big as some baleen whales.

Like baleen whales, most toothed whales are streamlined in appearance, but their body shapes differ considerably. Many, like the blunt-nosed sperm whale, are solid and bulky; others, including the strap-toothed whale and most dolphins, are sleek and tapering. Most toothed whales have a dorsal fin, but a few, such as the beluga, have only a raised hump. Beaked whales have a pair of conspicuous throat grooves, but other toothed whales have no ventral feeding grooves. Toothed whales are less often infested with barnacles and whale lice than baleen whales.

Above: While toothed whales have tended to gain teeth during evolution, some species have lost teeth. Orcas have up to 48 conical teeth, which are distributed evenly on each side of the upper and lower jaw.

Right: Linear scarring is common on the skin of many toothed whales, and is extensive in Risso's dolphin. It is caused by the teeth of other dolphins during mating or aggressive interactions.

Left: A striking feature of many toothed whales is a bulging forehead, or melon, as in these northern bottlenose whales. This structure plays a vital role in echolocation.

How Toothed Whales Feed

Whereas baleen whales consume mouthfuls of small schooling prey, toothed whales eat larger prey, one at a time. They feed mainly on cephalopods (squid, octopus, and cuttlefish) and fish, although some species also prey on warm-blooded animals. Others, such as belugas, sometimes forage for bottom-dwelling worms and crustaceans. Most dolphins use their conical, pointed teeth to grasp slippery prey such as fish, which they then swallow whole. Porpoises, on the other hand, dismember their prey with their slicing teeth.

Teeth, however, are not essential. Whalers have caught sperm whales with deformed jaws, but which were otherwise in excellent physical condition. Most beaked whales have no functional teeth. In mature male straptoothed whales, two teeth protrude upward from the lower jaw, folding around the upper jaw and preventing the mouth from opening more than a few inches. Recently it has been discovered that whales without functional teeth actually use suction to capture squid and fish. By rapidly distending the throat grooves and moving the tongue backwards like a piston, beaked whales such as Hubb's beaked whale create a powerful suction in their mouths, causing nearby fish, in an observer's words, to "vanish."

Feeding Patterns

Different toothed whales have widely differing feeding strategies. Daily behavior patterns of many species depend largely on what they eat. Some species laze and socialize during the day, and at night hunt fish and

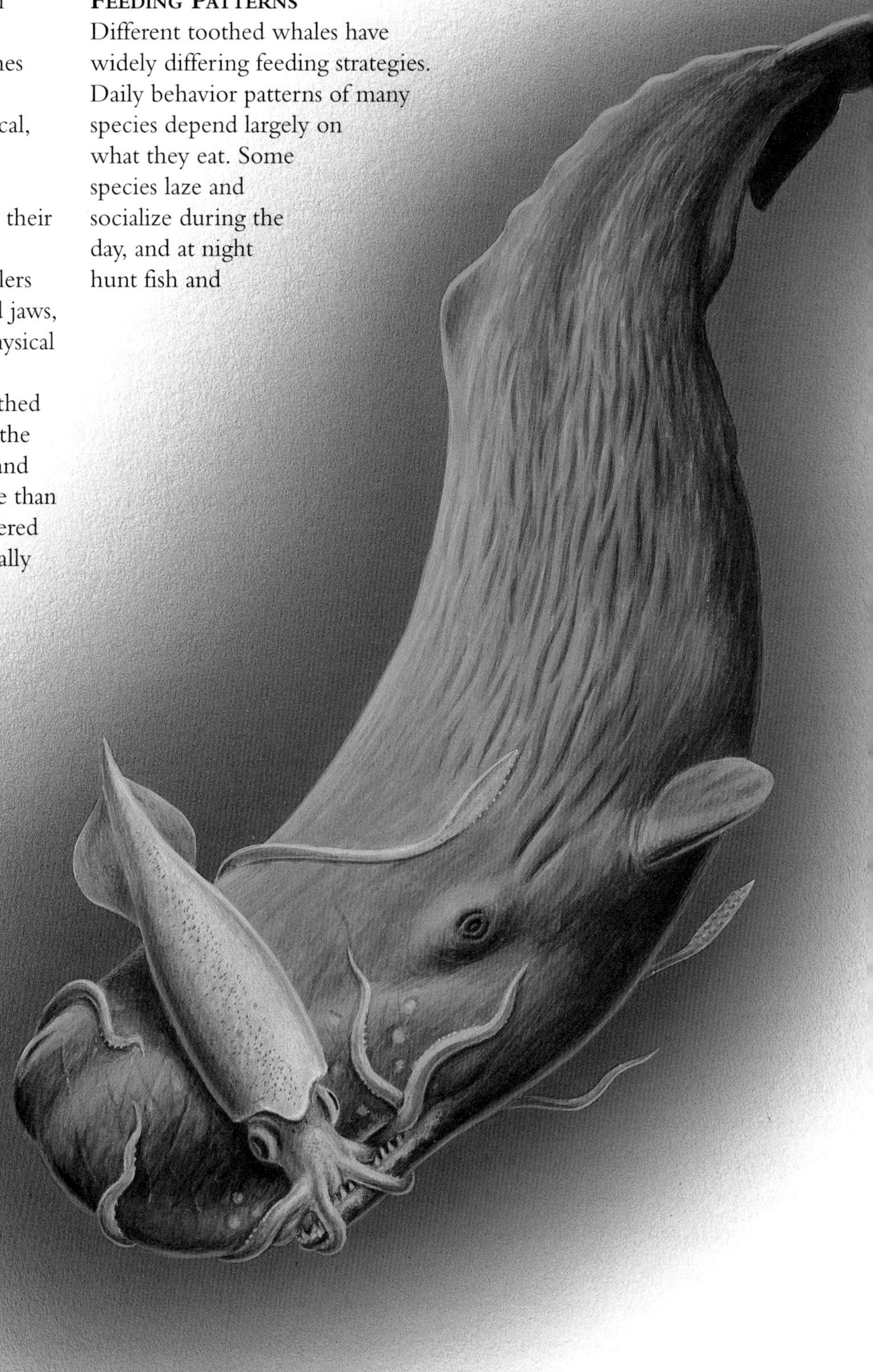

Sperm Whale Feeding

Sperm whales dive vertically to levels where squid congregate, down to 10,000 feet (3,000 m). No one knows how a slow-moving, 40-ton whale stalks fast-moving, sharp-sighted squid. Squid can exceed 30 feet (9 m) and whales often swallow them intact. How sperm whales subdue and swallow such large prey is a mystery. The white pigment around their mouths may act as a lure. A quick suction action might be used once the squid is within range.

squid that rise to the surface in darkness. Many dolphins tend to hunt during daylight, when schooling fish cluster, and relax and socialize at night. Whales that feed close to shore, where food supplies are more predictable than they are in the open ocean, do so in smaller groups than oceanic dolphins.

We can only speculate about how toothed whales identify locations where prey is abundant. Once they find these places, however, they have several adaptations that help them to capture the prey. As well as their excellent sight and hearing, they use echolocation, a remarkable natural sonar system shared by all toothed whales (see page 116.) Echolocation allows them to track individual prey, even when it is dark or the water is very murky. Some river dolphins depend so heavily on echolocation that they have almost lost the use of their eyes.

BELOW: Oceanic dolphins often move around in groups of many hundreds, pooling their combined senses to search for schooling prey that often congregates along such oceanographic features as submarine canyons and ridges.

Feeding in Groups

A fascinating aspect of toothed whales' behavior is their ability to coordinate group activities. Sometimes, for example, a pod of bottlenose dolphins will encircle a school of fish; or a family of orcas will divide the labor, each performing a separate task as the group harasses and attacks a solitary baleen whale, tearing away pieces of its flesh. It has recently been discovered that false killer whales also attack other whales in this way.

Herding prey is another way in which toothed whales cooperate in feeding. Many species herd their prey against the surface or against the shore before devouring it. Bottlenose dolphins take this to an extreme, by sliding up onto mud banks to catch fleeing fish. Other species, such as the dusky dolphin, herd baitfish into tight balls, and take turns to dash in and feed on them. Some toothed whales, such as male sperm whales in polar waters, do not conform to the group feeding pattern, and seem to be solitary hunters.

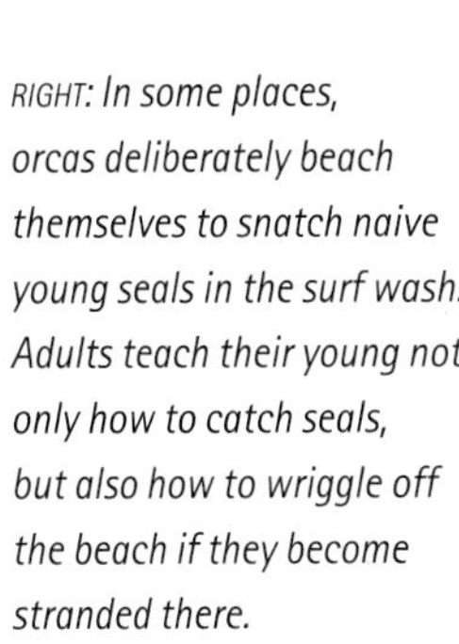

RIGHT: In some places, orcas deliberately beach themselves to snatch naive young seals in the surf wash. Adults teach their young not only how to catch seals, but also how to wriggle off the beach if they become stranded there.

The Sperm Whale Family

Above: Diving off Mexico, François Gohier photographed this sperm whale resting at the surface. The whale then dived vertically, disappearing for about 30 minutes, before resurfacing for another 15-minute rest.

At first glance there is a huge disparity in this group. The sperm whale, the largest toothed whale by far, grows to about 60 feet (18 m). The pygmy sperm reaches only 11 feet (3.4 m) and the dwarf sperm is a mere 9 feet (2.7 m) long, making it one of the smallest animals to be dignified with the term "whale." All three species have a large melon (in male sperm whales, a quarter of the body length), a short, narrow lower jaw tucked under the head, and no functioning teeth in the upper jaw.

The Sperm Whale

The sperm whale, or cachalot, is a most intriguing whale. Its distinctive blow slants forward at 45°, making it easy to distinguish at sea. It has a dorsal hump rather than a fin.

Found in all the oceans to the edge of the polar ice, it feeds predominantly on squid (in some areas on fish) along continental shelf edges, around oceanic islands, over seamounts, and in areas of upwelling in deep water.

Sperm whales are unusual in that males grow to nearly twice as long and weigh up to three times as much as females. They also live largely separate and different lives. Females and very young animals remain in "nursery" schools in temperate to equatorial waters throughout the year; young males live in "bachelor" schools in the same waters. In summer, mature males migrate to squid-rich polar waters, returning in winter to mate and socialize with the females. Sperm whales have a low reproductive rate, with females calving every four to six years. Female calves remain with their group for life, in a matrilineal, or female-dominated, society.

Sperm whales were intensively whaled during the 19th century for oil, including the superb spermaceti oil contained in their melons. They inspired the fear and respect of open boat whalers, many of whom lost their lives hunting them. Ambergris, a waxy substance formed in the whales' stomachs, like a pearl in an oyster, was a valuable component of perfumes. Although industrial whaling continued during the 20th century, sperm whales are still relatively abundant. Much knowledge of their diet, migrations, and life history has come from whaling records.

Pygmy and Dwarf Sperm Whales

Little is known of pygmy and dwarf sperm whales. Although they have definite dorsal fins, their small size, slow, unobtrusive movements, and indistinct blow make them difficult to sight at sea. Consequently what is known comes mostly from strandings. Their diet consists largely of squid and cuttlefish, fish, and small crustaceans. Both species occur in temperate to tropical waters, where they apparently feed along the slopes of continental shelves, diving to at least 1,000 feet (300 m). Widely distributed in all major oceans, they strand occasionally, most notably off South Africa, Australia, and south-eastern USA, and are usually seen in groups of fewer than 10.

RIGHT: Because of their small size and unobtrusive habits, both pygmy and dwarf sperm whales are rarely sighted at sea. This photograph of a pygmy sperm whale was taken while it was being held in a dolphinarium in Florida.

Narwhals, Belugas, and Beaked Whales

Narwhals and Belugas

These two related species are found only in Arctic and subarctic waters, where their lives are interwoven with the seasonal changes of the sea ice. Both narwhals and belugas are found close to land, often in bays and fiords, and have long been hunted by indigenous people.

The beluga is one of the most distinctive of whales, with its white skin, lack of dorsal fin, flexible neck, and expressive face. Calves, born in spring and summer, are gray; some animals turn white by the age of five.

Belugas feed on a variety of prey, from bottom-dwelling mollusks to fish and zooplankton. There are five distinct populations throughout the Arctic and subarctic, and some of these are threatened by pollution, habitat alteration, and whaling. The smallest and most vulnerable population is in the Gulf of Saint Lawrence, Canada. Polar bears and orcas are their natural predators.

Belugas follow the spring melt, congregating in large herds during the summer in estuaries and shallow coastal waters. They sometimes become trapped and drown when their inlet freezes over, a phenomenon known as a "savssat." Whalers knew belugas as "sea canaries" for their ability to produce an array of loud chirps and whistles.

Narwhals, which are smaller and more ice-adapted than their larger cousins, the belugas, rarely venture below the Arctic Circle. They prey on squid and on such fish as cod and halibut. Living in family groups of up to 20, narwhals aggregate and calve in midsummer while close inshore and then follow the advancing ice edge out to sea when winter begins. They may winter in permanently open pools in the sea ice known as polynyas. Narwhals and belugas are often seen together.

ABOVE: *If stranded, belugas seem unique in their ability to wait patiently for the next high tide to float off, although they may be attacked by polar bears while waiting.*

Both narwhals and belugas have a thickened ridge on their backs that may help them to break through thin ice to surface and breathe. They are heavily hunted throughout their range and preyed on by polar bears and orcas. The tusk probably plays a role in sexual competition between males. In one instance, a female appeared to have been inadvertently speared to death by a male competing with other suitors for her favors.

RIGHT: *The extraordinary tusk of the mature male narwhal, renowned as the "unicorn whale," was once the gift of kings and is still highly prized by hunters. Viewed from the head, the tusk always spirals to the left and may reach a length of 10 feet (3 m).*

Beaked whales

The 20 species of beaked whales make up the least known group of cetaceans. All are small to medium-size deepwater species with unobtrusive habits that make them difficult to identify, much less study. Their characteristic physical features are the lack of a central notch in the tail flukes, a single pair of throat grooves, a dorsal fin placed well back on the body, and a lower jaw that extends to or past the upper jaw. Size varies from the 42 foot (12.8 m) Baird's beaked whale to the 11 foot (3.7 m) Peruvian beaked whale.

Their apparent rarity may simply reflect their deep-sea habitat and reclusive habits. Some species, such as the southern bottlenose and Arnoux's beaked whales, are relatively abundant, and may number in the hundreds of thousands in Antarctic waters in summer. Others, however, are undoubtedly rare. For example, Longman's beaked whale is known from only two skulls, one from Somalia and the other from Queensland, Australia. New species are still being found, one as recently as 1991.

Beaked whales are all deep divers that feed predominantly on squid. Some species may dive as deep as sperm whales do. They have many fewer teeth than other whales, a feature that is characteristic of a squid diet. In most species, females have no functional teeth and males often have only one or two pairs in the lower jaw, which are sometimes exaggerated to the point of being tusks. Teeth appear to be used in fights or in mating, and beaked whales are often heavily scarred with parallel tracks. Little is known of their social lives but as many as 50 beaked whales have been seen together acting in a coordinated and gregarious manner.

BELOW: A group of Arnoux's beaked whales in the Southern Ocean. This rarely sighted whale has a distinctive beak and displays highly visible body scars caused by aggressive male behavior related to mating.

THE DOLPHIN FAMILY

The family Delphinidae, the oceanic dolphins and their relatives, contains the greatest number of species—at least 33 at the latest count—and the greatest diversity of any cetacean family. However, the number of dolphin species is uncertain. For example, while bottlenose dolphins are currently recognized as one species worldwide, differences in size, color, and habitat lead some scientists to believe that there may actually be two or three species. This group also includes orcas and their smaller relatives (such as pygmy killer whales) and pilot whales. Some researchers prefer to classify the killer whales and pilot whales as a family but, on the basis of anatomical and other similarities, they are closely related to the dolphins.

A RANGE OF VARIATION

Dolphins range in size from orcas, which reach more than 30 feet (9.5 m), to the black dolphins of Chile, at a little more than 5 feet (1.6 m). Geographically, some range worldwide, as do orcas; others, such as Hector's dolphin, which is found only around New Zealand, are restricted. Many are deep-ocean species, while a few, such as the tucuxi of the Amazon and the Irrawaddy dolphin of Australasia, haunt tropical rivers and tidal mangrove areas. Some, such as Fraser's dolphin, are strictly tropical; others, such as the northern right whale dolphin (one of only two dolphin species to lack a dorsal fin), are found only in cool water.

Social organization among dolphins is complex and highly structured. In many species, family groups stay together for life. Dolphins may form temporary groups of many thousands, apparently related to their feeding behavior. Cooperative behavior is very useful when herding prey, such as small schooling fish, or avoiding predators, such as sharks. In general, large concentrations of prey can attract large groups of animals. Many oceanic dolphins are nomads that roam the deep sea in large groups in search of schooling fish and squid; coastal and estuarine dolphins, which have a more predictable food supply, are more sedentary and form much smaller groups.

RIGHT: Members of the dolphin family display a beautiful and dramatic variation in their skin pigmentation. As this spotted dolphin mother and her calf show, these markings can change with age.

LEFT: Dolphins dig for buried fish. Those adapted to a fish diet have narrower heads than squid-eaters. Tooth number varies according to diet—squid-eaters have fewer teeth, while oceanic fish-eaters may have 250 or more teeth.

Porpoises and River Dolphins

Porpoises

There are only six species of porpoise. All are small animals, the largest being little more than 7 feet (2.1 m) long. The vaquita, at slightly less than 5 feet (1.5 m), is the smallest of all cetaceans. Porpoises typically have small flippers and no beak and, except for the finless porpoises, all have a dorsal fin. Unlike the conical teeth of dolphins, the teeth are flattened to cutting edges, which enables porpoises to slice their prey. Porpoises usually form smaller social groups than dolphins do.

For such a small group, they are distributed remarkably widely around the globe. Several are basically coastal in their habitats. The vaquita, which occurs only in the northern part of the Gulf of California, is the most restricted in its range. Severely threatened by gillnet fisheries, it is one of the rarest and most endangered cetaceans. The harbor porpoise, on the other hand, is common along the North Atlantic and North Pacific coasts, where it bottom feeds in turbid water. Finless porpoises share much of the habitat of the Irrawaddy dolphin, inhabiting the warm shallow coasts, estuaries, and rivers of Asia but not penetrating south to Australia. Burmeister's porpoise prefers the cooler waters of the coasts along the southern half of South America, extending farther north on the Pacific coast due to the cold Humboldt Current. Dall's porpoise inhabits the cooler waters of the North Pacific, from Japan to California.

The spectacled porpoise is the least known porpoise. Its distribution, in the cool waters of the Southern Ocean, makes it difficult to study, and there have been few sightings at sea. Occasional strandings suggest that the spectacled porpoise may live in coastal waters, but a pattern of strandings and sightings at subantarctic islands points more strongly to

RIGHT: Dall's porpoise is the most striking of the porpoises, both in color and shape. It is usually found close to land, but sightings have occurred well offshore. Renowned as the fastest of all cetaceans, its skeletal adaptations allow heavy muscling for propulsion. It is also a relatively deep diver.

a circumpolar distribution. Almost nothing is known of its diet, biology, and behavior. Only one or two at a time have ever been sighted.

River Dolphins

Several species of river dolphin are also among the rarest and most threatened cetaceans. The obvious similarities among the five existing species may represent converging evolutionary paths from unrelated ancestors rather than close evolutionary relationships. As with many cetacean groups, their classification is still under debate. River dolphins are regarded as the most primitive group of cetaceans.

All river dolphins show specialized riverine habitat adaptations: broad pectoral fins to aid maneuverability; and a mobile neck that allows them to move their heads from side to side, possibly for scanning with echolocation. The Yangtze River dolphin and the La Plata dolphin each has a single dorsal fin; the other species have merely a dorsal ridge. Another unusual development in this group is their small eyes: some of them, such as the Ganges River dolphin, are functionally blind. They live in water that is almost permanently muddy, and rely totally on echolocation to find prey.

The La Plata dolphin is regarded as the most primitive of the group and occurs in nearshore waters along the Atlantic coast of South America, but the other river dophins have colonized some of the greatest of rivers—the Amazon, the Ganges, the Indus, and the Yangtze. They have apparently adapted to the cycles of flooding and drought that characterize these rivers. For example, during the rainy season, the Amazon River dolphin may even leave the river and forage in flooded grasslands; it has been filmed swimming among tree trunks in the flooded Brazilian rain forest.

ABOVE: River dolphins, such as this Yangtze River dolphin, have elongated, narrow beaks containing many small teeth. This reflects an adaptation to a fish diet, although these dolphins also eat mollusks, crustaceans, and even turtles.

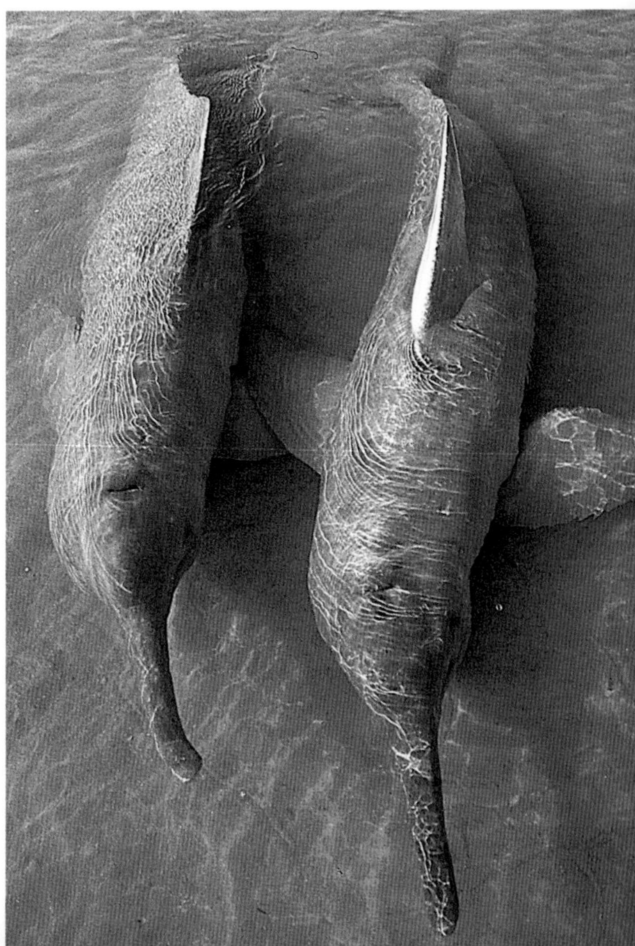

RIGHT: The Amazon River dolphin inhabits the muddy waters of the Amazon and Orinoco River basins of South America.

Identifying Whales

The world of whales displays a rich diversity. Whales vary greatly in their size, shape, and color, as well as in their distribution, ecology, behavior, and breeding patterns. There are numerous differences between species, often subtle, which allow them to be identified. This chapter examines the distinctive features of many species.

How to Use the Whale Identification Guide

The Identification Guide is a practical introduction to many of the world's important whale species. You can use it not only to identify whales you see in the field but also to learn in advance about those you are most likely to encounter. Information is included about the habitat and distribution of each species, which is particularly useful if you are planning to go whale-watching and want to know what species occur in your region.

The guide is divided into two main sections, one on baleen whales and one on toothed whales; and each of these sections, in turn, is divided into families, and then into species. Included are 48 cetacean species in all—those whales most likely to be sighted, as well as some of the more unusual species. Whales that are rarely sighted, or have never been seen alive, have been omitted. Each entry includes the following features:

Two Sections
This guide treats the two suborders in separate color-coded sections. The baleen whales have blue banding and the toothed whales have green.

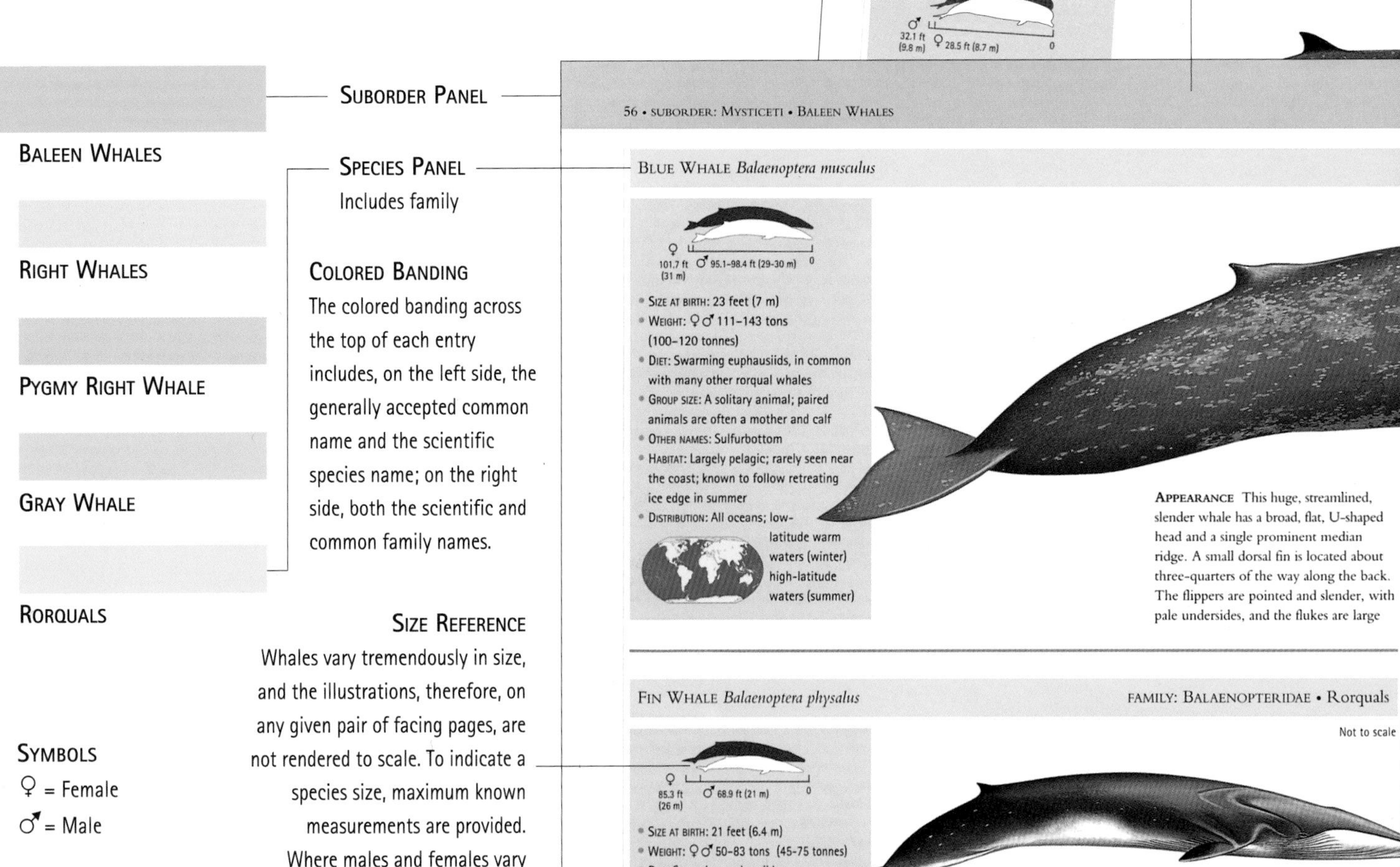

64 • suborder: Odontoceti • Dolphins

Northern Bottlenose Whale *Hyperoodon ampullatus* Family: Ziphiidae

♂ 32.1 ft (9.8 m) ♀ 28.5 ft (8.7 m) 0

56 • suborder: Mysticeti • Baleen Whales

Blue Whale *Balaenoptera musculus*

♀ 101.7 ft (31 m) ♂ 95.1–98.4 ft (29–30 m) 0

- Size at birth: 23 feet (7 m)
- Weight: ♀♂ 111–143 tons (100–120 tonnes)
- Diet: Swarming euphausiids, in common with many other rorqual whales
- Group size: A solitary animal; paired animals are often a mother and calf
- Other names: Sulfurbottom
- Habitat: Largely pelagic; rarely seen near the coast; known to follow retreating ice edge in summer
- Distribution: All oceans; low-latitude warm waters (winter) high-latitude waters (summer)

Appearance This huge, streamlined, slender whale has a broad, flat, U-shaped head and a single prominent median ridge. A small dorsal fin is located about three-quarters of the way along the back. The flippers are pointed and slender, with pale undersides, and the flukes are large

Fin Whale *Balaenoptera physalus* Family: Balaenopteridae • Rorquals

Not to scale

♀ 85.3 ft (26 m) ♂ 68.9 ft (21 m) 0

- Size at birth: 21 feet (6.4 m)
- Weight: ♀♂ 50–83 tons (45–75 tonnes)
- Diet: Swarming euphausiids; some fish such as capelin and herring
- Group size: Groups of 6–10 animals; can also occur in pairs or single animals
- Other names: Common rorqual, razorback, finn, finback
- Habitat: Generally open ocean, can be seen near the coast; migration geared to season and food supply
- Distribution: From the tropics to polar waters, in all oceans

Appearance A distinctive color pattern is the most noticeable feature of this large, sleek, streamlined whale. Body color is a dark gray to black, with the throat, belly, and undersides of the flippers and tail flukes being white. The head has an asymmetrical pigmentation: the right lower jaw is white, while the left is mostly dark. Baleen plates are creamy white for the first third of the right side; the rest are dark gray, often with yellow to cream stripes. A light gray "chevron" pattern may occur behind the head.

Reproduction Gestation period is 11 months, and a single young is born mid-winter. Sexual maturity for Southern Hemisphere males is 62 feet (19 m), and females 65.6 feet (20 m). Northern Hemisphere whales are smaller: males mature at 57–60 feet (17.4–18.3 m), and females at 60–62 feet (18.3–19 m).

Suborder Panel

Baleen Whales

Right Whales

Pygmy Right Whale

Gray Whale

Rorquals

Species Panel
Includes family

Colored Banding
The colored banding across the top of each entry includes, on the left side, the generally accepted common name and the scientific species name; on the right side, both the scientific and common family names.

Size Reference
Whales vary tremendously in size, and the illustrations, therefore, on any given pair of facing pages, are not rendered to scale. To indicate a species size, maximum known measurements are provided. Where males and females vary in size significantly, outlines drawn to scale are included.

Symbols
♀ = Female
♂ = Male

Specifications
A bulleted list of facts about each species is included for fast fact finding.

Distribution Map
Provides at-a-glance information on the worldwide distribution of each species.

Illustration
A finely detailed color illustration depicts the form, coloration, and markings of each species to help identify it in the field. As such features vary among individuals, the illustration gives the most representative example.

Appearance A physical description of each species appears in the text beneath the illustration to help readers make accurate identifications from what may be only fleeting glimpses in the field.

Reproduction The lengths at sexual maturity, where known, are provided to assist readers in distinguishing adults from juveniles.

Weight and Length Both English and metric figures are given. Birth sizes indicate the minimum lengths of species; adult lengths, the maximum.

Diet The main prey known to be taken by each species are listed.

Group Size The typical group size for each species aids in identification.

Other Names If a species is known by more than one common name, the alternative names are listed.

Habitat The environments in which the species is known to live are provided.

Distribution Both text and a map describe the range of each species. It is very helpful to know where whale species are likely to be seen when you are planning to undertake any field trips to go whale-watching.

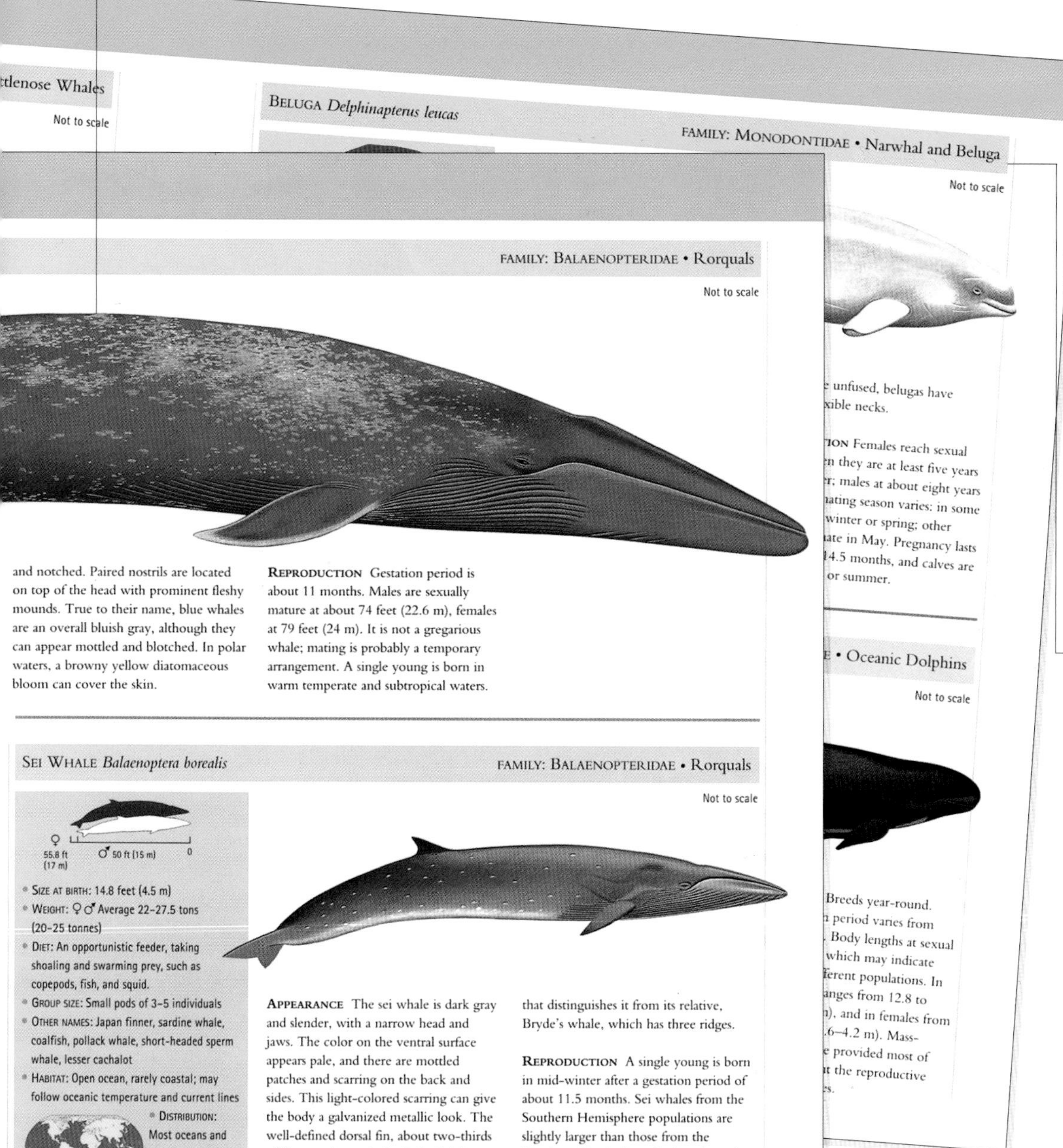

Toothed Whales

Sperm Whale

Small Sperm Whales

Beaked & Bottlenose Whales

Narwhal & Beluga

Oceanic Dolphins

Porpoises

Amazon River Dolphin

Yangtze & La Plata Dolphins

Ganges & Indus River Dolphins

Description
Appearance and Reproduction

NORTHERN RIGHT WHALE *Eubalaena glacialis*

FAMILY: BALAENIDAE • Right Whales

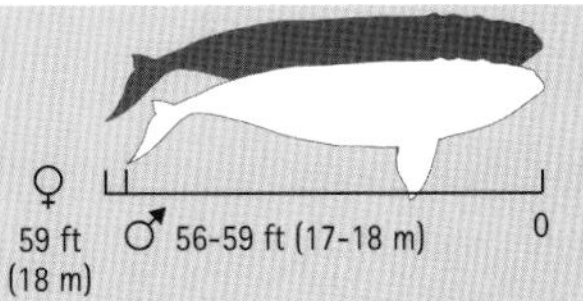

- SIZE AT BIRTH: 15–20 ft (4.5–6 m)
- WEIGHT: ♀♂ 40–80 tons/tonnes
- DIET: A specialized feeder; prefers small planktonic animals like copepods and krill
- GROUP SIZE: 1–3; occasionally larger groups (10–12) form on breeding or feeding grounds
- OTHER NAMES: Black right whale, Biscayan right whale
- HABITAT: Temperate and subpolar waters; sometimes coastal areas and shallow bays
- DISTRIBUTION: North Pacific, west coast of USA, Japan, and eastern and western sides of the North Atlantic

Not to scale

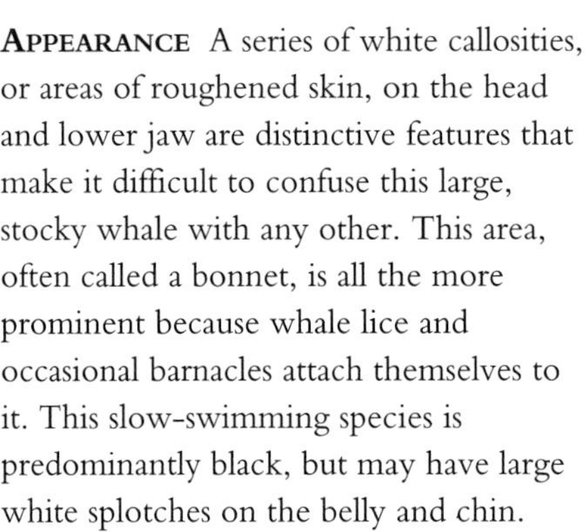

APPEARANCE A series of white callosities, or areas of roughened skin, on the head and lower jaw are distinctive features that make it difficult to confuse this large, stocky whale with any other. This area, often called a bonnet, is all the more prominent because whale lice and occasional barnacles attach themselves to it. This slow-swimming species is predominantly black, but may have large white splotches on the belly and chin. Right whales have massive heads, up to one-quarter of the total body length. They lack a dorsal fin, and their flippers are broad and fan-shaped.

REPRODUCTION Gestation period is unknown, possibly 12 months. Males are sexually mature at 46–50 feet (14–15 m), females at 43–50 feet (13–15 m). Contact between the sexes is restricted to mating. Calving is probably at three-year intervals.

BOWHEAD WHALE *Balaena mysticetus*

FAMILY: BALAENIDAE • Right Whales

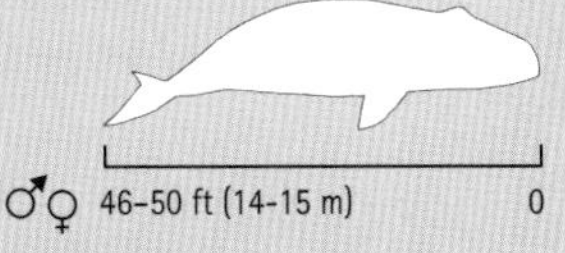

- SIZE AT BIRTH: 13 ft (4 m)
- WEIGHT: ♀♂ 50–60 tons/tonnes
- DIET: Primarily a surface feeder; eats very small crustaceans, including copepods, steropods, and krill
- GROUP SIZE: Average group size is 3 or fewer; 50 or more during migration
- OTHER NAMES: Greenland right whale, Greenland whale
- HABITAT: Arctic and subarctic waters
- DISTRIBUTION: North Atlantic Ocean; Bering, Beaufort, Chukchi, and Okhotsk seas

Not to scale

APPEARANCE This large, rotund, black whale has a massive head and a white chin patch. Like the right whales, it lacks a dorsal fin. The mouthline has a bowed appearance, emphasized by a strongly arched narrow upper jaw. The baleen of bowheads is the longest of any whale; the middle plates measure 14 feet (4.3 m) and are dark and blackish with fine, paler fringes. Recognition at sea is often by the characteristic bushy V-shaped blow, small rounded flippers and what appears to be a light gray to white band around the tail stock. Bowheads can break through sea ice in order to breathe.

REPRODUCTION Gestation period is 12–16 months. Males are sexually mature at 37½ feet (11.5 m) and females at 43–46 feet (13–14 m). Calving occurs in mid-winter, when a single young is born. Occasionally, twins are born.

Pygmy Right Whale *Caperea marginata*

FAMILY: NEOBALAENIDAE • Pygmy Right Whale

Not to scale

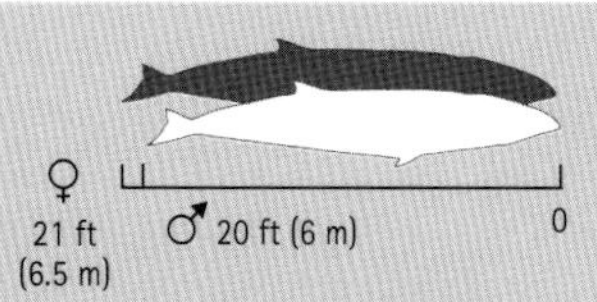

- Size at birth: Approximately 6½ ft (2 m)
- Weight: Very few have been weighed; ♀ estimated at 3.5 tons/tonnes ♂ estimated at 3.1 tons/tonnes
- Diet: The fine bristles of the baleen suggest very small prey, such as copepods
- Group size: Single or pairs
- Other names: None
- Habitat: Between latitudes of 30°S and 52°S
- Distribution: Stranding information provides the only clues to the possible migrations of this species. Most strandings have occurred on the southern coasts of Australia and South Africa

Appearance This small, streamlined animal is rarely sighted at sea. It shares some features with right and bowhead whales, such as a strongly bowed lower jaw, but there are also differences. It possesses a dorsal fin, and the flippers are more like those of the rorquals, being narrow and rounded. The body color varies, from black or gray on the back to a lighter gray or white on the belly. The baleen plates are narrow and number 210–230 on each side. The baleen are yellowish white, with a brown margin, ending in a fringe of fine, soft bristles. The species name of this whale, *marginata*, refers to the marginal band on the baleen.

Reproduction Little information is available on the reproductive history of this rare whale. Calving probably occurs in the fall–winter period, possibly with an extended breeding season.

Gray Whale *Eschrichtius robustus*

FAMILY: ESCHRICHTIDAE • Gray Whale

Not to scale

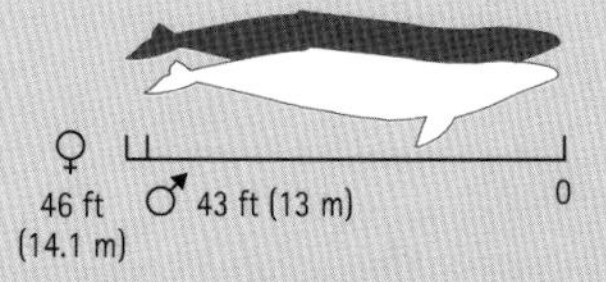

- Size at birth: 15 ft (4.6 m)
- Weight: ♀♂ 14–35 tons/tonnes
- Diet: A seafloor feeder, eating shrimp-like amphipods, polychaete worms, and mollusks
- Group size: Generally 1–3; traveling groups can contain up to 16; good feeding conditions can attract hundreds of whales
- Other names: Mussel digger, hard head, devil fish, gray back
- Habitat: Coastal waters, usually less than 33 feet (10 m) deep, and above the continental shelf
- Distribution: Western and eastern sides of the North Pacific

Appearance The gray whale has a relatively small, narrow, triangular head, and a series of bumps along the rear third of the dorsal ridge instead of a true dorsal fin. The flippers are pointed and paddle-like, with a notched tail fluke measuring 10 feet (3 m) from tip to tip. Overall body color is mottled gray with numerous encrusted patches of yellowish white or orange barnacles and whale lice. The extent of these parasites can indicate the general health of an individual. The blow is "heart-shaped," vertical to about 10-15 feet (3–4.5 m), and loud.

Reproduction Gestation period is about 13.5 months, with approximately two years between pregnancies. Males are sexually mature at 36½ feet (11.1 m) and females at 38½ feet (11.7 m). Young are born during a brief period of 5–6 weeks beginning in late December.

BLUE WHALE *Balaenoptera musculus*

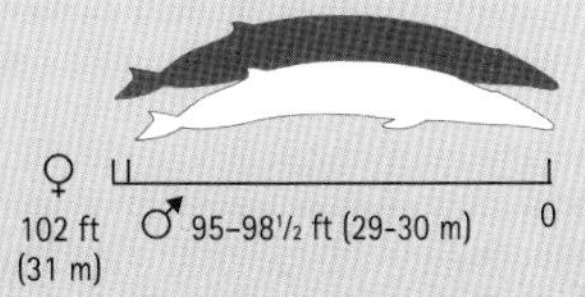

- SIZE AT BIRTH: 23 feet (7 m)
- WEIGHT: ♀♂ 100–120 tons/tonnes
- DIET: Swarming euphausiids, in common with many other rorqual whales
- GROUP SIZE: A solitary animal; paired animals are often a mother and calf
- OTHER NAMES: Sulfurbottom
- HABITAT: Largely pelagic; rarely seen near the coast; known to follow retreating ice edge in summer
- DISTRIBUTION: All oceans; frequents low-latitude warm waters (winter), high-latitude waters (summer)

APPEARANCE This huge, streamlined, slender whale has a broad, flat, U-shaped head and a single prominent median ridge. A small dorsal fin is located about three-quarters of the way along the back. The flippers are pointed and slender, with pale undersides, and the flukes are large

FIN WHALE *Balaenoptera physalus*

Not to scale

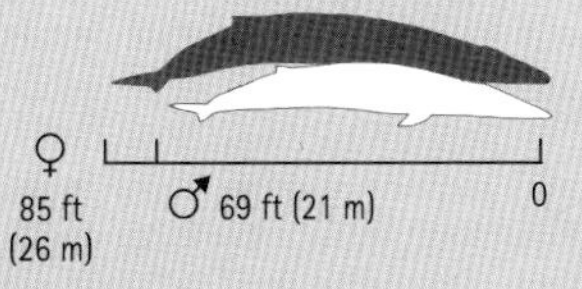

- SIZE AT BIRTH: 21 feet (6.4 m)
- WEIGHT: ♀♂ 45-75 tonnes/tons
- DIET: Swarming euphausiids; some fish such as capelin and herring
- GROUP SIZE: Groups of 6-10 animals; can also occur in pairs or single animals
- OTHER NAMES: Common rorqual, razorback, finn, finback
- HABITAT: Generally open ocean, can be seen near the coast; migration geared to season and food supply
- DISTRIBUTION: From the tropics to polar waters, in all oceans

APPEARANCE A distinctive color pattern is the most noticeable feature of this large, sleek, streamlined whale. Body color is a dark gray to black, with the throat, belly, and undersides of the flippers and tail flukes being white. The head has an asymmetrical pigmentation: the right lower jaw is white, while the left is mostly dark. Baleen plates are creamy white for the first third of the right side; the rest are dark gray, often with yellow to cream stripes. A light gray "chevron" pattern may occur behind the head.

REPRODUCTION Gestation period is 11 months, and a single young is born mid-winter. Sexual maturity for Southern Hemisphere males is 62 feet (19 m), and females 65½ feet (20 m). Northern Hemisphere whales are smaller: males mature at 57–60 feet (17.4–18.3 m), and females at 60–62 feet (18.3–19 m).

Not to scale

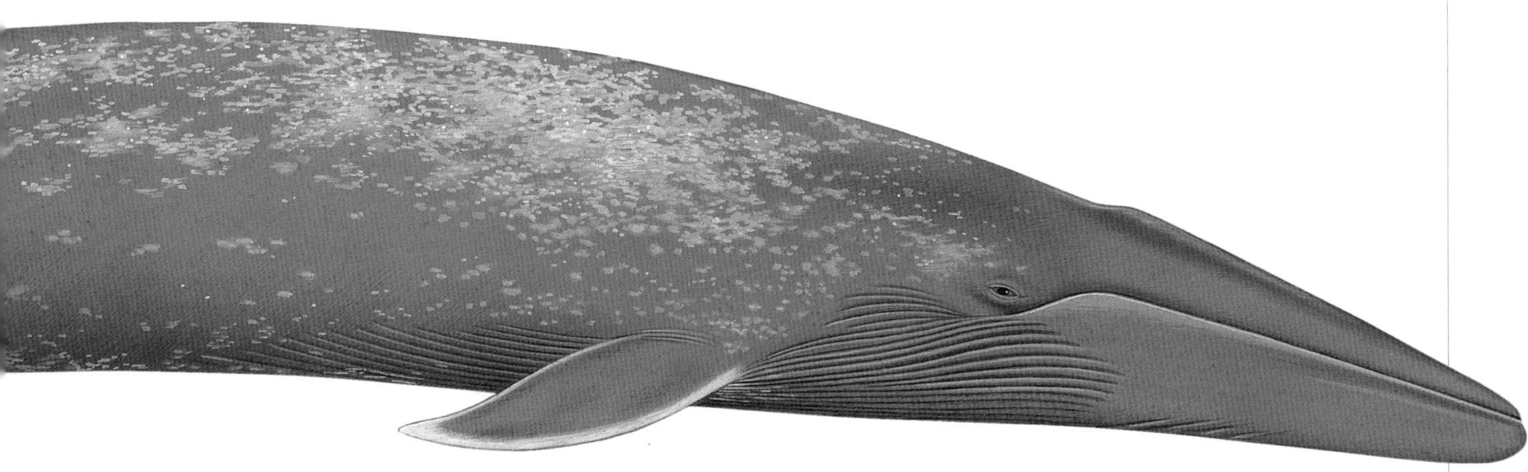

and notched. Paired nostrils are located on top of the head with prominent fleshy mounds. True to their name, blue whales are an overall bluish gray, although they can appear mottled and blotched. In polar waters, a browny yellow diatomaceous bloom can cover the skin.

REPRODUCTION Gestation period is about 11 months. Males are sexually mature at about 74 feet (22.6 m), females at 79 feet (24 m). It is not a gregarious whale; mating is probably a temporary arrangement. A single young is born in warm temperate and subtropical waters.

SEI WHALE *Balaenoptera borealis*

FAMILY: BALAENOPTERIDAE • Rorquals

Not to scale

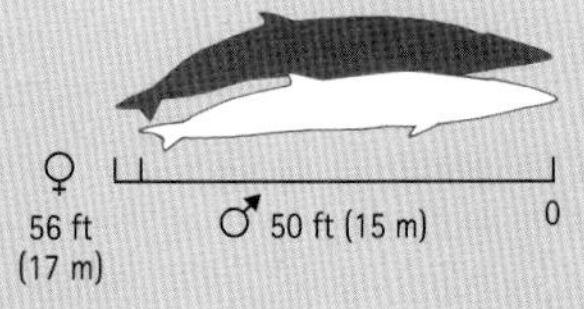

- SIZE AT BIRTH: 15 feet (4.5 m)
- WEIGHT: ♀♂ Average 20–25 tons/tonnes
- DIET: An opportunistic feeder, taking shoaling and swarming prey, such as copepods, fish, and squid
- GROUP SIZE: Small pods of 3–5 individuals
- OTHER NAMES: Japan finner, sardine whale, coalfish, pollack whale, short-headed sperm whale, lesser cachalot
- HABITAT: Open ocean, rarely coastal; may follow oceanic temperature and current lines
- DISTRIBUTION: Most oceans and seas, but rarely in polar areas

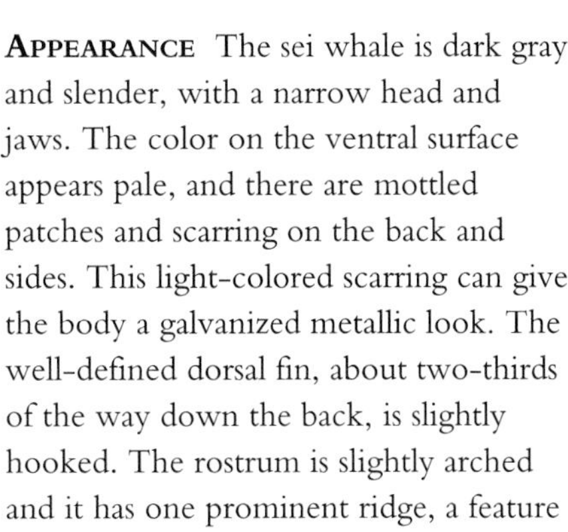

APPEARANCE The sei whale is dark gray and slender, with a narrow head and jaws. The color on the ventral surface appears pale, and there are mottled patches and scarring on the back and sides. This light-colored scarring can give the body a galvanized metallic look. The well-defined dorsal fin, about two-thirds of the way down the back, is slightly hooked. The rostrum is slightly arched and it has one prominent ridge, a feature that distinguishes it from its relative, Bryde's whale, which has three ridges.

REPRODUCTION A single young is born in mid-winter after a gestation period of about 11.5 months. Sei whales from the Southern Hemisphere populations are slightly larger than those from the Northern Hemisphere. Both males and females are sexually mature at about 92–95 percent of their adult length.

BRYDE'S WHALE *Balaenoptera edeni*

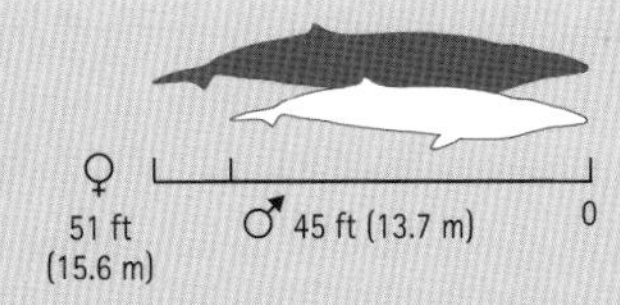

- SIZE AT BIRTH: 10–13 feet (3–4 m)
- WEIGHT: ♀♂ 16–18 tons/tonnes
- DIET: Generally larger size prey, often shoaling fish species; will also feed on krill
- GROUP SIZE: Over a few square miles, aggregations of 10–23 can be seen; mostly found alone or in pairs
- OTHER NAMES: None
- HABITAT: Some resident inshore animals, others offshore and migratory. All prefer warm waters above 68°F (20°C)
- DISTRIBUTION: Worldwide in tropical and temperate oceans

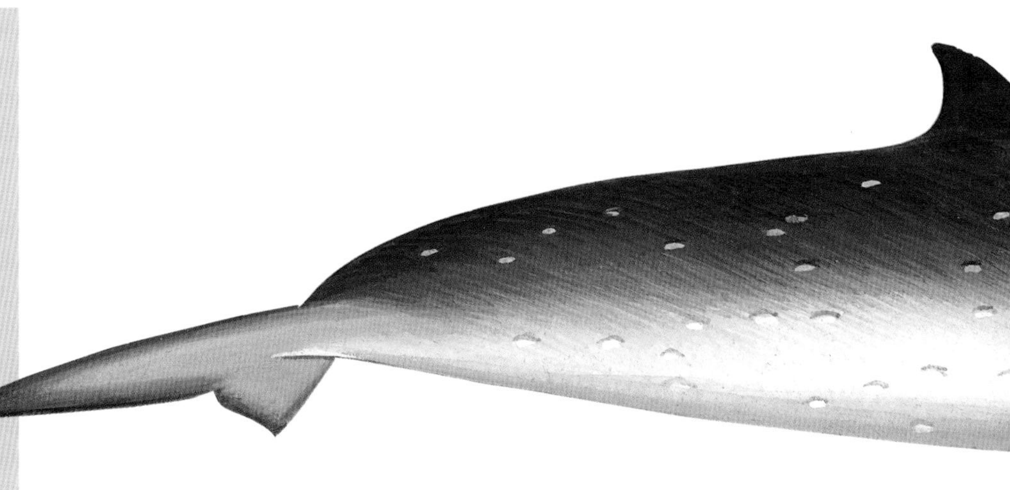

APPEARANCE Bryde's whale (which is pronounced *brood-ess*) is often confused with the sei whale, because it is quite similar in both size and appearance. However, the major difference is that Bryde's whale possesses three head ridges. In general, this whale is dark gray, with some white on the throat and chin. The dorsal fin is well-defined and sickle-shaped. It is positioned about two-thirds of the way down the back. Stocky in its appearance, this species has pointed, relatively short flippers, and rather pale gray to black baleen bristles.

HUMPBACK WHALE *Megaptera novaeangliae*

FAMILY: BALAENOPTERIDAE • Rorquals

Not to scale

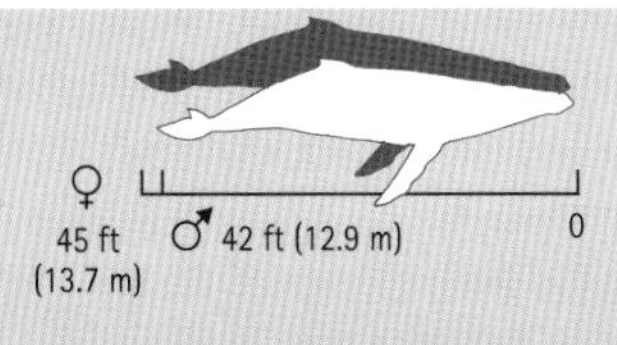

- SIZE AT BIRTH: Average of 14 feet (4.3 m)
- WEIGHT: ♀♂ 25–30 tons/tonnes
- DIET: Krill, generally euphausiids; also some schooling fish, such as mackerel and herring
- GROUP SIZE: 1–3 when migrating; can gather in larger numbers when feeding or breeding
- OTHER NAMES: None in English; *baleine a bosse* in French, *rorcual jorobado* in Spanish
- HABITAT: Considered relatively shallow-water animals, humpbacks migrate thousands of miles between the tropics and polar regions each year
- DISTRIBUTION: Widely distributed around the world

APPEARANCE Highly visible, and probably the most familiar of the large whales, the humpback is a very acrobatic animal, and it occasionally breaches quite spectacularly. It has a stout black-and-white body and the characteristic long flippers generally have white undersides. The dorsal flukes are large, and the undersides have a mixed pattern of black and white, a feature that is useful in identifying individual animals. As with other rorquals, the ventral area, from the chin to the abdomen, contains a series of pleats or grooves that allow the throat to expand while the animal is feeding.

REPRODUCTION Young are born in warm waters during late fall and winter after an extensive migration. Gestation period is 11-11.5 months. Sexual maturity in males is reached at 38 feet (11.5 m), and in females at 40 feet (12 m).

Not to scale

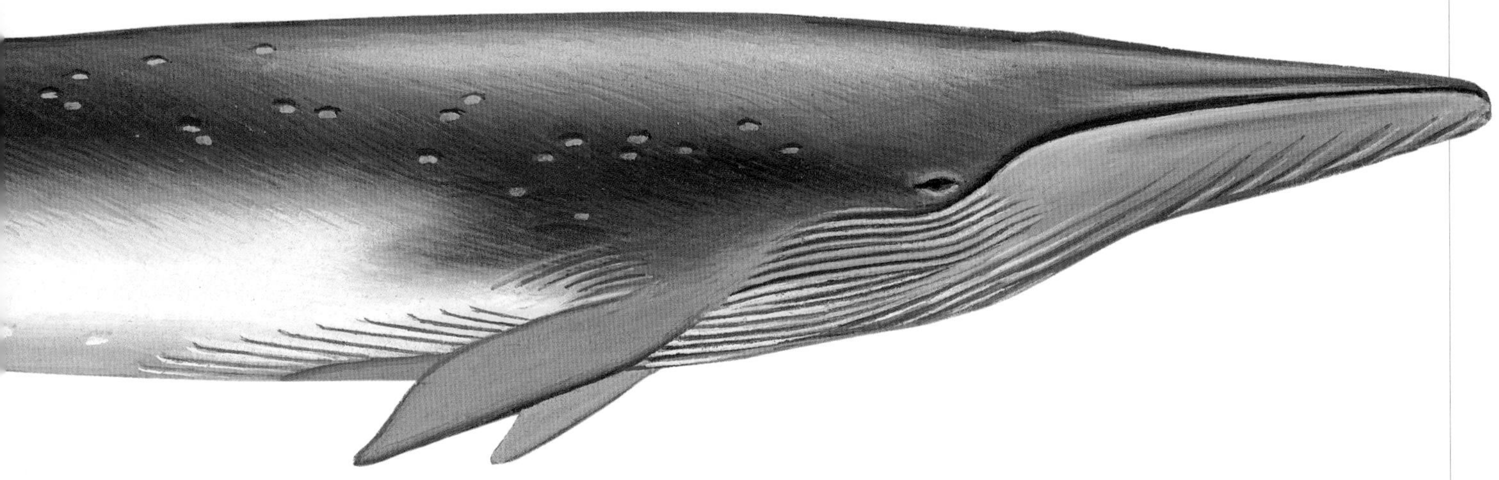

REPRODUCTION The existence of inshore and offshore forms of this species makes it difficult to define a particular breeding season. Calves are born after a 12-month gestation period, then probably suckled for about six months. Males can reproduce at 38-41 feet (11.6-12.4 m), females at 40-42 feet (12-12.8 m).

MINKE WHALE *Balaenoptera acutorostrata*

FAMILY: BALAENOPTERIDAE • Rorquals

Not to scale

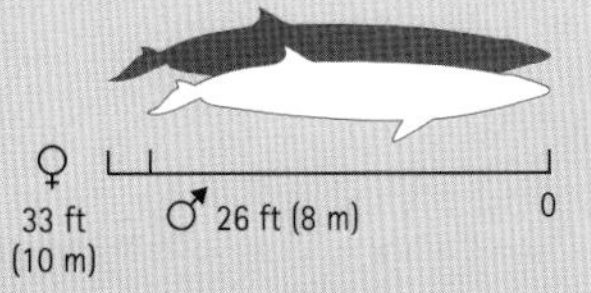

- SIZE AT BIRTH: 8–9 feet (2.4–2.8 m)
- WEIGHT: ♀♂ 8–13 tons/tonnes
- DIET: Preferred prey is krill; also some fish, and occasionally small, free-swimming mollusks
- GROUP SIZE: Generally solitary or groups of 2–3; larger aggregations when feeding
- OTHER NAMES: Lesser rorqual, pikehead
- HABITAT: Generally open ocean; can be found near the ice edge in polar areas
- DISTRIBUTION: Worldwide, with populations in the Southern Hemisphere, and the North Pacific and North Atlantic oceans

APPEARANCE The smallest of the rorquals and the second smallest of the baleen whales, the minke has a pointed head and prominent median ridge. Its tall, sickle-shaped dorsal fin is about two-thirds of the way down the back. Generally a dark slate gray, the color changes to a paler gray or white on the belly. Some shading occurs on the sides, and in some animals a prominent white band can be found across each flipper. Behind the head, there may also be a paler area that resembles a small cape.

REPRODUCTION Mating probably occurs in late winter. A single young is born in low-latitude waters, after a 10-month gestation period. At sexual maturity, Southern Hemisphere whales are larger than Northern Hemisphere ones. The average length is 23 feet (7 m) for males, 24 feet (7.3 m) for females.

SPERM WHALE *Physeter macrocephalus*

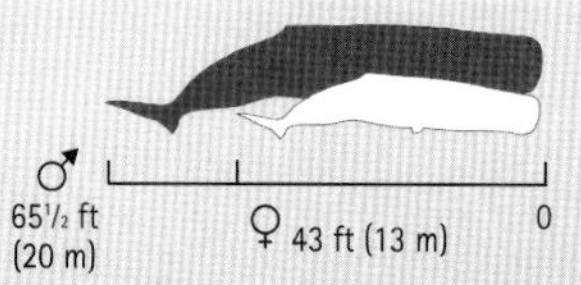

- SIZE AT BIRTH: 13 feet (4 m)
- WEIGHT: Ranges from ♂ 45 ton/tonnes to ♀ 20 tons/tonnes
- DIET: Almost exclusively cephalopods (squid and octopus)
- GROUP SIZE: Occurs in family groups of 10–20 animals
- OTHER NAMES: Cachalot, lesser sperm whale, short-headed sperm whale, lesser cachalot
- HABITAT: Oceanic; prefers deep waters, especially around volcanic islands
- DISTRIBUTION: All oceans, females and young prefer water above 59°F (15°C); adult males also inhabit polar waters

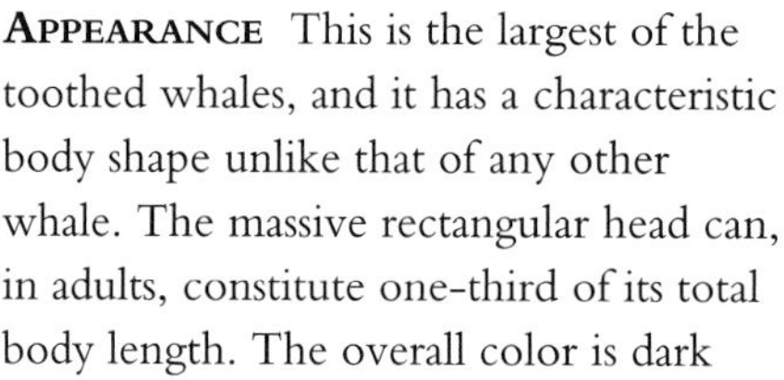

APPEARANCE This is the largest of the toothed whales, and it has a characteristic body shape unlike that of any other whale. The massive rectangular head can, in adults, constitute one-third of its total body length. The overall color is dark brown, gray, or occasionally black, and there is a light gray ventral patch. Older animals, especially males, often bear scars on the head resulting from fights with other males, and there may also be sucker marks of large squid. The 50 large conical

PYGMY SPERM WHALE *Kogia breviceps*

FAMILY: KOGIIDAE • Small Sperm Whales

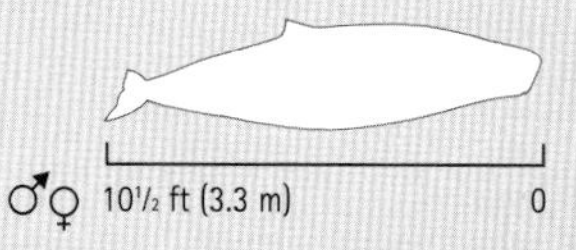

- SIZE AT BIRTH: 4 feet (1.2 m)
- WEIGHT: ♀♂ 900 lb (400 kg)
- DIET: Primarily oceanic squid; some small numbers of fish and deep-sea shrimp
- GROUP SIZE: Small groups of fewer than 5 individuals; a difficult species to observe at sea, but frequently found stranded
- OTHER NAMES: None
- HABITAT: Oceanic; tends to stay close to or over the continental slope
- DISTRIBUTION: Probably occurs in widely distributed areas, including temperate, subtropical, and tropical seas

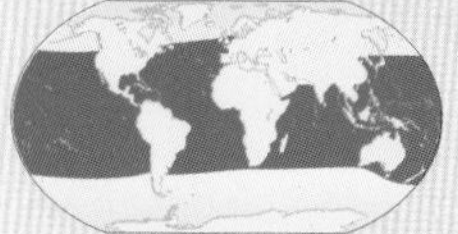

Not to scale

APPEARANCE A large bulbous snout gives this small, robust whale its shark-like appearance. The short, narrow mouth under the head has 12–16 curved, needle-shaped teeth on each side of the lower jaw. In adults, the head takes on a rectangular shape. Viewed from above, the dorsal surface of the body is dark bluish gray. The ventral surface is a paler, often slightly pinkish, color. A small dorsal fin is located behind the mid-point of the back. This species is difficult to distinguish at sea from its nearest relative, the dwarf sperm whale.

REPRODUCTION The little that is known about the pygmy sperm whale's reproduction has been obtained from stranded animals. Calving is probably annual, and the gestation period is about 11 months. Sexual maturity is reached at 9–10 feet (2.7–3 m).

Not to scale

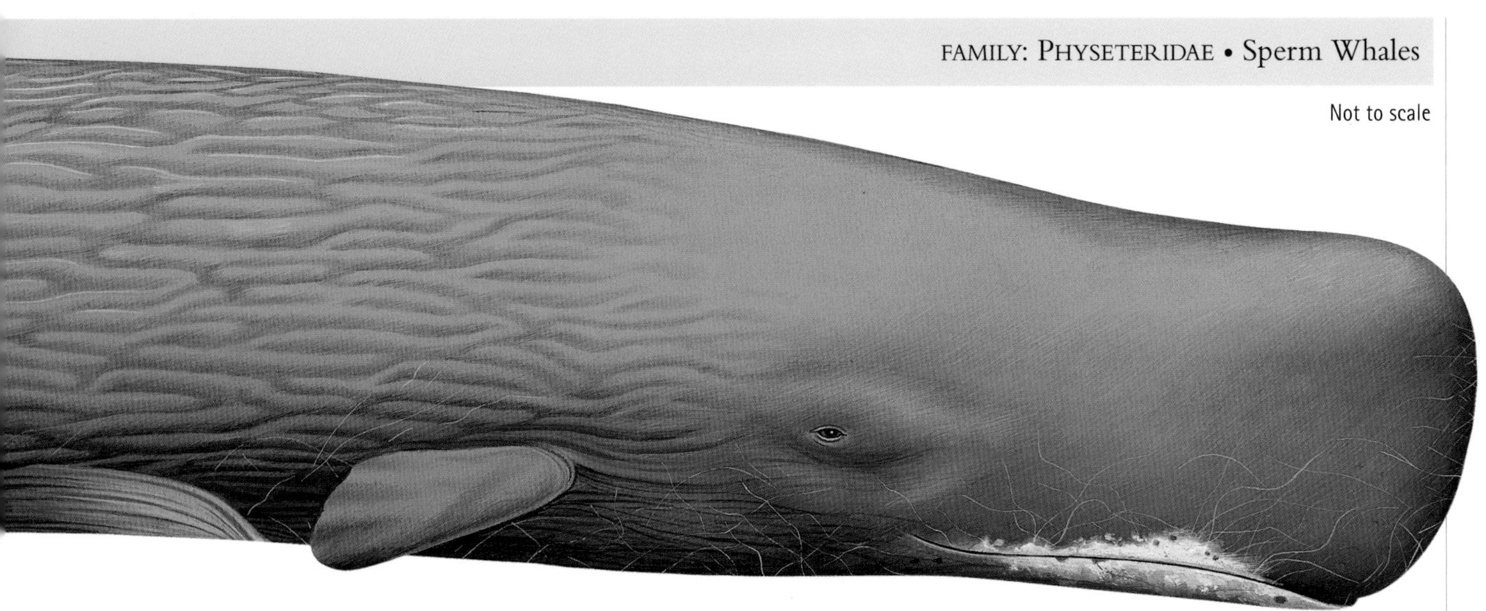

teeth, often carved by whalers in the art of scrimshaw, are arranged in parallel rows on both sides of the lower jaw.

REPRODUCTION This is a slow-breeding species with calves born in summer and fall after a gestation period of 14-15 months. Sperm whales exhibit extreme sexual dimorphism in favor of the males. Females can reproduce at about 26–29½ feet (8–9 m); males when they are 36–39 feet (11–12 m) long.

DWARF SPERM WHALE *Kogia simus*

FAMILY: KOGIIDAE • Small Sperm Whales

Not to scale

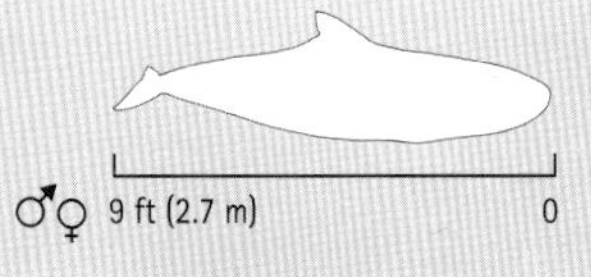

- SIZE AT BIRTH: About 3 feet (1 m)
- WEIGHT: ♀♂ 463 lb (210 kg)
- DIET: The very small mouth of this species indicates that the prey is small; it is thought to be mainly tiny cuttlefish
- GROUP SIZE: Up to 10 individuals, including calves, females, and males
- OTHER NAMES: Until relatively recently this species was included with *K. breviceps*
- HABITAT: Known mostly from strandings, it seems to live exclusively on or near continental slopes

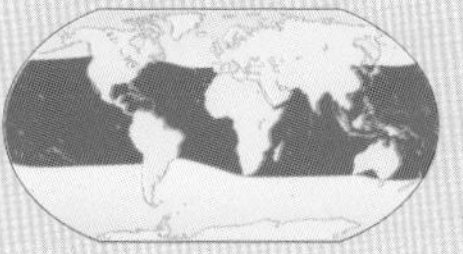

- DISTRIBUTION: Sporadic; in tropical and temperate seas

APPEARANCE The dwarf sperm whale is very similar in appearance to the pygmy sperm whale; the major differences occur in the head area. The adult dwarf sperm whale's short snout is blunt and squarish, and there are one or two short, irregular grooves on the throat behind the tiny mouth. It also possesses far fewer teeth; there are only 7–12 in each side of the lower jaw. Some teeth (about three pairs) can also occur in the tip of the upper jaw. The dorsal fin is tall and broad-based, with a concave trailing edge, and resembles that of dolphins.

REPRODUCTION Little is known about many aspects of this species' reproductive behavior. Gestation is about nine months and calving occurs over a period of several months during summer. Both sexes are about 6½–7½ feet (2–2.2 m) long when they reach sexual maturity.

BAIRD'S BEAKED WHALE *Berardius bairdii*

FAMILY: ZIPHIIDAE • Beaked and Bottlenose Whales

Not to scale

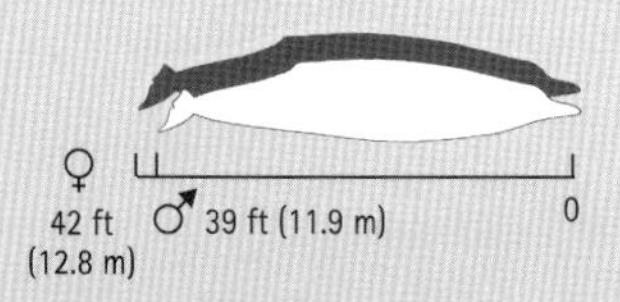

- SIZE AT BIRTH: 15 feet (4.5 m)
- WEIGHT: ♀♂ 11–12 tons/tonnes
- DIET: Mostly bottom-dwelling organisms, such as squid, skate, and crustaceans
- GROUP SIZE: A social animal, often gathering in groups of up to 50 individuals
- OTHER NAMES: Bottlenose whale; in Japan where most exploitation takes place it is called *tsuchi-kujira* or *tsuchimbo*
- HABITAT: Generally restricted to above the continental slope and oceanic seamounts
- DISTRIBUTION: North Pacific Ocean (including California), and the Japan, Okhotsk, and Bering seas

APPEARANCE The largest member of its family, Baird's beaked whale is an impressive animal, with a long, well-defined beak and a bulging forehead. The lower jaw is longer than the upper jaw, making the front pair of teeth clearly visible, even when the mouth is closed. There is another pair of slightly smaller teeth farther back in the lower jaw. The relatively slender body is a uniform brownish gray, with a pattern of scratches and marks that become more numerous as the animal ages. The underside, especially around the throat, is often covered with irregular blotches of white.

REPRODUCTION The peak season for calving is March–April, and the estimated gestation period is 17 months. Females are about 34½ feet (10.5 m) long when they are ready to breed; males are slightly smaller at 33 feet (10 m).

BLAINVILLE'S BEAKED WHALE *Mesoplodon densirostris*

FAMILY: ZIPHIIDAE • Beaked and Bottlenose Whales

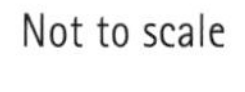

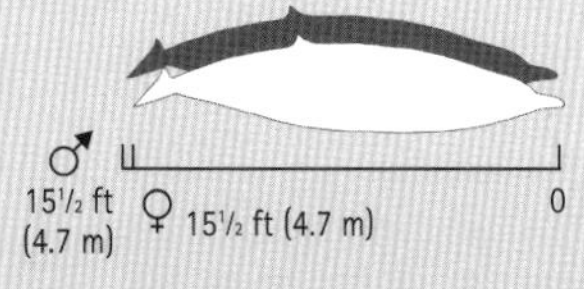

- SIZE AT BIRTH: 6½–8 feet (2–2.5 m)
- WEIGHT: ♀♂ 1 ton/tonne
- DIET: Possibly squid and some fish
- GROUP SIZE: Pods of 3–7 individuals have been recorded; single animals and pairs have also been sighted
- OTHER NAMES: Dense beaked whale, Atlantic beaked whale
- HABITAT: Warm temperate to tropical waters, mostly offshore in deep water
- DISTRIBUTION: This species has the widest distribution of all the *Mesoplodons*, and has been recorded in all oceans

APPEARANCE An adult male Blainsville's beaked whale is striking and distinctive in its appearance. Two massive teeth are located on prominent raised arches on each side of the lower jaw. These forward-projecting teeth can protrude higher than the flattened forehead, and are often covered with barnacles. Males of this species are largely dark all over. Females, on the other hand, are generally dark above and paler (usually white) below. The flippers and flukes appear gray-black on the dorsal surface. Prominent oval scarring and scratches are a feature of the overall body patterning. Beaked whales are rarely sighted at sea and are difficult to identify.

REPRODUCTION Little is known of the reproductive biology of this or any of the *Mesoplodon* species. Age at sexual maturity is thought to be about nine years.

Hubb's Beaked Whale *Mesoplodon carlhubbsi*

FAMILY: ZIPHIIDAE • Beaked and Bottlenose Whales

Not to scale

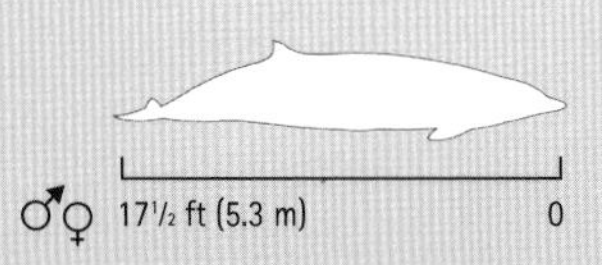

- Size at birth: Average of 8 feet (2.5 m)
- Weight: ♀ Only known from the weight of one animal: 3,157 lb (1,432 kg)
- Diet: Squid and deepwater fish
- Group size: Not known; most strandings are of single animals
- Other names: Arch-beaked whale
- Habitat: Cold temperate waters; probably in association with deep subarctic current systems
- Distribution: North Pacific Ocean, around Japan and California

Appearance Adult males of this species are more easily identified than females because they have a white "cap" in front of, and around, the blowhole. The tips of the rostrum and lower jaw are also white. Males also possess a large, flattened, tusk-like tooth on each side of the lower jaw. Both sexes are an overall dark gray to black. Females appear paler on the sides, with white on the ventral surface. Scarring and scratches that cover the body are thought to be inflicted during conflict between adult males. This species was described as recently as 1963. Most of the information about it has been obtained from stranded animals.

Reproduction Because this species is so rare, virtually nothing is known of its length at maturity, or its gestation period. Calving is thought to occur in mid-summer.

Cuvier's Beaked Whale *Ziphius cavirostris*

FAMILY: ZIPHIIDAE • Beaked and Bottlenose Whales

Not to scale

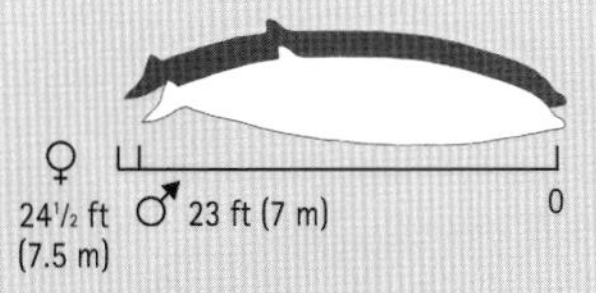

- Size at birth: About 9 feet (2.75 m)
- Weight: ♀♂ 3 tons/tonnes
- Diet: Principally squid and deepsea fish
- Group size: Occurs singly or in groups of 2–7 individuals
- Other names: Goose-beaked whale
- Habitat: A deep-water animal; rarely seen near the coast
- Distribution: A widely distributed and probably common species, found in all seas except polar waters

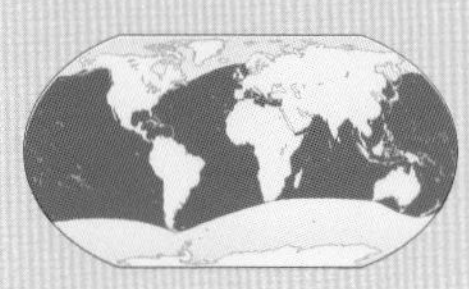

Appearance Cuvier's beaked whale has a pair of V-shaped throat grooves and a slightly upturned mouthline. Its small beak appears continuous with the melon. A small, falcate dorsal fin is set about two-thirds of the way along the back. The pigmentation pattern varies from one individual to another, probably reflecting geographical race or age. Males lighten as they grow older; the head and nape eventually change from a gray–brown to white. General body color can be acorn brown, tan, light brown, or gun-metal blue. The two conical teeth in the front of the lower jaw erupt only in the males.

Reproduction Females can reach sexual maturity at 16½ feet (5.1 m), but most may be longer than this. Males are probably longer—18 feet (5.5 m) or even more—at sexual maturity. Season of birth and gestation period are unknown.

NORTHERN BOTTLENOSE WHALE *Hyperoodon ampullatus* FAMILY: ZIPHIIDAE • Beaked and Bottlenose Whales

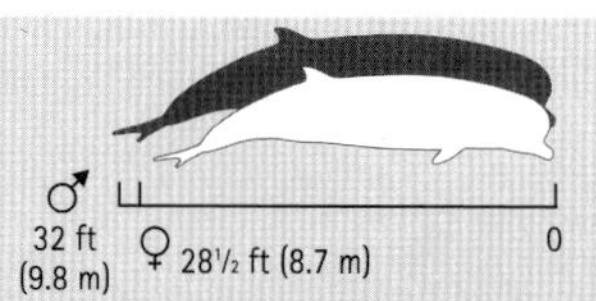

Not to scale

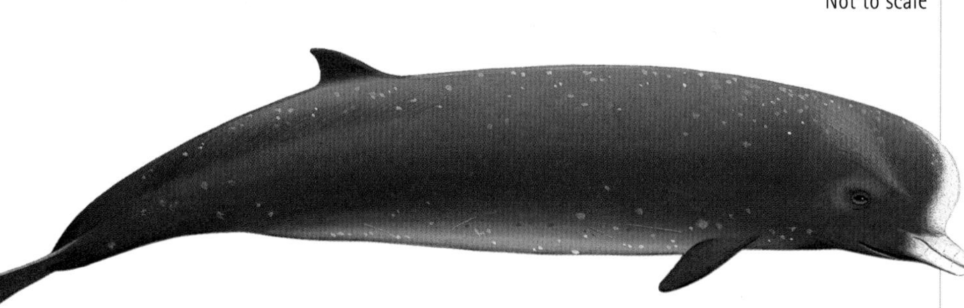

SIZE AT BIRTH: 11½ feet (3.5m)
WEIGHT: ♀♂ Estimated at several tons
DIET: Specialist squid feeder; occasionally sea cucumbers, sea stars, and prawns
GROUP SIZE: Pod size usually 4–10; being gregarious, several groups often in one area
OTHER NAMES: *Andehval* (Norwegian), *butskopf* (German)
HABITAT: Deep waters of 28-63°F (-2-17°C) on the continental shelf edge and slopes
DISTRIBUTION: North Atlantic–west from New England to Greenland, and east from the Straits of Gibraltar to Svalbard

APPEARANCE A distinctive head shape gives this species its common name. It has a prominent squarish melon (most notable in the males) and a long, tubelike snout. The dorsal fin is small, sickle-shaped, and set well back on the body. There is little color variation over the body, which is dark grayish brown on the back, changing to a lighter shade on the belly. Some individuals also develop a rather blotchy appearance, and the head area, in particular, gradually becomes paler. There are two conical teeth in the tip of the lower jaw, which erupt only in males. There may also be 10–20 vestigial teeth in the gums of the upper and lower jaws.

REPRODUCTION On average, males are 24½ feet (7.5 m) when sexually mature; females are slightly shorter at 22½ feet (6.9 m). Calves are born April–June after a gestation period of about 12 months.

NARWHAL *Monodon monoceros* FAMILY: MONODONTIDAE • Narwhal and Beluga

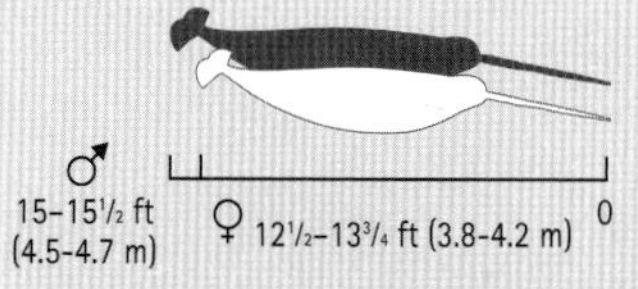

Not to scale

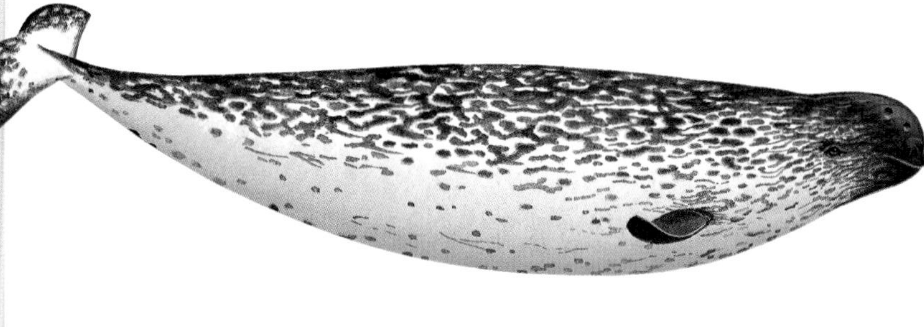

SIZE AT BIRTH: 5 feet (1.6 m)
WEIGHT: ♀♂ 1.6 tons/tonnes
DIET: Squid and shrimp; some fish, such as Arctic cod and Greenland halibut
GROUP SIZE: Immediate group of 2–10; pods can number in the thousands in a large area
OTHER NAMES: *Kelleluak, kakortok,* and *quilalugaq* (Inuit)
HABITAT: Deep fiords in Arctic and subarctic waters; generally near ice
DISTRIBUTION: Above Arctic Circle, from central Canadian Arctic to Greenland and to the central Russian Arctic; sometimes migration between areas occurs

APPEARANCE The narwhal male's most prominant feature is its conspicuous tusk, a modified tooth that reaches a length of about 6½ feet (2 m). Many other features vary with age—most notably the tail flukes, which change shape as the animal grows, gradually becoming semicircular, with the curve on the trailing edges. There is no dorsal fin, and the body is stocky with short pectoral fins. Color also varies: calves are a uniform gray but later develop white patches on the belly that gradually spread to the sides. Adults are a mottled black-brown on light gray.

REPRODUCTION On average, females reach sexual maturity at 11 feet (3.4 m); males at 13 feet (3.9 m). There is a gestation period of about 14–15 months and calving occurs at the height of summer in July–August. Females reproduce about every three years.

Beluga *Delphinapterus leucas*

FAMILY: Monodontidae • Narwhal and Beluga

Not to scale

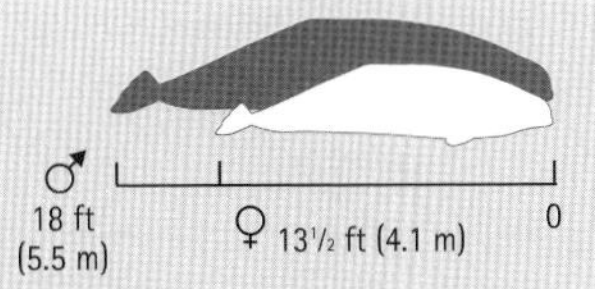

Size at birth: 5 feet (1.6 m)
Weight: ♀ 0.4–1 ton/tonne
♂ 1.5 tons/tonnes
Diet: Various: fish, mollusks, zooplankton and other invertebrates
Group size: A highly social species, rarely alone, generally in family-size groups; can also occur in the thousands
Other names: White whale, sea canary
Habitat: Arctic and subarctic waters; shallow coastal waters and estuaries in summer; other times, near the ice edge
Distribution: Circumpolar; in most ice-free Arctic waters

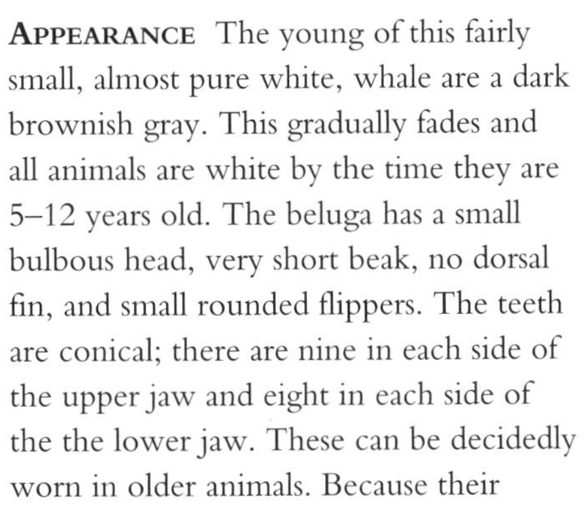

Appearance The young of this fairly small, almost pure white, whale are a dark brownish gray. This gradually fades and all animals are white by the time they are 5–12 years old. The beluga has a small bulbous head, very short beak, no dorsal fin, and small rounded flippers. The teeth are conical; there are nine in each side of the upper jaw and eight in each side of the the lower jaw. These can be decidedly worn in older animals. Because their vertebrae are unfused, belugas have relatively flexible necks.

Reproduction Females reach sexual maturity when they are at least five years of age, or later; males at about eight years of age. The mating season varies: in some areas it is late winter or spring; other populations mate in May. Gestation lasts for about 14–14.5 months, and calves are born in spring or summer.

False Killer Whale *Pseudorca crassidens*

FAMILY: Delphinidae • Oceanic Dolphins

Not to scale

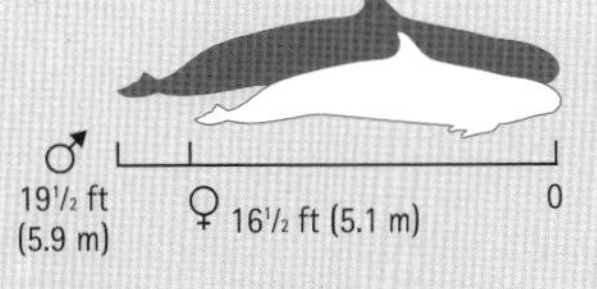

Size at birth: Varies; 5–6 ft (1.6–1.9 m)
Weight: ♀1 ton/tonne ♂ 2 tons/tonnes
Diet: Mostly squid and some large fish, such as tuna; known to attack other whales
Group size: This species is known to occur in groups of 50 of more; mass strandings are common
Other names: Often called blackfish, as are a few other similar-sized whales
Habitat: Largely open ocean; tropical to warm temperate waters
Distribution: Worldwide

Appearance The upright dorsal fin of this slim, medium-size whale is slightly rounded at the tip, and located midway along the back. The head has a rounded snout, which overhangs the lower jaw. There are 7–12 pairs of conical teeth in each of the upper and lower jaws. General body color is black, with lighter areas on the chest and head. The flippers are quite distinctive; each has a broad hump on the leading edge.

Reproduction Breeds year-round. Estimated gestation period varies from 12 to 15.5 months. Body lengths at sexual maturity also vary, which may indicate the existence of different populations. In males, the length ranges from 13 to 15 feet (3.9–4.5 m), and in females from 12 to 14 feet (3.6–4.2 m). Mass-stranded whales have provided most of what we know about the reproductive biology of this species.

ORCA *Orcinus orca*

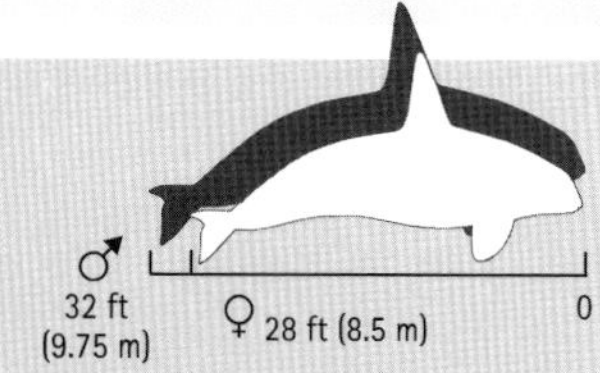

- SIZE AT BIRTH: 6½–8 feet (2–2.5 m)
- WEIGHT: ♀ 7.5 tons/tonnes
  ♂ 10.5 tons/tonnes
- DIET: Extremely diverse; often other marine mammals, such as dolphins, large whales, and seals; also fish, birds, dugongs, and even turtles
- GROUP SIZE: Stable pods of 3–25
- OTHER NAMES: Killer whale, blackfish, grampus
- HABITAT: Broad range: from coastal to open sea, and from equator to polar areas
- DISTRIBUTION: The most cosmopolitan of all cetaceans, it occurs in all oceans and seas

APPEARANCE This large, distinctively patterned toothed whale has a very tall dorsal fin (especially in males), rounded head, and blunt snout. The flippers are large and paddle-like and, in the males, can grow up to 6½ feet (2 m). It is easily recognized by its clearly defined black-and-white body pattern. The flippers and dorsal surface of the tail flukes are black, as is most of the back. White occurs on the ventral surface from the lower jaw to the urinogenital area. There is also a white oval patch above and behind each eye. There are 10-12 large recurved teeth in each half of both jaws.

REPRODUCTION Males are about 19 feet (5.8 m) long when they reach sexual maturity; females are about 16 feet (4.9 m). Gestation period is thought to be 12–16 months, with most calves born between October and March.

SHORT-FINNED PILOT WHALE *Globicephala macrorhynchus*

FAMILY: DELPHINIDAE • Oceanic Dolphins

Not to scale

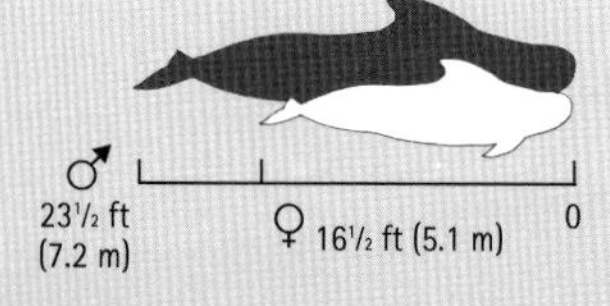

- SIZE AT BIRTH: Southern, 4½ feet (1.4 m); northern, 6 feet (1.8 m)
- WEIGHT: ♀ 1.4 tons/tonnes
  ♂ 3.9 tons/tonnes
- DIET: Largely squid and octopus; some fish
- GROUP SIZE: Rarely seen alone; generally 40 animals in a pod
- OTHER NAMES: Blackfish, Pacific pilot whale, short-headed sperm whale, lesser cachalot
- HABITAT: Deep oceans; tropical, subtropical and warm temperate; common strandings indicate it can come close to the coast
- DISTRIBUTION: All oceans within its water temperature limits

APPEARANCE This small- to medium-size whale has a bulbous head and a low, rounded dorsal fin, set well forward. The sickle-shaped flippers measure up to 19 percent of the body length. The overall color is gray-black, but many animals also have a lighter anchor-shaped patch on the chest, a gray-white saddle in front of the dorsal fin, and a gray streak behind the eyes. It is easily mistaken at sea for the long-finned pilot whale.

REPRODUCTION Lengths at sexual maturity vary, and this variation is most marked in two different forms that occur off Japan. For females, the size varies from 10½ to 13 feet (3.2–4 m); in males, the difference is even greater: from 14 to 18 feet (4.2–5.5 m). Calving is in fall–winter for the northern form, and in spring–autumn for the southern form. Gestation period is about 15 months and the nursing period is at least two years.

FAMILY: DELPHINIDAE • Oceanic Dolphins

Not to scale

PYGMY KILLER WHALE *Feresa attenuata*

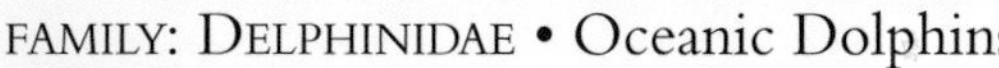

FAMILY: DELPHINIDAE • Oceanic Dolphins

Not to scale

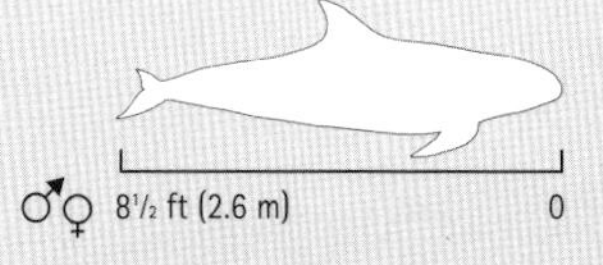

- SIZE AT BIRTH: Estimated at 31½ inches (80 cm)
- WEIGHT: ♀♂ 330–375 lb (150–170 kg); ♂ may be slightly bigger
- DIET: Squid and a variety of fish; evidence suggests they attack other cetaceans
- GROUP SIZE: From 50 to several hundred individuals
- OTHER NAMES: None
- HABITAT: Deep tropical and subtropical oceanic waters
- DISTRIBUTION: Worldwide in warm waters

APPEARANCE This species is similar in size to most of the true dolphins, but it lacks the dolphins' beak and has a rounded melon head. The front half of the body is robust and narrows to a slightly slimmer shape from the dorsal fin. The fin is high and fairly pointed, and the flippers are rounded at the tip and curved along the leading edge. Body color is dark gray to blue-black, with a darker capelike pattern extending from the top of the head back toward the dorsal fin. The lips and the tip of the lower jaw are white. There are 8–11 pairs of teeth in the upper jaw and 11–13 pairs in the lower jaw.

REPRODUCTION Because this species is not a mass strander, and has not been directly hunted, little is known of its life history. Sexual maturity is reached when the animals are about 6½ feet (2 m) long. The gestation period is unknown.

COMMON DOLPHIN *Delphinus delphis*

FAMILY: DELPHINIDAE • Oceanic Dolphins

Not to scale

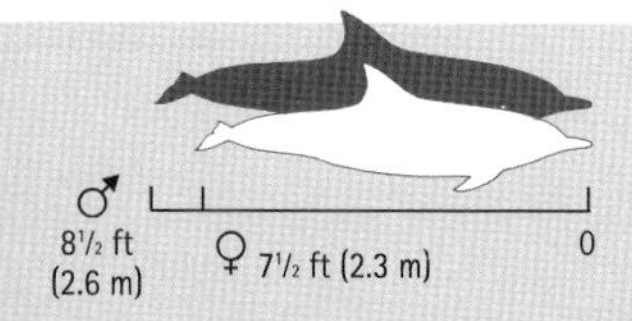

- **SIZE AT BIRTH:** 31½–33½ inches (80–85 cm)
- **WEIGHT:** ♀♂ 165 lb (75 kg)
- **DIET:** A wide variety of fish, including schooling species, such as herring, anchovies, and sardines
- **GROUP SIZE:** Can occur in large pods, often numbering in the thousands
- **OTHER NAMES:** Whitebelly porpoise, saddle-backed dolphin
- **HABITAT:** Deep offshore warm waters in tropical and temperate areas
- **DISTRIBUTION:** Warm waters worldwide; includes most oceans and seas

APPEARANCE The common dolphin is slender and streamlined. Its long beak is separated from the melon by a distinct crease. The color pattern is striking, with a dark brown to black dorsal surface, including appendages, and a white ventral surface. This is offset by yellow front flank patches, and light gray rear flanks and tail stock. A narrow dark stripe runs forward from the black eye surround to the front of the melon. Striping also occurs between the chin and flippers. Each side of each jaw has 80–100 small pointed teeth.

REPRODUCTION A number of different populations and stocks may account for variations in both length at sexual maturity and breeding seasons. Females, on average, become sexually mature at about 6 feet (1.8 m); males at 6½ feet (2 m). Gestation period is 11–12 months and births occur all year round.

PANTROPICAL SPOTTED DOLPHIN *Stenella attenuata*

FAMILY: DELPHINIDAE • Oceanic Dolphins

Not to scale

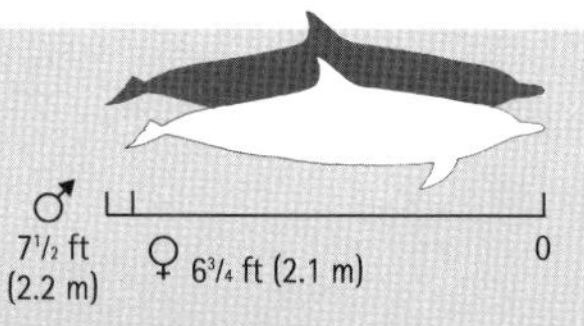

- **SIZE AT BIRTH:** 34 inches (87 cm)
- **WEIGHT:** ♀♂ 262 lb (119 kg)
- **DIET:** A surface-water feeder, takes squid and flying fish
- **GROUP SIZE:** Large variation in school size, from a few individuals to thousands
- **OTHER NAMES:** Spotted dolphin
- **HABITAT:** Tropical oceans with warm surface temperatures
- **DISTRIBUTION:** In a band each side of the equator, varying in latitude from 25°N to 15°S off South America, and from 40°N to 40°S in the Atlantic

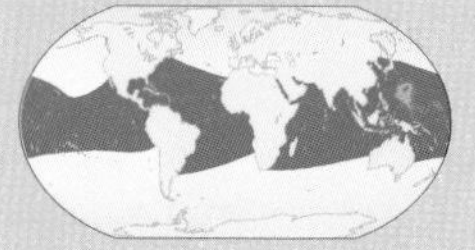

APPEARANCE The pantropical spotted dolphin is a slender animal. The extent of the white spotting depends on the age and/or geographical region of the individual. Spots appear after birth, and become bigger and more numerous with age. An overall dark gray background forms a cape-like pattern from the top of the head to halfway down the animal, then sweeps up behind the dorsal fin. The ventral surface is a lighter gray. It has 40 small teeth on either side of each jaw.

REPRODUCTION The gestation period of 11–12 months indicates that mating and calving probably occur at the same time of year. The season depends on location of the group, usually May and September. These animals are quite old and large when they begin to breed: about 12 years and 6½ feet (1.9 m) for males; 9 years and 6 feet (1.8 m) for females.

SPINNER DOLPHIN *Stenella longirostris*

FAMILY: DELPHINIDAE • Oceanic Dolphins

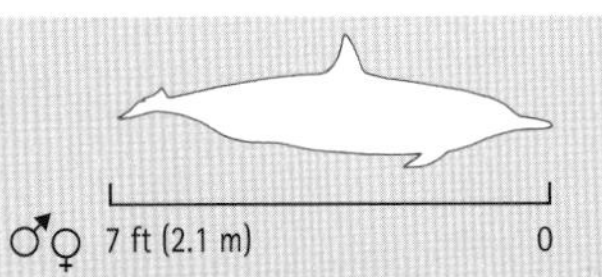

- SIZE AT BIRTH: Average 30 inches (77 cm)
- WEIGHT: ♀♂ Average size 165 lb (75 kg)
- DIET: Prefers fish and squid found well below surface level
- GROUP SIZE: As in other *Stenella* species, from a few animals to hundreds; some mixing of schools with other dolphins
- OTHER NAMES: *Stenella clymene* is also known as the spinner dolphin; four distinct forms of *S. longirostris* are recognized
- HABITAT: Tropical and subtropical waters north and south of the equator
- DISTRIBUTION: All oceans

Not to scale

APPEARANCE The spinner is a particularly slender dolphin with a long, thin beak. There are several distinct forms of this species, and individuals differ. The dorsal fin can vary from slightly sickle-shaped to erect and triangular. Some spinners are an overall monotone gray; others are gray with a white belly. Still others show a three-part color pattern: gray cape, light gray sides, and a white belly. Most spinner dolphins have dark eye-to-flipper stripes, and dark lips and beak tip. The teeth are sharply pointed, with 45–65 in each side of the upper and lower jaws.

REPRODUCTION Most life history has been obtained from a single population. These dolphins reach sexual maturity when they are 5–5½ feet (1.6–1.7 m) long, and breed annually in late spring or early summer. A single young is born

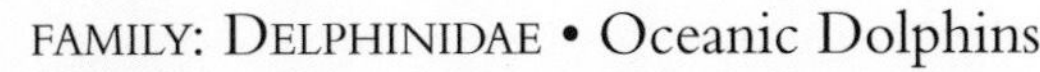

STRIPED DOLPHIN *Stenella coeruleoalba*

FAMILY: DELPHINIDAE • Oceanic Dolphins

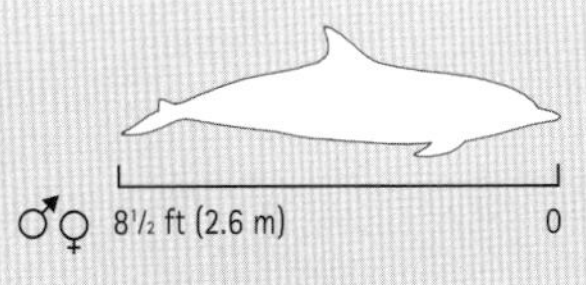

- SIZE AT BIRTH: About 3 feet (1 m)
- WEIGHT: ♀♂ Up to 330 lb (150 kg)
- DIET: Small prey over a foot (30 cm), consisting of mid-water fish and squid
- GROUP SIZE: Can be found in groups of thousands; most pods are 100–500
- OTHER NAMES: Euphrosyne dolphin
- HABITAT: Equatorial and subtropical waters; sometimes close to the coast where the water is deep, but open ocean is preferred
- DISTRIBUTION: Found in all the world's oceans, restricted only by surface water temperature of at least 71.6°F (22°C)

Not to scale

APPEARANCE The most distinctive feature of the striped dolphin is its color pattern. A dark stripe runs from behind the eye to the anus, forming a clear border between the white belly and light gray sides. A light gray spinal blaze also extends from the flank area to under the dorsal fin. A number of other stripes or dark bands run from the eyes to the flippers. Otherwise this dolphin is similar in shape to others in the *Stenella* and *Delphinus* groups. There are 40-55 small, sharp teeth in each tooth row.

REPRODUCTION Gestation is about 12–13 months. Breeding occurs during two seasons: summer and winter. Sexual maturity in both males and females is at about 7 feet (2.2 m). Although males are, on average, ready to breed at nine years of age, they do not become socially mature until they are at least 16.

FRASER'S DOLPHIN *Lagenodelphis hosei*

FAMILY: DELPHINIDAE • Oceanic Dolphins

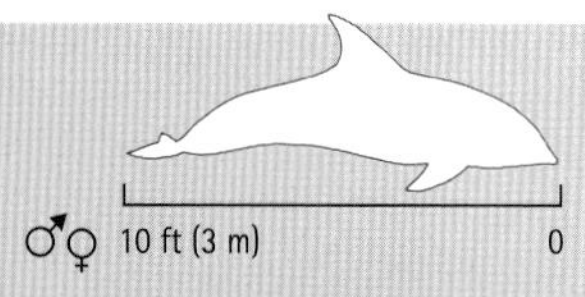

- SIZE AT BIRTH: Probably about 3 ft (1 m)
- WEIGHT: ♀♂ 440 lb (200 kg)
- DIET: Probably hunts at depths of more than 820 ft (250 m), taking a variety of fish, crustaceans, and squid
- GROUP SIZE: Pods can number 100 or more; often seen with other dolphin species
- OTHER NAMES: Originally called the sarawak dolphin
- HABITAT: Offshore; encountered near coasts only around oceanic islands
- DISTRIBUTION: Between latitudes 40°N and 40°S; a few sightings in Atlantic and Indian oceans

Not to scale

APPEARANCE Fraser's dolphin has a short but well-defined beak, a robust body, and short, pointed flippers and dorsal fin. Its most striking feature is the bold, dark gray striping: this occurs on the flippers and, especially, on the face and along the sides, giving the face a masked effect. The dark stripe is further accentuated by a cream border both above and below. The rest of the body is a dark brownish gray on the back and sides, and pink or white on the belly. As with many dolphin species, the patterns of the bands or stripes generally become more marked with age.

REPRODUCTION As this species was described only relatively recently, little is known about its reproductive behavior. Females are thought to become sexually mature when they are about 7½ feet (2.3 m). Breeding season, weaning age, and gestation period are unknown.

WHITE-BEAKED DOLPHIN *Lagenorhynchus albirostris*

FAMILY: DELPHINIDAE • Oceanic Dolphins

♂♀ 10 ft (3 m) 0

- SIZE AT BIRTH: 4–5 ft (1.2–1.6 m)
- WEIGHT: ♀♂ Unknown
- DIET: Varied; fish (capelin), squid, crustaceans
- GROUP SIZE: From a few individuals to dozens; often seen in groups of 1,000 or more
- OTHER NAMES: White-nosed dolphin, jumper, squidhound
- HABITAT: Widely scattered near the continental slope and along the shelf edge
- DISTRIBUTION: Northern and subarctic North Atlantic; in the east they are rare south of the UK; in the west, the southern limit is Cape Cod, USA

Not to scale

APPEARANCE The white-beaked dolphin has a short, thick beak that is clearly separate from the melon, a robust body, and a large sickle-shaped dorsal fin midway along its back. The overall color of the strongly patterned body is black to dark gray. There is white or light gray on the sides and dorsal surface of the tail stock, and forward of the dorsal fin. The undersides of the body and the beak are also white, which can sometimes appear mottled. The area between the eye and the flipper is often darkly spotted. Each half of each jaw contains 22–28 sharp teeth. Although larger and more robust, this species can be confused with the Atlantic white-sided dolphin.

REPRODUCTION Little is known about any aspect of this species' reproduction and life cycle. Calving is thought to occur in summer and early fall.

Pacific White-sided Dolphin *Lagenorhynchus obliquidens*

FAMILY: Delphinidae • Oceanic Dolphins

Not to scale

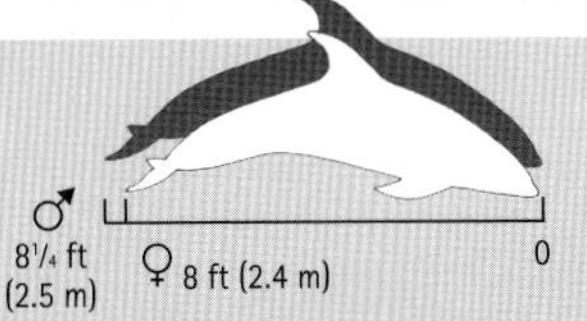

- Size at birth: 31–50 inches (80–124 cm)
- Weight: ♀♂ 165–200 lb (75–90 kg)
- Diet: Squid; schooling fish, such as anchovies and hake
- Group size: Large congregations numbering in the thousands; may split into small groups then reform into large pods
- Other names: Lags; in older texts it is called the Pacific striped dolphin
- Habitat: Offshore species; favors deep water of the continental slope and shelf
- Distribution: Continuous across the Pacific rim in the North Pacific Ocean, above 20°N

Appearance A characteristic feature of the Pacific white-sided dolphin is its distinctive dorsal fin, which is tall, strongly recurved, and bicolored. The front third of this fin is dark gray or black, and the rest a light gray. The flippers are similarly patterned. The body is grayish black on the back and paler gray on the sides; a thin black line sharply demarcates a white belly. Pale streaking starts from the top of the head and continues along the back to an enlarged gray patch on the sides of the tail stock. The beak is short and dark, which makes it difficult to detect, except at close quarters.

Reproduction Both males and females are sexually mature when they are 5½–7 feet (1.7–2.2 m) long. Calving and mating both take place from spring through to fall. Young are born after a gestation period of 10–12 months.

Atlantic White-sided Dolphin *Lagenorhynchus acutus*

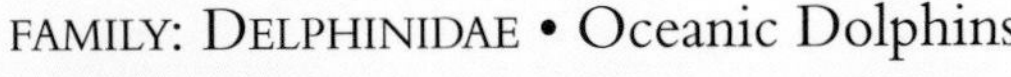

FAMILY: Delphinidae • Oceanic Dolphins

Not to scale

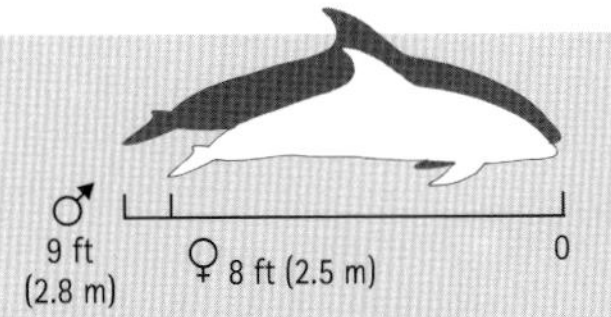

- Size at birth: 3½–4 feet (1.1–1.2 m)
- Weight: ♀♂ 400–520 lb (182–235 kg)
- Diet: Squid; small schooling fish, such as juvenile mackerel, herring, and sand lance
- Group size: Small groups to several hundred
- Other names: Lags, springers; both names also apply to other small dolphins
- Habitat: Continental shelf and shelf regions with water surface temperatures of 43–68°F (6–20°C)
- Distribution: Cold temperate and subpolar waters of the North Atlantic Ocean

Appearance This species has the typical body shape of the *Lagenorhynchus* group: a short well-defined beak; robust body; and a tall, sharply pointed dorsal fin. The body pattern is its most distinctive feature: the dorsal surface, including the upper jaw, flippers and flukes, is all black; the underside is white; and the sides a mixture of gray and white bands. The white underside is particularly noticeable when this dolphin leaps clear of the water. A narrow orange band behind the white can cause this species to be confused with the common dolphin, which is superficially similar.

Reproduction Males reach sexual maturity at a length of 7½–8 feet (2.3–2.4 m); females at about 7 feet (2.2 m) long. Mating is thought to take place in summer, and the young are born about 10–12 months later.

TUCUXI *Sotalia fluviatilis*

FAMILY: DELPHINIDAE • Oceanic Dolphins

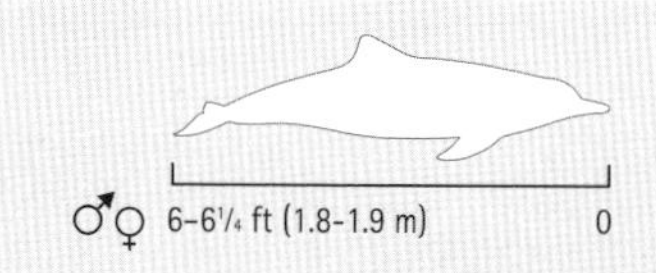

- SIZE AT BIRTH: About 2½ feet (75 cm)
- WEIGHT: ♀♂ 77–88 lb (35–40 kg)
- DIET: Rivers—prey varies from invertebrates, such as crabs and prawns, to fish; coast—mostly pelagic fish and cephalopods
- GROUP SIZE: Generally single animals, or small groups; family units of up to 10
- OTHER NAMES: None
- HABITAT: Deep channels of large rivers and shallow coastal waters
- DISTRIBUTION: North-eastern South America; Brazil–Colombia and the Orinoco and Amazon river systems

Not to scale

APPEARANCE The tucuxi is a small, robust dolphin with an elongated snout and well-formed, rounded melon. Overall color is a bluish gray, fading on the flanks and ventral surface to pale gray and white. Some animals have a slight pinkish tinge on the belly and throat. A broad stripe runs from the eye to the flipper base. Flippers and flukes are large and broad, and the dorsal fin is characteristically triangular. At sea this species is sometimes confused with the bottlenose dolphin, which is a much larger animal with a larger dorsal fin. Teeth numbers vary; usually there are 26–35 pairs in each jaw.

REPRODUCTION Limited data is available. In some parts of this species' range, females become sexually mature at about 4½ feet (1.3 m) long. Gestation is thought to be 10 months, and calving generally coincides with flood periods.

INDO-PACIFIC HUMP-BACKED DOLPHIN *Sousa chinensis*

FAMILY: DELPHINIDAE • Oceanic Dolphins

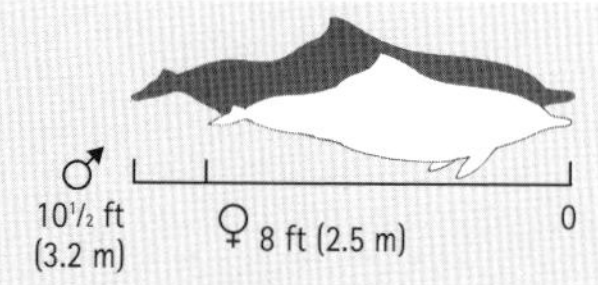

- SIZE AT BIRTH: About 3 feet (1 m)
- WEIGHT: ♀♂ 625 lb (285 kg)
- DIET: Schooling fish such as mullet, sea bream, and grunts
- GROUP SIZE: Groups of 5–7 animals; occasionally combine to form larger groups
- Other names: *Parampuan laut* in Malaya
- HABITAT: Mangrove channels and shallow water less than 65½ feet (20 m) deep; will enter rivers and estuaries
- DISTRIBUTION: Northern Australia; southern China; Indonesia; coastal Indian Ocean to South Africa

Not to scale

APPEARANCE A highly variable species, the Indo-Pacific hump-backed dolphin has a robust body and elongated snout or beak. It is so-named because its dorsal fin sits on a distinct hump, or ridge, midway along the back. There is also a ridge, or keel, above and below the tail stock. Color pattern varies with age and population: in some areas, adults are an overall dark gray, lead-like color, and the young are lighter gray; in other regions, adults are very pale, almost white. The number of teeth in each side of the upper and lower jaws varies between 27 and 38.

REPRODUCTION Very little is known. The breeding season is probably protracted, with a peak in summer. Only two sexually mature animals, both from South Africa, have been measured. They were an 8 foot (2.5 m) female, and a male measuring 9 feet (2.8 m).

ROUGH-TOOTHED DOLPHIN *Steno bredanensis*

FAMILY: DELPHINIDAE • Oceanic Dolphins

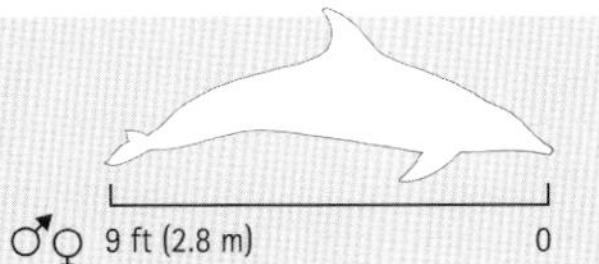

Not to scale

- SIZE AT BIRTH: Unknown
- WEIGHT: ♀♂ Up to 330 lb (150 kg)
- DIET: Squid, free-swimming octopus, and a variety of fish
- GROUP SIZE: Pods of up to 100 have been observed; most are probably fewer than 50
- OTHER NAMES: Delfin de pico largo
- HABITAT: A deep-water species, found beyond the continental shelf in tropical and subtropical seas
- DISTRIBUTION: Probably a widely distributed species in areas with sea surface at 77°F (25°C) or more; between latitudes 40°N and 35°S

APPEARANCE The rough-toothed dolphin lacks a prominent melon. The head is conical and slopes evenly toward the tip of the snout. Its shape, along with its large eyes, gives this dolphin a somewhat reptilian appearance. The body is dark gray, with a narrow dorsal cape and white belly, lips, and lower jaw. White scratches and spots either from cookie-cutter sharks or other dolphins, are common body markings. The common name apparently describes the numerous wrinkles and ridges occurring on the teeth.

REPRODUCTION Populations seem to vary in their reproductive patterns. In the western North Atlantic, sexually mature males and females are, on average 7½ feet (2.3 m) long. In Japanese waters, they seem to be slightly shorter. The gestation period is unknown.

BOTTLENOSE DOLPHIN *Tursiops truncatus*

FAMILY: DELPHINIDAE • Oceanic Dolphins

Not to scale

- SIZE AT BIRTH: 3–4½ feet (1–1.3 m)
- WEIGHT: ♀♂ Varies enormously: 200–1,430 lb (90–650 kg)
- DIET: Inshore populations—variety of fish, squid, and octopus; offshore populations—bottom-dwelling and schooling fish
- GROUP SIZE: Highly variable; up to 100 inshore to several hundred in oceanic groups
- OTHER NAMES: Gray or black dolphin in North America; bottlenosed porpoise (erroneously)
- HABITAT: Wide variety: bays and lagoons in coastal areas; open ocean
- DISTRIBUTION: Widely distributed from tropical to temperate seas

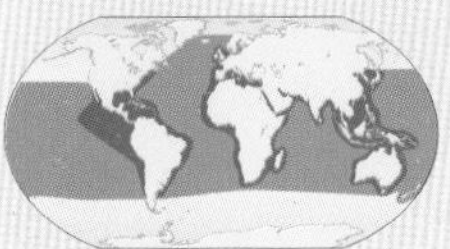

APPEARANCE Probably the most familiar of all dolphins, the bottlenose is a relatively large and robust dolphin. It has a well-formed melon, which is separated from the stocky snout by a marked crease. The dorsal fin, located near the middle of the back, is broad and triangular. The belly is off-white, and the sides of the head and body are a light gray, which gradually becomes deeper until it forms a dark bluish gray cape on the back. Striping occurs from the melon to the eyes, and also from the eyes to the flipper. As they get older, these dolphins develop a white tip on the snout.

REPRODUCTION This species undergoes a long adolescence: females do not begin to breed until they are 9–10 years old; males when they reach 10–13 years. Gestation lasts for about 12 months; a single young is born in spring or summer.

■ Primary range ■ Occasional range

IRRAWADDY DOLPHIN *Orcaella brevirostris*

FAMILY: DELPHINIDAE • Oceanic Dolphins

Not to scale

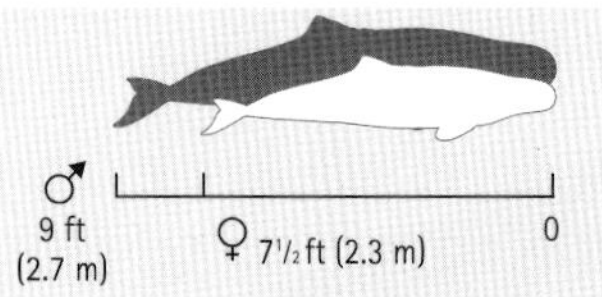

- SIZE AT BIRTH: About 3 feet (1 m)
- WEIGHT: ♀♂ 200–330 lb (90–150 kg)
- DIET: Crustaceans and other invertebrates; also fish
- GROUP SIZE: Generally small groups up to 6; groups of 15 have been observed
- OTHER NAMES: Pesut, lumbalumba
- HABITAT: Found only in warm waters of the tropics and subtropics; prefers rivers and shallow coastal areas
- DISTRIBUTION: South-East Asia and northern Australia; the range of this species is, as yet, not fully known

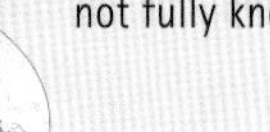

APPEARANCE With its blunt, rounded head, lack of a beak, and pale body color, the Irrawaddy dolphin resembles the beluga whale. However, while the beluga gradually turns white, the Irrawaddy dolphin remains gray—darker above, and paler below. It also possesses a small dorsal fin, which lies behind the midpoint of the body. Some unfused neck vertebrae allow the head free movement. The flippers are quite large, with curved leading edges. There are 17–20 peglike teeth in each tooth row of the upper jaw, and 15–18 in each row of the lower jaw.

REPRODUCTION Many aspects of the life history of this species are poorly understood. What little we do know has been obtained from captive animals. The evidence suggests that mating occurs in spring and early summer. Gestation period seems to be about 14 months.

RISSO'S DOLPHIN *Grampus griseus*

FAMILY: DELPHINIDAE • Oceanic Dolphins

Not to scale

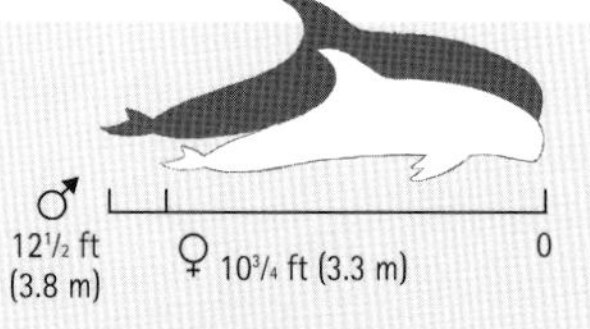

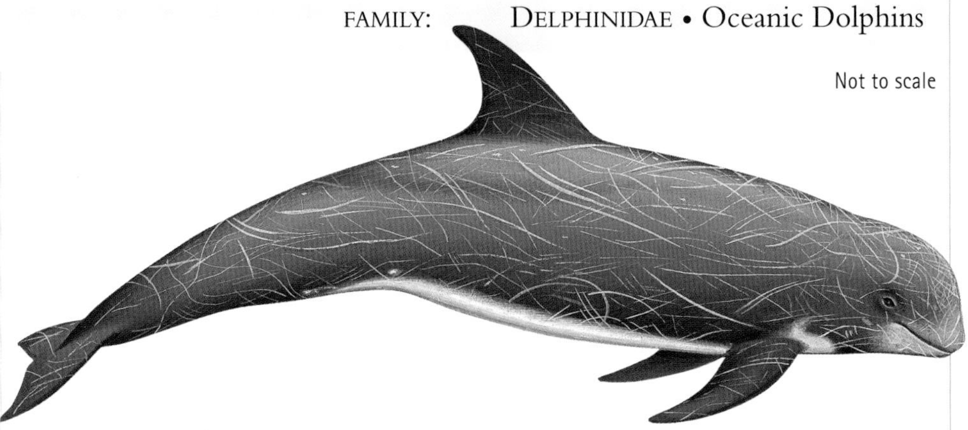

- SIZE AT BIRTH: 4–5 feet (1.2–1.5 m)
- WEIGHT: ♀♂ 880–1,100 lb (400–500 kg)
- DIET: Largely squid; some fish
- GROUP SIZE: Small groups up to 12; also sighted in large pods numbering thousands, and often with other dolphin species
- OTHER NAMES: Grampus, gray grampus
- HABITAT: Deep water
- DISTRIBUTION: Most tropical and warm temperate oceans and seas; avoids the polar oceans; northern limits are Newfoundland and Shetland, the Gulf of Alaska, and the northern Indian Ocean

APPEARANCE Adult Risso's dolphins are easily recognized by the extensive white scarring and blotching that covers what is otherwise a gray body. These scratches can sometimes be so extensive that some animals, especially older ones, appear almost white. The flippers and dorsal fin are generally a darker shade of gray than the rest of the body, and there is an anchor-shaped white chest patch. A robust-looking dolphin, it has a large, blunt head and no beak, which gives it a somewhat squarish profile. The flippers are long and sickle-shaped with pointed tips.

REPRODUCTION Both sexes become sexually mature at about 8½ feet (2.6 m) long. Young are born after a gestation period of 13–14 months. Calving generally occurs in summer, although there is some variation among the different populations.

Northern Right Whale Dolphin *Lissodelphis borealis*

FAMILY: DELPHINIDAE • Oceanic Dolphins

Not to scale

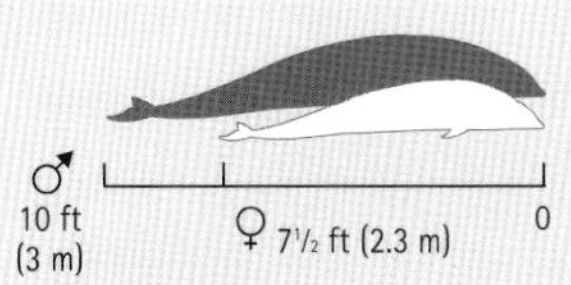

- SIZE AT BIRTH: Unknown; estimated at about 3 feet (1 m)
- WEIGHT: ♀♂ 253 lb (115 kg)
- DIET: Market squid; lantern fish; other surface and mid-water species of fish
- GROUP SIZE: Occurs in large numbers from a few hundred to thousands; often seen traveling with other dolphin species
- OTHER NAMES: Pacific right whale dolphin
- HABITAT: Open ocean, favors deep-water areas of 46.4–66.2°F (8–19°C)
- DISTRIBUTION: North Pacific Ocean, between 30° and 50°N in the west, and 35° and 51°N in the east

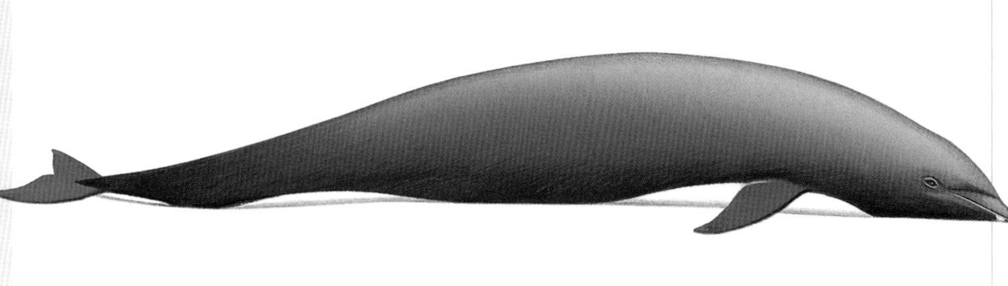

APPEARANCE Slender and strikingly patterned, the northern right whale dolphin lacks a dorsal fin, and has small flippers and tail flukes. Its largely black body has a white band running from the throat, along the ventral surface, to the flukes. The rear border of the flukes is white below and light gray above. The lower jaw carries a white patch just behind the tip. The extent of these black-and-white markings can vary among individuals, with the area of white often being far more extensive. The teeth are present in both the upper and lower jaws, and number 40–49 in each side.

REPRODUCTION Males become sexually mature at about 7 feet (2.2 m), and females at about 6½ feet (2 m). Little else is known of the life history. There is some evidence that the peak calving period is around winter to early spring.

Hector's Dolphin *Cephalorhynchus hectori*

FAMILY: DELPHINIDAE • Oceanic Dolphins

Not to scale

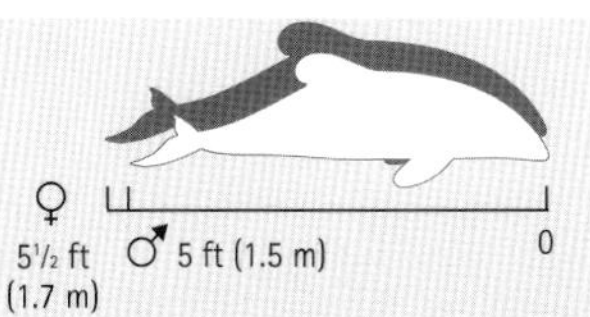

- SIZE AT BIRTH: 23–27 inches (60–70 cm)
- WEIGHT: ♀♂ 110–132 lb (50–60 kg)
- DIET: A variety of small fish, from both the surface and sea floor
- GROUP SIZE: Generally small groups of 2–8 animals that occasionally come together in larger pods
- OTHER NAMES: None
- HABITAT: Shallow water, usually less than 984 feet (300 m) deep; near the shoreline
- DISTRIBUTION: Found only in New Zealand waters, with greatest concentrations around the South Island

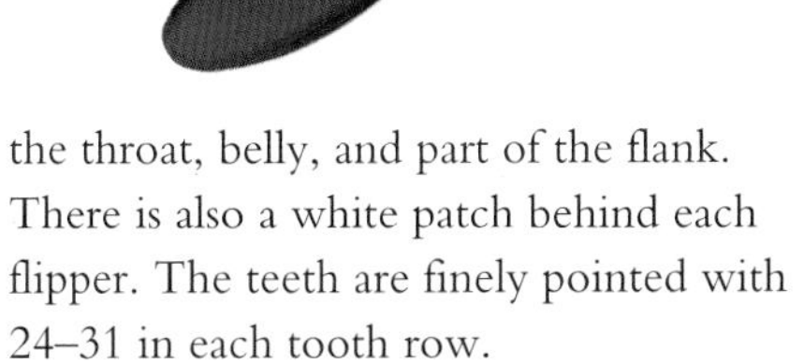

APPEARANCE Typical of its genus, Hector's dolphin is a small, stocky animal with a blunt head and a low, rounded dorsal fin. The color combinations of black, white, and gray give this species its distinctive appearance. Most of the torso is gray, with black on the tail, dorsal fin, side of the head around and back from the eye, and tip of the lower jaw. White appears largely on the ventral surface, extending from the lower jaw back along the throat, belly, and part of the flank. There is also a white patch behind each flipper. The teeth are finely pointed with 24–31 in each tooth row.

REPRODUCTION Very little is known of this species' life history. Sexual maturity is reached at about 4 feet (1.2 m) in males, and about 4½ feet (1.4 m) in females. Calving occurs during spring and early summer.

DALL'S PORPOISE *Phocoenoides dalli*

FAMILY: PHOCOENIDAE • Porpoises

Not to scale

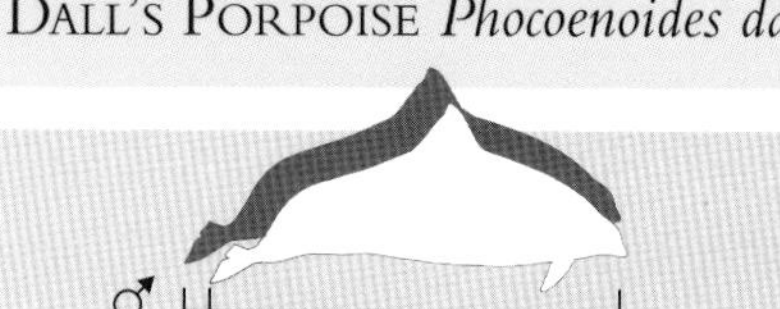

- SIZE AT BIRTH: 37–40 inches (95–100 cm)
- WEIGHT: ♀♂ 440 lb (200 kg)
- DIET: Surface and midwater prey, such as squid and lanternfish; in coastal areas it favors schooling fish, such as hake
- GROUP SIZE: Generally small groups of 2–12; larger groups form for activities such as feeding and social interaction
- OTHER NAMES: None
- HABITAT: Cold waters off the continental shelf and slope
- DISTRIBUTION: North Pacific and adjacent waters between about 30°N and 62°N

APPEARANCE This striking black-and-white patterned porpoise, similar in color to the spectacled porpoise, has a wide girth and a triangular dorsal fin. In contrast to its robust body, the head and beak are small, as are the flippers and flukes. Most of the body is a rich black. A large patch of white occurs on the flank and ventral area, and there is a smaller patch on the trailing edge of the dorsal fin. The teeth are extremely small and spadelike; there are 23–28 in each tooth row. Despite its bulky appearance, this porpoise is a particularly fast swimmer.

REPRODUCTION Males reach sexual maturity when they are about 6 feet (1.8 m) long. Females can breed when they are 5½ feet (1.7 m) long. Young are generally born in summer, after a gestation period of approximately 11.5 months.

SPECTACLED PORPOISE *Australophocaena dioptrica*

FAMILY: PHOCOENIDAE • Porpoises

Not to scale

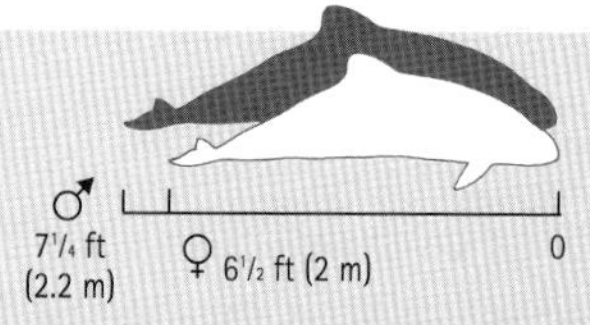

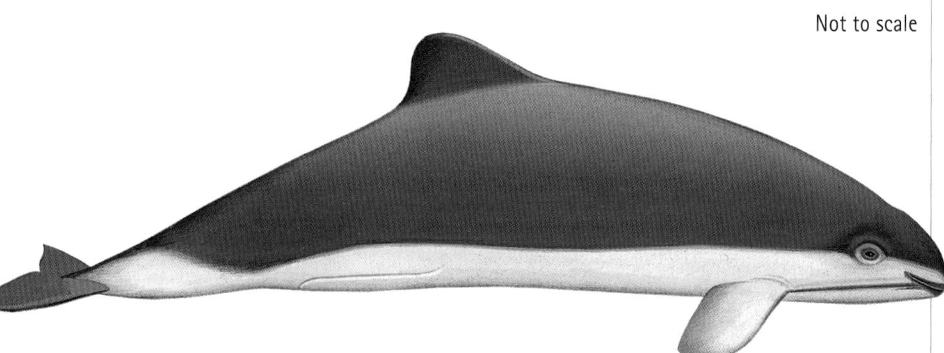

- SIZE AT BIRTH: Probably about 3 feet (1 m)
- WEIGHT: ♀♂ Unknown as no adults have been weighed
- DIET: Unknown
- GROUP SIZE: A difficult species to identify at sea unless closely observed; has been seen alone or in pairs
- OTHER NAMES: Bicolour porpoise tonina (in Chilean waters)
- HABITAT: Sightings have occurred in rivers and channels as well as offshore waters
- Distribution: Probably has a circumpolar distribution in subantarctic latitudes

APPEARANCE The largest of the porpoise group, this species has the characteristic stocky body shape, blunt snout, and short or non-existent beak. The dorsal fin is quite large, triangular, and rounded at the tip. Like Dall's porpoise, it has distinctive black-and-white markings, and the pattern is strongly demarcated, with black dorsal and white ventral surfaces. The teeth are spadelike; the upper jaw contains 17–23 pairs, and the lower jaw 16–20. Strandings have been recorded from the southern coast of eastern South America, and around some offshore subantarctic islands.

REPRODUCTION As this species is rarely sighted, there is almost no life history information available on it. Some length measurements of pregnant females have been taken and these were about 6 feet (1.8 m) on average.

Harbor Porpoise *Phocoena phocoena*

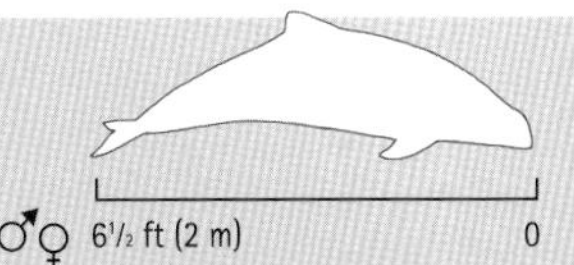

- Size at birth: 27–35 inches (70–90 cm)
- Weight: ♀♂ 88–132 lb (40–60 kg)
- Diet: Small schooling fish, such as herring or anchovy, which often occur on the bottom
- Group size: Usually small, fewer than 8; can be larger when feeding or migrating
- Other names: Common porpoise, porpoise (English); *marsopa* (Spanish); *pourcil* (French)
- Habitat: Bays and estuaries containing murky waters caused by tidal races or coastal upwellings
- Distribution: Northern Hemisphere waters in temperate and subarctic areas

Not to scale

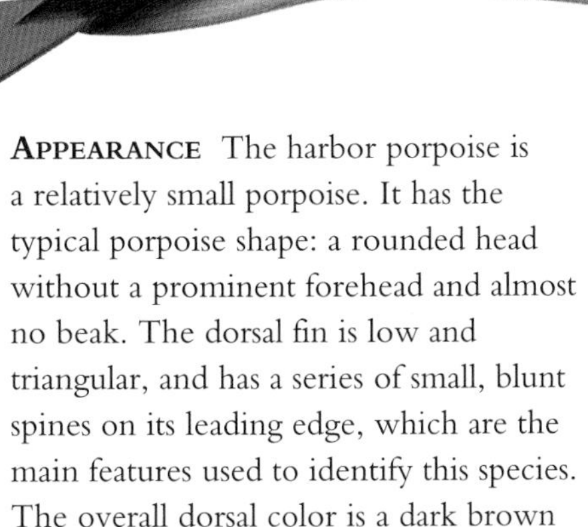

Appearance The harbor porpoise is a relatively small porpoise. It has the typical porpoise shape: a rounded head without a prominent forehead and almost no beak. The dorsal fin is low and triangular, and has a series of small, blunt spines on its leading edge, which are the main features used to identify this species. The overall dorsal color is a dark brown or dark gray, which fades to a whitish color on the belly. A thin, gray stripe extends from the flipper to the area near the gape of the mouth. There are 21–25 pairs of spadelike teeth in the lower jaw and 22–28 in the upper jaw.

Reproduction Both males and females are sexually mature when about 5 feet (1.5 m) long. The young are born during the summer after a gestation period of 11 months. Females generally calve each year.

Vaquita *Phocoena sinus*

♀ 5 ft (1.5 m) ♂ 4½ ft (1.4 m) 0

Not to scale

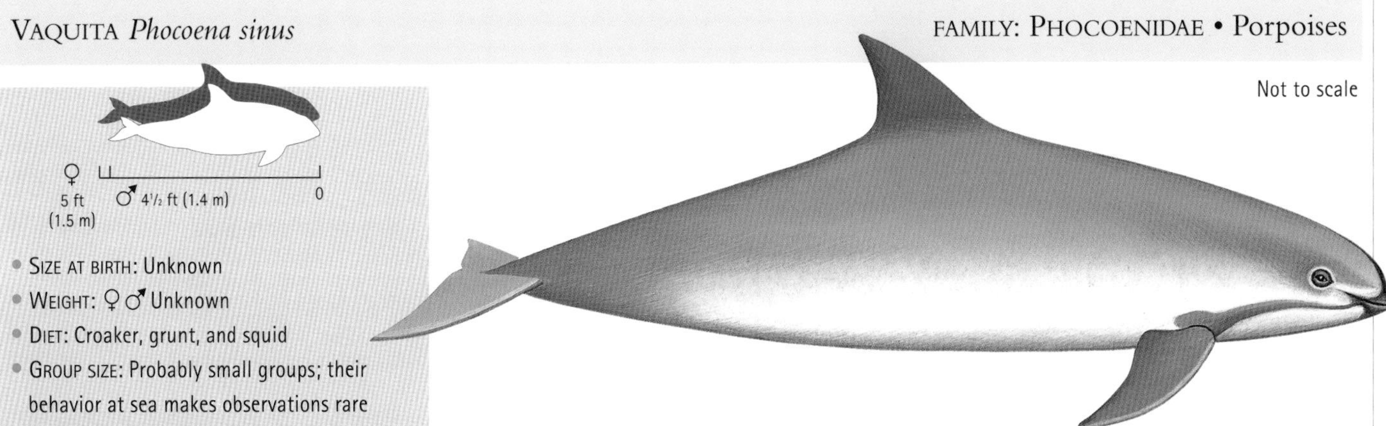

- Size at birth: Unknown
- Weight: ♀♂ Unknown
- Diet: Croaker, grunt, and squid
- Group size: Probably small groups; their behavior at sea makes observations rare
- Other names: Originally cochito, a general term for all dolphins in Mexican waters
- Habitat: Shallow waters, even in mangrove areas, and those of a general murky appearance
- Distribution: Limited to Mexico, the northern gulf of California, and the Colorado River delta

Appearance A very small cetacean, the vaquita is believed to be the smallest of all the dolphins and porpoises. The upper surface of the body is gray, while the belly area is a paler whitish color. The flippers are dark and there is a dark eye patch as well as a dark mouth, which gives the distinct impression that this porpoise has lips. Like the other porpoises, it has a triangular dorsal fin. The vaquita's, however, is taller in comparison to that of the other porpoises. The teeth are spade-shaped; there are 20–21 pairs in the upper jaw, and 18 in the lower jaw.

Reproduction Because this species is so rare, and consequently very difficult to observe at sea, virtually nothing is known about its life history. It is considered to be extremely endangered, with the main reason being its highly restricted distribution.

AMAZON RIVER DOLPHIN *Inia geoffrensis*

FAMILY: INIIDAE • Amazon River Dolphin

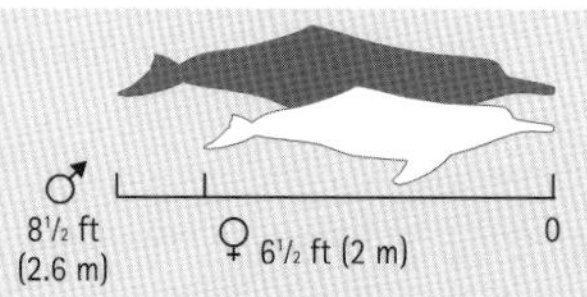

- SIZE AT BIRTH: 31½ inches (80 cm)
- WEIGHT: ♂ 350 lb (160 kg), ♀ 220 lb (100 kg)
- DIET: A large variety of fish, both bottom-dwelling and schooling; crustaceans
- GROUP SIZE: Essentially solitary; fluctuating river depths can force animals into groups
- OTHER NAMES: Boto (sometimes spelled bouto); *tonina* (Spanish)
- HABITAT: Turbid waters of river channels; forests and grasslands during floods
- DISTRIBUTION: Drainage basins of the Amazon and Orinoco rivers in tropical South America

Not to scale

APPEARANCE Mainly pink, the Amazon River dolphin has a long beak with more than 100 teeth, and a steep, bulbous forehead, or melon. Instead of a true dorsal fin, it has a wide-based dorsal ridge or hump about two-thirds the way down the body. Both flippers and flukes are broad, with the latter having frayed rear margins. This species is unique in having differentiated teeth. The front ones are conical, like those of most dolphins; the rear teeth are more like molars, with an inside flange. This suggests that they chew their food, rather than swallowing it whole, as other dolphins do.

REPRODUCTION Males reach sexual maturity at about 6½ feet (2 m) long; females at 6 feet (1.8 m). Gestation period is thought to be about 10–11 months, with births occurring between May and July, during peak water levels.

YANGTZE RIVER DOLPHIN *Lipotes vexillifer*

FAMILY: PONTOPORIIDAE • Yangtze and La Plata Dolphins

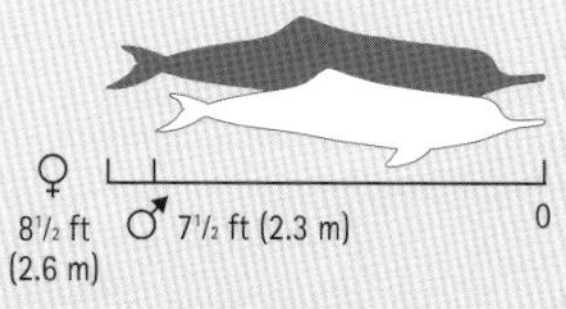

- SIZE AT BIRTH: About 37 inches (95 cm)
- WEIGHT: ♂ 265 lb (125 kg), ♀ 350 lb (160 kg)
- DIET: Various fish species
- GROUP SIZE: Generally in groups of six or fewer; individuals and pairs sometimes seen
- OTHER NAMES: Baiji, Chinese river dolphin
- HABITAT: Slow-moving river areas with established sandbars, an environment in which human activities, such as fishing and boating, threaten this species
- DISTRIBUTION: Middle and lower reaches of the Yangtze River, China

Not to scale

APPEARANCE The Yangtze River dolphin is predominantly a dark bluish gray. Its long, narrow beak is slightly upturned, and it has a steep, rounded forehead. The dorsal fin is low and triangular, and the flippers are broad and rounded. The dark color on its back gradually fades down the sides toward the belly, lower jaw, and the dorsal surface of the flippers and flukes, where it becomes a light gray or white. There are also some white markings on the face and sides of the tail stock. Each tooth row contains 31–38 conical teeth.

REPRODUCTION Because this species is so rare—it is considered one of the rarest cetaceans, with a population numbering only in the hundreds—there is little biological information available on it. It is thought that calves are born between February and April.

La Plata Dolphin *Pontoporia blainvillei*

FAMILY: Pontoporiidae • Yangtze and La Plata Dolphins

Not to scale

♀ 5¾ ft (1.75 m) ♂ 5 ft (1.5 m) 0

- Size at birth: About 30 inches (75 cm)
- Weight: ♀ 117 lb (53 kg), ♂ 95 lb (43 kg)
- Diet: Largely bottom-dwelling prey such as shrimp (especially by young dolphins); squid, octopus, fish and crustaceans
- Group size: Probably does not form large groups
- Other names: Fransiscana
- Habitat: Primarily a marine species in shallow inshore waters
- Distribution: Coastal waters of eastern South America, from Peninsula Valdes in Argentina to the Doce River in Brazil

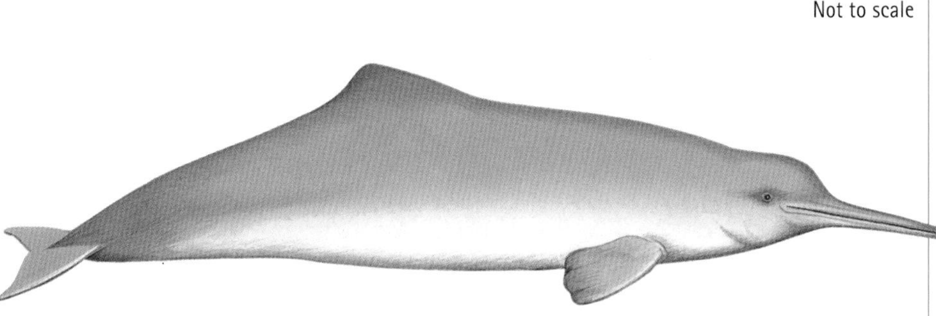

Appearance This marine dolphin is closely related to the river dolphins. Females are larger than males, but are otherwise similar. Both have a long, narrow beak that grows with age, a triangular dorsal fin, rounded at the tip, and prominent spatulate flippers. The overall color is gray, darker on the back than on the ventral surface. There are probably more than 200 teeth, with 51–58 in each row. Research suggests that different forms occur in different parts of its range; the northern form being smaller than the southern. Few of these animals have been observed alive.

Reproduction Females weigh about 77 pounds (35 kg) at sexual maturity; males weigh slightly less at 64 pounds (29 kg). The gestation period lasts for approximately 11 months with births occurring in November and December.

Ganges River Dolphin *Platanista gangetica*

FAMILY: Platanistidae • Ganges And Indus River Dolphins

Not to scale

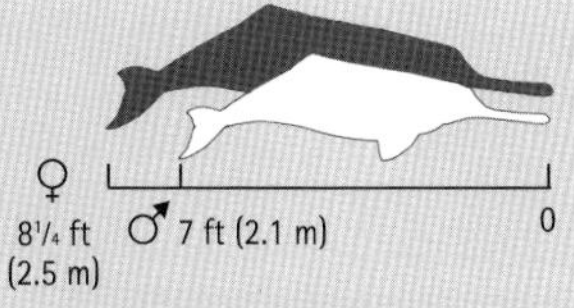

- Size at birth: 25½–35½ inches (65-90 cm)
- Weight: ♀♂ 185 lb (85 kg)
- Diet: A variety of vertebrate and invertebrate prey, such as fish, crustaceans and mollusks
- Group size: Small groups are the norm; also seen in pairs and alone
- Other names: Susu or Ganges susu; blind river dolphin; gangetic dolphin; also a variety of local names
- Habitat: Largely slow-moving river waters; some areas in fast-moving, clear rivers
- Distribution: India, Bangladesh, parts of Nepal and Bhutan river systems

Appearance The very long, slender beak of this species contains 26–39 backward-curving teeth in each side of the upper and lower jaws. The anterior teeth are longer than the rear, and these extend outside the closed mouth like a pair of forceps. This feature, combined with the small, rounded melon set off from the fat, chunky body, contributes to the strange appearance of this relatively small dolphin. Its overall body color is gray, and there are some pinkish areas on the belly. The very tiny eyes, set in a fold of skin just above the corner of the mouth, are barely visible.

Reproduction Little life history information is available on this species. The estimated gestation period is about 8–9 months. Young can be born any time, although there are probably peaks in December–January and March–May.

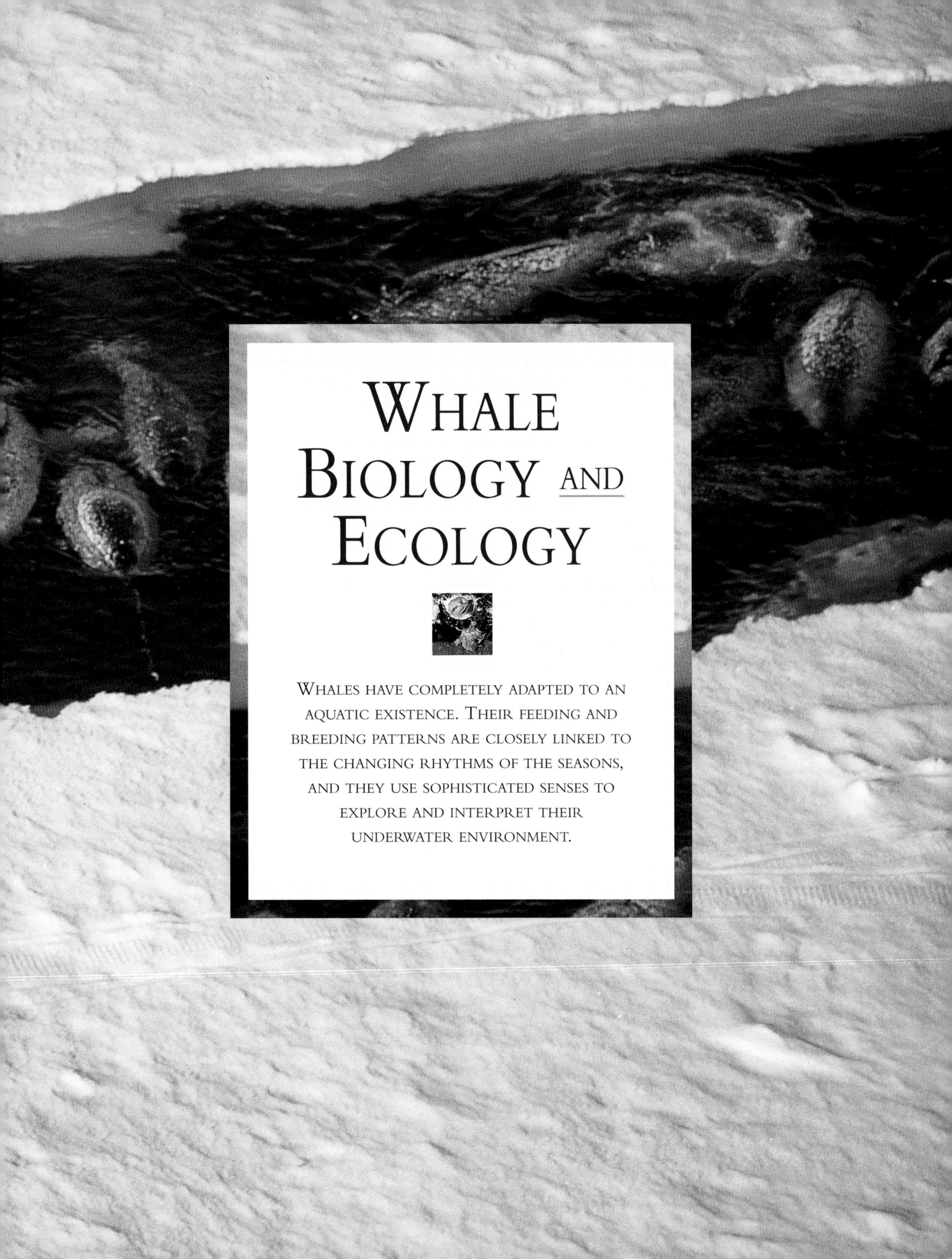

WHALE BIOLOGY AND ECOLOGY

WHALES HAVE COMPLETELY ADAPTED TO AN AQUATIC EXISTENCE. THEIR FEEDING AND BREEDING PATTERNS ARE CLOSELY LINKED TO THE CHANGING RHYTHMS OF THE SEASONS, AND THEY USE SOPHISTICATED SENSES TO EXPLORE AND INTERPRET THEIR UNDERWATER ENVIRONMENT.

How Whales Move

As you watch a whale swim, it seems to move effortlessly, but this is misleading. Whales require a great deal of energy to move their large bodies through the water—but they use it more efficiently than most other animals. Water provides resistance to movement, and whales overcome this in interesting ways. Until recently, scientists were puzzled by the speeds at which some dolphins were able to travel; according to their calculations, these dolphins had only a fraction of the amount of muscle they needed to move so fast. Like well-designed ships, whales' bodies produce "laminar flow," which means that the fluid they displace as they move flows smoothly from their front to their rear, producing

ABOVE: Closeness to its mother gives this humpback calf reassurance and protection. Calves possibly "slipstream" when close to their mothers: by staying close, they may use her laminar flow, reducing their own energy output.

Dolphin Propulsion

Cetaceans derive their propulsive power from the vertical flexing of the body and tail flukes; they use the pectoral fins for steering. Until recently it was thought that most power was produced during the upstroke, which occurs as the flukes are lifted by the contraction of the large muscles on top of the backbone. However, it now seems possible that the downstroke may be equally important, and not, as was previously believed, merely a passive return to the start of a new upstroke.

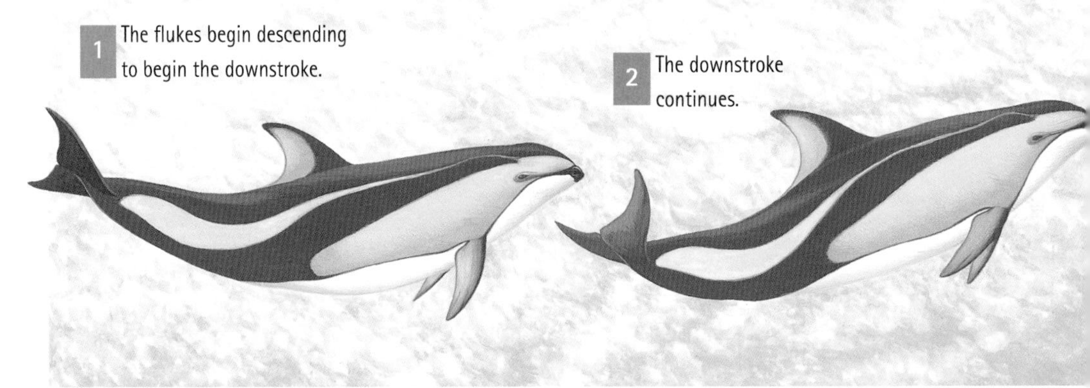

RIGHT: Hourglass dolphins porpoise while they ride the wake of a passing boat. Wave riding is quite an energy-efficient form of travel, but dolphins also appear to surf for pleasure.

minimum drag or turbulence. The streamlined shape of the cetacean's body, and its smooth, rubbery, flexible skin, which has few folds or wrinkles, promote laminar flow, at least as far back as the shoulder, the widest part of the body. Behind the shoulder, turbulence may form, but even this, for technically complex reasons, may ultimately reduce overall drag.

The Role of Skin

Certain properties of cetacean skin could also contribute here. At speed, or during rapid maneuvers, when turbulence develops, temporary ridges, or folds, form in the skin. These may well absorb and reduce the energy of the turbulence. This explanation, however, is highly speculative, and it is possible that these folds could *increase* drag. Also, the outer layer of a whale's skin contains oily compounds, which may "lubricate" the body as it moves through the water. A whale can shed this outer layer up to 12 times a day, and this could enhance the body's streamlining by limiting the growth of barnacles and other parasites that induce drag.

How Fast can Cetaceans Swim?

Dall's porpoises are the sprint champions, reaching speeds in excess of 31 mph (50 kph), although most species commonly cruise at between 5.5 mph (9 kph) and 10.5 mph (17 kph). Baleen whales pursued by whalers have attained 18.6 mph (30 kph), possibly in desperation, and there have been some impressive feats of strength and endurance—a fin whale traveled 2,300 miles (3,700 km) at an average of 10.5 mph (17 kph). However, sustained high-speed swimming is extremely costly in energy, and most routine swimming speeds are probably fairly low.

Attaining Speed

Small cetaceans use several methods to increase their speed or reduce effort, such as porpoising or bowriding. The familiar rhythmic airborne leaping of dolphins is called porpoising. While they are in the air, dolphins are free of water resistance and so are able to breathe efficiently while moving at high speed. This helps them to conserve energy. Oceanic dolphins are constantly on the move in search of scattered prey, and they often porpoise while traveling. Dolphins also use the water displaced by a boat or a large whale to enhance their speed, by bowriding on the pressure wave that it creates. You may see them jostling for position, each seeking to occupy the precise point at which the wave has sufficient thrust to sweep them forward with little effort.

3 The downstroke is completed.

4 The upstroke then begins.

5 Completing the upstroke, the dolphin prepares for the next downstroke, and the sequence is repeated.

Breathing, Diving, and Buoyancy

You may well be unaware that a whale is close by until you see or hear its blow. When a whale exhales, its pent-up breath can emerge loudly and explosively. This "blow" is a cloud of vapor that forms when condensed air from within the lungs, combined with oil droplets from inside the breathing passage and also water lying around the blowholes, meets cooler, outside air. The spectacular sight and sound of the tell-tale spout was once eagerly sought by whalers; today, whale-watching enthusiasts look out for it with equal anticipation. Experienced observers can often identify a whale's species by the size, shape, and angle of its blow alone, although some species' blows can be almost invisible, even at very close range.

Breathing and Blowholes

Unlike humans, cetaceans control their breathing completely voluntarily, but they need to surface regularly in order to breathe. The blowhole is often the first part of a whale to appear above the surface. After it blows, a whale immediately inhales very rapidly before diving again.

Whales' breathing patterns vary according to species, and are influenced by how active an individual is. While resting at the surface, a whale may blow quietly and invisibly, but when swimming fast, it can begin to blow while it is still underwater, and then inhale as soon as its blowhole breaks the water's surface.

The size of a cetacean's lungs is small in relation to the animal's overall size. Instead of relying on large lung capacity, whales exchange gases very efficiently, replacing about 80 percent of the air in their lungs each time they blow and inhale. In this respect they are about three times as efficient as land mammals.

Cetaceans also transport and store oxygen very efficiently in their bodies. They have proportionately more blood than other mammals. They also have a richer supply of the proteins that store oxygen: hemoglobin in the blood, and myoglobin in the muscles. The extra amount of both these proteins is what gives whale muscle its characteristic dark burgundy color.

ABOVE: A sperm whale plunges vertically to feed in the ocean depths. The remoras clinging to the whale for protection and transport may be capable of tolerating depths as extreme as those to which sperm whales dive.

Diving Ability

A number of physiological mechanisms enable whales to dive and remain underwater for long periods. As they dive, they are able to slow their heartbeat, and in doing so, save oxygen. At the same time, blood flows away from non-essential organs and toward vital ones, such as the brain and heart.

ABOVE: The powerful blast of a blue whale's blow cannot easily be confused with that of another species. It can rise higher than 30 feet (9 m) and may be visible for many miles. This whale can remain submerged for 30 minutes.

Water pressure increases with depth, which poses a known danger to human divers, but whales have developed a remarkable ability to avoid "the bends." This phenomenon occurs when pressurized air enters the bloodstream. As a diver ascends, the water pressure lessens, and the dissolved nitrogen component of the air expands, forming dangerous bubbles in the diver's bloodstream. When a whale dives, the increasing water pressure causes its lungs to collapse, and the remaining air is driven into the windpipe, where little of it can get into the bloodstream. Also, as a whale dives, blood flows into the small cavities inside the ear and equalizes the pressure in the inner and outer ear. By contrast, human divers must constantly equalize the air pressure in their sinus cavities while descending and ascending.

MAINTAINING BUOYANCY

Most whales have net negative buoyancy, and they will sink unless they compensate for this by holding some air in their lungs. Sperm whales dive vertically, descending as deep as 10,000 feet (3,000 m), where they may remain for an hour, or even two, in complete darkness and under enormous pressure. When it reaches the desired depth, a sperm whale may swim horizontally as it hunts for squid. When it has found and consumed sufficient prey, it then ascends vertically and lies motionless on the surface, where it blows continuously to reoxygenate its blood and muscles before it once again plunges vertically downward.

According to one theory, sperm whales have developed a special buoyancy mechanism that enables them to spend so much of their lives moving vertically. This theory says that, as the whale dives, the increased water pressure and reduced temperature cause the spermateci oil in its huge head to become denser. The whale therefore becomes heavier, making it easier to descend. When it next ascends, the pressure lessens and the oil becomes lighter and the whale rises effortlessly to the surface.

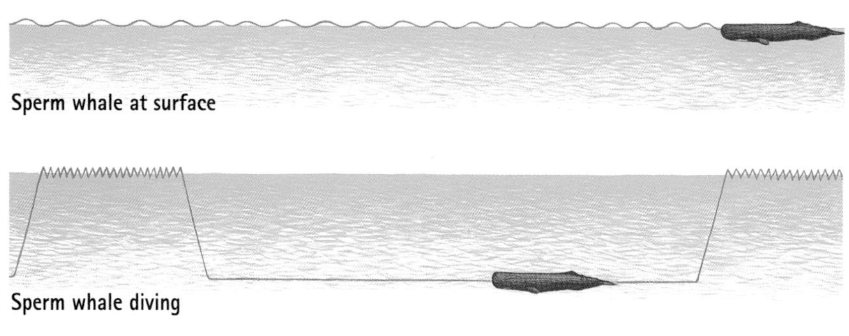

DIVE INTERVAL

Diving and breathing patterns vary between species and also depend on the animal's activity. Each small "crest" represents the whale surfacing in order to breathe. Sperm whales may dive to 10,000 feet (3,040 m), which the vertical scale does not show, although they average 1,000–2,500 feet (304–760 m). This is much deeper than either fin whales or dolphins, which rarely dive below 300 feet (92 m). The horizontal scale shows time elapsed during dive, not distance, which may vary.

Reproductive Cycles

One factor that affects the conservation of cetaceans is that they grow slowly. They do not become sexually mature for several years, and usually give birth to a single calf that remains dependent for some time, often for years. A low reproductive rate means that whales recover slowly from whaling and other setbacks. On the positive side, they are relatively long-lived, which allows females to produce many young during a lifetime. One consequence of Antarctic whaling was that fin whales became sexually mature earlier—at six instead of 10 years of age. As numbers declined, so did the competition for food, and this allowed the remaining whales to feed and grow more rapidly. A similarly early onset of sexual maturity occurred with sei whales. In effect, these two species responded to heavy whaling by increasing their reproductive rate.

LEFT: Whale catcher from the Norwegian factory ship KOSMOS, in Antarctic waters in about 1930. While fin and sei whales increased their reproductive rate in response to heavy whaling, the metabolic stresses involved may have caused them to age faster and die younger.

Baleen Whales

Baleen whales reach puberty reasonably early—at five to seven years of age. In many species, attainment of sexual maturity is closely related to body size, and for most, the timing of reproduction is linked to the seasons. Baleen whales, more than toothed whales, are tied to a pattern of annual migrations: to feeding areas in summer, and breeding areas in winter. Because of the physical demands of producing, suckling, and caring for a calf, especially while

Size Comparison

Weighing in at 2.75 tons (2.5 tonnes) and measuring about 23 feet (7 m) long, a newborn blue whale calf is more than 33 times heavier than the average adult human and about half the weight of an adult African elephant. An average adult blue whale would weigh roughly the same amount as about 1,300 people or 20 African elephants.

Left: A sperm whale cow with her rare albino calf. The low reproductive rate of this species allows females to invest many years of care in each calf.

migrating, females usually have a rest period of about two years before calving again. Changes in the length of days or in the water temperature, or even certain behavioral stimuli, can trigger ovulation hormonally.

In Southern Hemisphere humpbacks, the peaks of both ovulation and sperm production coincide in July, which suggests that mating also peaks at this time. January is their peak time in the Northern Hemisphere. The gestation period for rorqual whales is around 10-12 months; for gray whales it is 13.5 months. Females conceive during one winter breeding season, and return to calve the following year. Bryde's whales remain year-round in warmer water, and may mate at any time of the year.

Right whales generally calve every three years and humpbacks, every two to three years, However, some humpbacks calve only once in five years and other females have been seen with a new calf in three consecutive years. Males are sexually active every breeding season.

Toothed Whales

Some species of oceanic dolphins may have two annual breeding peaks: in spring and fall. Most toothed whales have a break of at least two years between calvings. Smaller species have a nine to 11 month gestation period, and they feed their calves for 18-24 months. The gestation period for pilot whales is about 12 months, and for sperm whales 16-17 months. Long-finned pilot whales calve, on average, every five years, but they display an unusual pattern: as females age, they calve less often, and spend longer feeding each successive calf.

Many female pilot whales stop breeding at about 40 years; belugas at about 21 years, and orcas at 27. These examples of menopause are very rare in non-human mammals. Since they live far longer than this, older females may have other roles to play, such as caring for other females' young. This appears to include actually feeding the calves of other whales, as pilot whale females over 50 years old—10 years past calving age—can still produce milk.

Development and Growth of Calves

Left: An orca calf swims with a group of older female relatives. These "aunts," which could include older sisters, may assist the calf to the surface immediately after birth and form a protective social network that will endure for life. However, the bond between the calf and its mother is particularly strong.

The most dangerous time of a calf's life is while it is being born. At this stage it is almost completely defenseless; it is at risk from predators, and could die from drowning, disease, and excessive heat loss. However, once they are born, young whales are well enough developed to be able to swim with their mothers and to withstand the surrounding water temperature. Whales sometimes give birth to twins, but these rarely survive.

During gestation, a calf grows from a mere speck of a fertilized egg up to, in the case of a blue whale, a fetus weighing 2.75 tons (2.5 tonnes). In the later stages of pregnancy, this fetus will increase by 220 lb (100 kg) a day, and during its seven-month suckling period the calf grows by 17 tons (15.4 tonnes), at a rate of 180 lb (82 kg) a day. In minke and sei whales the lactation period lasts from four to five months; in fin whales it lasts six months; and for humpbacks, 10.5 months.

Newborn calves cannot hold their breath for very long, so mothers often suckle them in short bouts. Whale milk is very rich, nearly 40 percent fat, and copious. As calves grow, their mothers suckle them less frequently, but for longer periods. If a calf is too persistent, a cow may refuse it milk by rolling on her back. She will even physically suppress a boisterous calf. This may be an energy-conserving tactic—the mother will need to replenish a calf's energy loss from her own limited supply of milk.

As they grow, calves become bolder and venture farther away from their mothers. Southern right whale cows permit their calves to associate with certain other females with

Below: Claire, a well-studied southern right whale, rests at the surface with her calf. In baleen whales, the close bond, so important during the calf's early life, is completely severed at weaning. For right whale calves, this is at about 10 months of age.

ABOVE: A week-old humpback whale calf remains close to its mother. Within three months it must be large enough and strong enough to accompany its mother on its first migration to Antarctic waters.

calves, but not other cows without calves, even threatening them if they approach. In this way, calves learn about social relationships.

Growing Up

Whales do not form nuclear families, as humans do: males play very little part in their offsprings' upbringing. In some highly social species, such as sperm and pilot whales, females may suckle and care for each other's calves, and even defend them against predators. Most cows are very protective of their young. Some, however, are less vigilant—one southern right whale that was observed lost two calves in succession, and her third was severely mauled by a large shark.

After their first year, toothed and baleen whales lead very different lives. Young toothed whales normally remain with their mother's group, at least until puberty, when the males of many species join other groups. Most toothed whales suckle their young for between one and two years; bottlenose dolphins do so for up to four years. Some older female sperm whales suckle their last one or two calves for as long as 15 years. Once baleen whales are weaned, they have little or no further contact with their mothers. The immediate post-weaning period can be dangerous and lonely for young baleen whales, but most of them soon form the social contacts they need in order to survive.

Play and Training

Whale calves often play, and they learn adult behaviors by mimicking them. Early socializing is vital for young whales as an important way to learn survival and other essential cooperative skills. Female orcas teach their young to hunt seals and other prey, an ability that contributes to the wellbeing and survival, not only of the calves, but also of the entire pod.

The Senses: Sight, Smell, and Taste

LEFT: *A bottlenose dolphin being fed at Monkey Mia in Western Australia. Many cetaceans see well in or out of water, and are able to compensate for the refraction at the water's surface.*

Scientists used to think that cetaceans had poor eyesight, but for most species they have been proved wrong. The cetacean eye is well adapted to low-light conditions, and can tolerate a great range of light intensity, from bright daylight to the extreme gloom of deep water. Some river dolphins, however, which live in a muddy environment, have almost dispensed with sight, although they can still distinguish between light and dark.

There is reason to believe that some species of dolphins have good color vision. Although water is usually a semi-opaque medium that quickly filters colors other than green and blue, the sometimes colorful markings on many dolphins and whales suggest that these species can recognize them at close quarters.

Whales use sight to examine their immediate environment, to look at objects of interest, and to capture prey at close range. Sight is particularly important for baleen whales, which lack the ability to echolocate (see page 116). It is also probably invaluable in helping them to avoid predators. The eyes of pygmy sperm whales can turn backward, perhaps for this very reason.

Many whales—including large species such as southern right whales—have their eyes set at the widest part of their head, and appear to have binocular vision. This means that their eyes, like those of humans, work together to focus on objects. Sperm whales, which have a huge head and eyes set well back, probably have only monocular vision in each eye. The bottlenose dolphin, which has excellent binocular vision, also has the unique ability to move each eye independently of the other.

Sense of Smell

For land mammals, both taste and smell are important for detecting chemical stimuli. The sense of smell, in particular, is useful for identifying substances that are some distance away. The structures that enable land mammals to detect smells do not operate in water, although fish, particularly sharks, do have external receptors that enable them to sense chemicals carried through the water. However, in cetaceans this ability seems to be much less well developed, or completely absent. Toothed whales have no olfactory equipment at all, but baleen whales do have olfactory nerves and sensors in their brains. While it is very unlikely that baleen whales are able to detect any smells underwater, it is possible that their olfactory sense comes into play when they rise to the surface to breathe, enabling them sometimes to smell plankton on the wind.

The Importance of Taste

All cetaceans do seem to use taste. It is obvious that some dolphins can distinguish between the tastes of different fish species. They also seem to be able to taste traces of other

BELOW: Many species of whales "spyhop," raising their heads vertically from the water to see above the surface. This enables them to see much further than they would below the surface.

dolphins' urine and feces, allowing them to follow a "taste trail" where other dolphins have recently passed. They may also use taste to locate food and to determine its freshness. Taste, too, is probably a means of sexual communication for dolphins; bottlenose dolphins appear to "sniff" the genital area of females to find out if they are in estrus. Taste may also play a part in whale navigation: fresh water from the mouths of rivers, the presence of living organisms such as plankton, or the chemical composition of some areas could give different parts of the ocean their own particular, recognizable taste.

The Senses: Touch and Hearing

A newborn calf's first sensations are probably the shock of entering the water, and then the feel of its mother's skin as she nudges it to the surface to take its first breath. In the next few months, frequent physical contact will reinforce the bond between mother and calf. In most species touch remains an important lifelong means of social communication. Even very large right whales touch each other quite gently as a form of social contact; some other species, such as humpbacks, appear to communicate more by sound than by touch. Courting whales often nibble or caress each other gently, but they may also resort to forceful physical contact and rough, and probably painful, behavior such as raking each other with their teeth. Gregarious social species, such as dolphins and orcas, maintain physical contact within their groups, even while swimming at high speeds.

Above: Whales use touch to explore their environment. Calves of many species, such as these young spotted dolphins in Little Bahama Banks, off Florida, often drape seaweed or pieces of driftwood over themselves. Antarctic minke whales have been seen balancing blocks of ice on their heads.

At well-frequented beaches in British Columbia in Canada, orcas appear to derive great pleasure from rubbing off flaking skin on the pebbly bottom. Such sensory stimulation is sometimes sexual in nature. For example, a male bottlenose dolphin may use its penis to explore objects, or a whale might rub its body against an inflatable boat that is similar in texture to a whale's skin. Touch may also have more routine applications, such as sensing the correct moment to open the blowhole when surfacing, or sensing disturbances to laminar flow (see page 82) while swimming.

Sound and Hearing

In a dense medium such as water, sound travels four times as fast, and very much farther, than it does in air. The ear canal of a baleen whale is blocked by a waxy plug, which may transmit sound to the inner ear. In toothed whales, the ear canal is open, but we cannot be certain whether these whales hear through this canal, through the bones of the skull, or through the fatty deposits in the lower jaw.

All whales and dolphins seem to have excellent hearing. They can not only hear distant sounds, but also recognize the direction from which they came. Cetacean ear bones are surrounded by air-filled foam that reflects

Left: This gray whale calf, in Baja California, enjoys the gentle feel of a human hand. Cetaceans' skin is soft and well supplied with nerves, which makes it very sensitive to touch. Even the largest whale may shiver at the lightest of touches.

sound, and this enables a whale to detect the difference between the strength of the sound in each ear. This is only one of many complex adaptations within the cetacean ear that indicate how important the sense of hearing is.

Another sense, one cetaceans might possess, allows some animals to detect perturbations in the earth's magnetic field. Many birds and sea turtles definitely have this ability, which they use for long-distance navigation. Crystals of the magnetic mineral magnetite, which are found in these and many other animals, have also been found in a number of toothed whales, as well as in one humpback whale, which suggests that cetaceans, too, may have this valuable "sixth sense."

RIGHT: While sight, taste and touch mainly provide information about what is nearby, hearing is probably the most important of all the senses, because it can also convey information from a distance. This singing male humpback whale off Hawaii can communicate with distant whales, even in darkness or murky water.

THE DYNAMICS OF WHALE POPULATIONS

Wild populations of whales are not fixed and stable. While there is usually an overall balance between births and deaths in a given whale population, numbers vary over time depending upon such factors as the availability of food, predation, the movement of individuals among populations, and the presence of whaling ships and fishing boats.

FOOD SUPPLY AND PREY

Large-scale natural events, such as climatic changes and variations in ocean currents, also affect whale populations. For example, El Niño activity in the South Pacific, in which the southeast trade winds fail, can cause fish populations to collapse, and can have complex, lasting effects on whale ecology. Prey species are also at risk from disease and the destruction of their coastal habitat by storm or flood.

If left undisturbed and given an adequate food supply, a population of whales may reach a state of equilibrium. When their numbers are very high, the competition for food is more intense, so the reproductive rates decline. However, when their numbers are low and food is abundant, whales grow faster and reach reproductive age earlier, which leads to an increase in their overall reproductive rate.

REPRODUCTIVE RATES

Whales have inherently low reproductive rates because they mature slowly, have long pregnancies (up to 15 months in sperm whales), and give birth to only one calf at a time. Many species also need to have a "rest" year between calves, or will care for a calf for some years before mating again. Right whales calve only every three years, while toothed whales, such as bottlenose dolphins or pilot whales, calve only every four to five years or longer. While these characteristics are comparable with those of the African elephant, they differ greatly from other, smaller mammals. Rodents, such as mountain voles in the western United States, can produce up to 15 young in a year, and are sexually mature at three weeks of age.

Whales reach sexual maturity relatively late in life. The older an animal matures, the less chance it has of surviving to reproductive age. Although it is still uncertain how long whales live, their longevity normally offsets this late sexual maturation. However, the heavy impact of commercial whaling dramatically increased death rates far beyond the whales' capacity to recover their numbers. This resulted in dramatic long-term population crashes. In species where numbers were severely depleted by whaling, as in the case of blue whales in the Southern Hemisphere, individuals may have difficulty finding a mate and their populations may never recover.

ABOVE: Although spinner dolphins occur in very large schools and number in the millions, they are still vulnerable to catastrophic events. Many hundreds of thousands have died in purse seine tuna nets.

During periods of heavy whaling the largest whales were prime targets: female baleen whales and male sperm whales were the hardest hit. Apart from unbalancing the

RIGHT: Southern right whales have one of the lowest reproductive rates of baleen whales: one calf per cow every three years. For more than 100 years after heavy whaling ceased, their populations scarcely seemed to increase and their numbers remained desperately low.

BELOW: Pacific gray whales, such as this large group off the Mexican coast, almost became extinct as a result of 19th-century whaling. They have since recovered and now number more than 20,000.

normally equal ratio of males to females, these were also the most reproductively experienced whales. Male baleen whales then had to compete to mate with fewer females, which led to fewer births. Also, because these females were younger and inexperienced, the chance of survival for those calves that were produced was even further reduced. In the case of male sperm whales, which don't reach sexual maturity until about 27 years of age, the surviving young males lacked the gradually acquired social and sexual skills needed to reproduce successfully.

Problems of Assessing Populations

Low reproductive rates make recovery from population disturbances long and slow. Unfortunately, cetacean population dynamics is not an exact science. Variations in the rates of population increase and decrease may not be detectable until too late and the population has already crashed. Apart from difficulties in estimating birth, death, and dispersal rates, the absolute size of populations is nearly impossible to establish because surveys used to calculate abundance are necessarily based on assumptions (such as that whales are evenly distributed over the survey area), which are often false. Hence, we may yet discover too late that the cessation of whaling or the control of overfishing was not soon enough for some species of whale.

Whale Migration

ABOVE: Orcas spyhopping in Antarctic sea ice in August. One theory to explain baleen whale migrations is that they leave polar waters to avoid winter predation by orcas, which might feed selectively on young baleen calves, if they were on hand.

Whale migration is a seasonal phenomenon. During the long, bright days of polar summers, whales feed on a rich variety of abundant marine life. In the polar winter, when food becomes scarcer, many animals move away to breed and rear their newborn young in warmer waters. This regular to-and-fro movement between feeding and breeding areas is known as the migratory cycle.

Baleen Whale Migrations

Of all whale migrations, those of baleen whales are the most predictable and the ones that have been most closely observed. But the reasons for these long, and somewhat arduous journeys is not perfectly clear. It is often assumed that newborn calves cannot survive in the cold winter waters, and that reduced food supplies in winter in feeding grounds cannot sustain the whale populations. Yet narwhals and some orcas, whose calves are smaller than baleen calves and should, at least theoretically, be more vulnerable to heat loss, remain in polar waters all year-round, and breed there. In Antarctic waters, there is ample food in winter to sustain millions of seals and penguins, as well as numerous minke whales. And although Southern Hemisphere humpbacks always migrate to tropical waters in order to breed, in any one year half of the adult females remain in the Southern Ocean during winter. These are probably whales that are in the resting phase of their breeding cycle.

Shortening days seem to be the trigger for the whales' departure, but other factors may also play a part. Different groups of Southern Hemisphere humpbacks, for example, leave Antarctic waters at different times during fall. The first to depart are females with suckling calves, which are on the verge of becoming independent; the last are pregnant females that need to gain extra weight to prepare them for the long journey. After up to three months in the tropics, newly pregnant females leave first, followed by immatures, adult males, and, last, cows with calves that are large enough to endure their first migration. Tropical breeding waters and migration routes are food-poor compared to polar waters, so there is little chance to feed on the move. Whales must subsist for up to eight weeks on the energy stored in their muscle, blubber, and body fat.

Whale Migration Map
Migration routes, breeding areas, and feeding areas of humpback and right whales, the baleen whales whose migrations are best known. Solid lines indicate regular migrations while dotted lines represent occasional migratory movement.

Humpback
Breeding areas

Humpback
Feeding areas

Right Whale
Breeding areas

Right Whale
Feeding areas

The Great Rorqual Migrations

Humpbacks in both hemispheres migrate huge distances. In the North Atlantic, humpbacks from feeding grounds as far apart as Maine in the USA, Greenland, and Iceland congregate to breed on shallow banks in the West Indies. Whales from a single Antarctic feeding ground may travel in successive years to such South Pacific breeding areas as New Caledonia, Tonga, and Australia's Great Barrier Reef. Some humpbacks move between Japan, Hawaii, and British Columbia, while one group, which every year travels from the Antarctic Peninsula across the Equator to Colombia, and back, has the longest regular migration of any mammal. Other rorquals have a similar migratory cycle, though we know little of the routes they take or the location of their breeding grounds.

Northern right whales may move from feeding grounds near Iceland to the east coast of the USA. Southern right whales migrate from the southern continents as far south as the Antarctic ice edge. The seasonal formation of sea ice in Arctic waters is the signal for bowheads to move to warmer parts.

Toothed Whale Migrations

Many toothed whales are nomadic, rather than truly migratory: their movements are dictated more by changing distributions of prey than by patterns of feeding and breeding. Two migrating species that forsake the polar regions in winter are bottlenose and long-finned pilot whales. As the cold sets in, the former set out for the tropics and the latter make for cool temperate regions. Whether a mature sperm whale makes a seasonal move depends on its sex: females, along with immature males and juveniles, do not move from warmer waters; adult males spend the summer months in polar areas, feeding on squid. In general, we know far less about the migrations of toothed whales than we do about those of baleen whales.

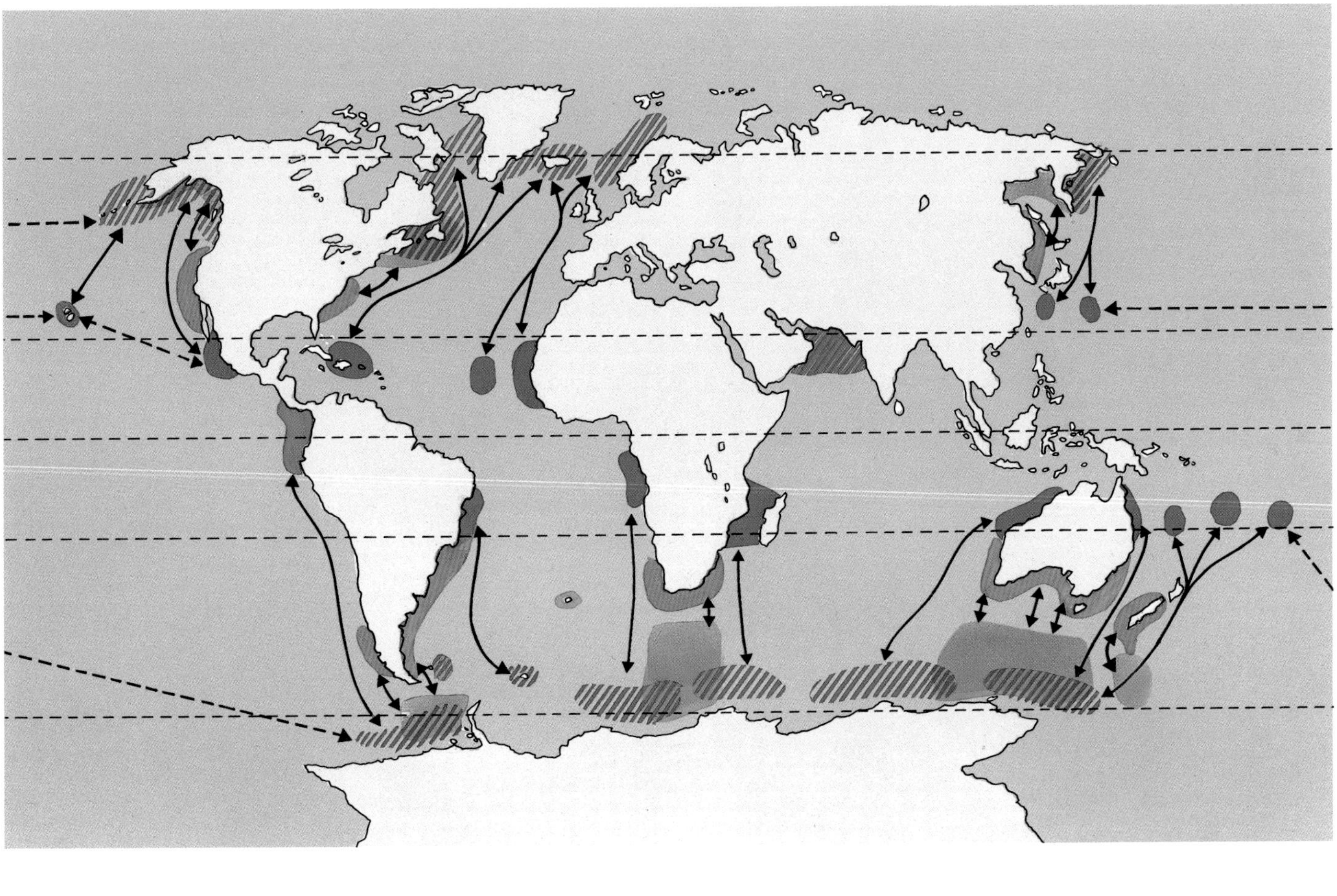

The Mechanics of Migration

LEFT: Fin whales are among the fastest and most powerful migratory travelers, moving between warm tropical waters, such as this lagoon in Baja California, Mexico , and Alaska.

BELOW: Humpback whales in Platypus Bay, Fraser Island, off the eastern coast of Australia. After breeding in the sheltered waters of the Great Barrier Reef, many humpbacks pause here for a few days before returning to the open sea for the long haul south to Antarctica.

The distances that many whales cover in the course of a migratory cycle are so great that each year they spend as much time in transit as they do in the feeding and breeding grounds that they travel between. They may need to swim for two to three months at a time, moving between icy cold and lukewarm waters, finding their way across apparently featureless oceans to destinations that may be mere reefs or tiny islands.

Fast or Slow?

Although they travel more or less constantly, both in daylight and darkness, migrating whales seldom swim non-stop. They may pause to rest, to socialize, or even to feed, although this happens rarely. Social interaction is as important to whales when they are traveling as when they are in their feeding and breeding grounds. During their migration, whales are often seen idling, or engaging in vigorous pre-mating behavior. Sometimes they will even swim against the flow of migration. As a result, there is considerable variation in overall migration speeds, not just from one day to the next, but also among individual groups and within different species.

We do know that humpbacks are slow migrators. The average speed of southern humpback migrations over many years—calculated by timing the peak of migration past various latitudes—was 34 miles (55 km) per day, or 1.4 miles per hour (2.25 kph). The fastest humpback migration on record—at an average speed of almost three miles per hour (5 kph)—was from Alaska to Hawaii.

The Energy Factor

The energy required to migrate long distances is enormous, particularly for females that produce a calf and then feed it during the journey. It takes up to 15 times as much energy to feed a calf as it does to produce a fetus. Blue, fin, and humpback females may double their weight during the feeding season, only to lose most of what was gained. In the course of a migration, a blue whale cow may shed up to 80 tons (72.6 tonnes). Toward the end of a migration, many individuals appear very depleted, and sometimes resort to feeding. Because of their poor physical condition, and therefore their low oil content, whales on a return migration to their feeding grounds were usually safe from attack by whalers.

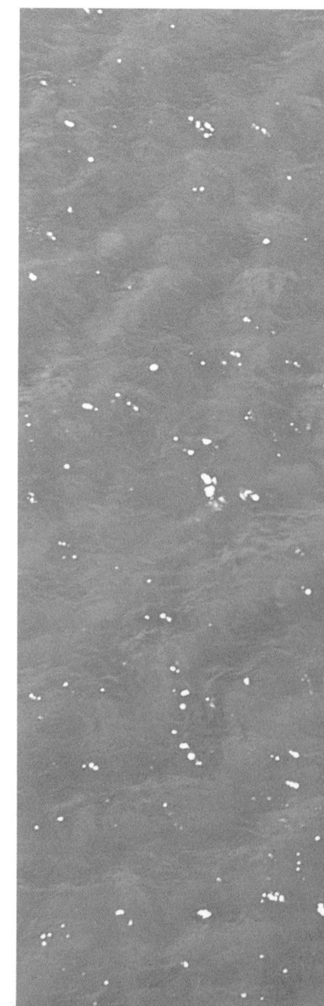

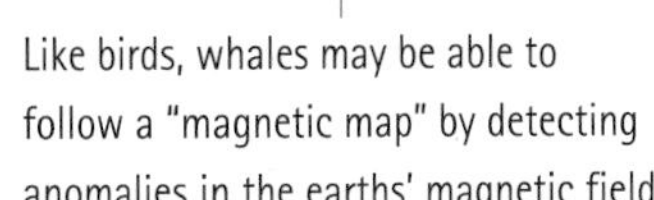

WHALE NAVIGATION

How whales navigate during their long migrations remains a mystery. There is an array of possible mechanisms, some of which we know are used by other migratory animals. It is possible that over millions of years a number of these strategies have become blended to give whales a kind of general navigational awareness. Unraveling the details is a major task for the future.

Predators, Parasites, and Diseases

LEFT: External parasites on whales include barnacles and crustaceans such as "whale lice" or cyamids. Both are more common on slower-swimming cetaceans. Cyamids feed on shedding skin or unhealed wounds, as on this injured northern right whale, which may have been entangled by a rope or net.

Whales live in a dangerous environment. They face a number of natural external threats and are subject to a range of debilitating, and sometimes fatal, diseases.

Predation—the killing of one animal by another—is probably the most constant external danger. Large sharks, such as great whites, regularly prey on smaller dolphins. Stories of dolphins pursuing groups of terrified sharks are merely imaginative flights of fancy. Whales, too, sometimes attack and kill other whales and dolphins. Orcas, also called killer whales, can stage coordinated assaults on other cetaceans, including blue whales and humpbacks. And it now seems likely that the orca's relatives, the false killer, pygmy killer, and pilot whales, also prey on other cetaceans. The tooth rake-marks found on the flukes of many baleen whales is a sign that orcas or other toothed whales have attacked them.

A whale's tail flukes are its best defence against large predators; lashing out with these, it can inflict a damaging blow to an assailant. Some whales group together when they sense danger. Adult sperm whales, for example, form protective rings, with their calves in the center and their flukes pointing outward.

Whale Parasites

It is the whale's lot to be infested by parasites, both external and internal. One of the most discomfiting of these is the tiny "cookie-cutter" shark, barely 20 inches (50 cm) long, which scoops out mouthfuls of flesh from the

BELOW: Some parasites are specific to certain host species. This barnacle, Cryptolepos rhachianecti, *favors gray whales. Cyamids can be seen here sheltering among the barnacles.*

ABOVE: *There is increasing evidence that sharks attack large whales. This southern right whale calf, along with several other calves and their mothers, was mauled by a large shark at a breeding area in South Australia. Great white sharks up to 18 feet (5.5 m) long are frequently seen prowling in this area.*

back and sides of a whale as if using an icecream scoop. Assaults such as these will not kill a whale, but they may weaken it and leave it open to infection or invasion by other parasites. Seagulls, for example, often perch on whales' backs, pecking at open wounds, which may lead to infections. Remoras, or sucker fish, attach themselves for a free ride. They may slow a whale down, but they do no harm.

Humpbacks, in particular, are subject to infestations of barnacles. In cooler waters, a whale may carry up to half a ton (0.45 tonnes) of barnacles. However, these usually drop off during migration to warmer areas. Cyamids, or "whale lice," cannot swim, so they must transfer from whale to whale during physical contact. One cyamid species lives only on humpbacks; others are found on various whales, suggesting that there is some social interaction between these whale species.

Internal parasites, which are common in all cetaceans, include tapeworms, nematodes, and flatworms. They occur in all body organs, including the lungs, brain, inner ear, kidneys, and intestines. They may be related to some serious whale diseases, and therefore could be an important, if indirect, contributor to whale deaths. Severe parasite infestations have been found in many stranded and hunted whales.

WHALE DISEASES

Cancers, pneumonia, bacterial infections, and ulcers are some of the diseases to which whales are susceptible. In recent times, an increasing number of viral infections has also been detected, and some of these are thought to be responsible for mass die-offs of dolphins and seals. Toothed whales frequently band together to give physical support and protection to sick or dying pod members; rather than abandoning them, a whole group will often strand. Baleen whales, which do not live in constant groups, show little evidence of such cooperative protective behavior.

Whale Behavior

The study of whale behavior encompasses everything they do, including their courtship and mating, their complex communications by means of clicks, whistles, and song; their echolocation abilities; and their tragic tendency to strand. This chapter also explores whale intelligence and social structures.

Social Organization Among Whales

The social organization of whales is the link that binds their group structure, behavior, and ecology. This complex and fascinating aspect of their lives is largely determined by three main priorities: feeding, reproduction, and avoiding predation. Group size among cetaceans is fluid in many species, but in most cases, the larger the gathering of prey, the larger the group will be. Formation of groups also facilitates mating, and there is safety in numbers when predators are about.

Baleen Whales

Baleen whales are usually seen in groups of fewer than 10, and such observations have led many scientists to conclude that small groups are the norm for these whales. Yet the numbers of most baleen whale species are still so reduced by whaling that reported sightings may have created a false picture of their societies. There are historical accounts of feeding groups of as many as 100 northern right whales, and recently, a group of 80 pygmy right whales was sighted—a species that was previously considered largely solitary. In 1996, 25 blue whales were observed feeding in a localized area off Antarctica. There is concern that blue whales may become extinct in the Southern Ocean because their desperately low numbers may hamper individual whales in the search for a mate.

Humpbacks and southern right whales, the best-studied baleen whales, are now revealing unexpectedly subtle and complex social ties. Instead of making short-term associations as previously believed, recent studies have shown that individual humpbacks form cooperative relationships that endure for many years. Usually, these are between females, or between a male and a female, rather than males together as they seem unable to put aside the aggression which is at the heart of their interactions during the breeding season. Male right whales in breeding areas form alliances in order to help each other to mate, while mothers associate with other preferred cows and calves. In the well-studied population at the Head of Bight in South Australia, about 70 whales congregate each winter. In such groups, individual variation in social behavior becomes apparent, and although it is not scientific to say so, "personality" and "likes and dislikes" seem to play a part in determining the nature of interactions among individuals.

RIGHT: In a peaceful meeting, a mature male sperm whale gently nuzzles adult females and young in a nursery school. During the breeding season, bull males move among many such schools.

ABOVE: Offshore spotted dolphins form schools of up to several thousand, while more coastal groups, such as this one in the Bahamas, off Florida, form smaller, close-knit groups.

Toothed Whales

Toothed whale groups are generally larger and more stable than those of the baleen whales. Like baleen whales, their group size is largely determined by feeding ecology. Coastal dolphins, with more patchy prey and more exposure to predators, form large groups that overlap—and interbreed—along coastlines.

LEFT: A group of southern right whales socializes during the breeding season in Australian waters. In this and other species, associations between individuals are known to persist over many years.

Oceanic dolphins travel in small, stable pods that amalgamate into large, temporary herds, sometimes of hundreds, or even thousands, seeking patches of widely dispersed prey, and facing many predators, such as sharks. Because river dolphins exist in a stable environment with evenly dispersed prey and few predators, they occur in small groups, or singly.

Most toothed whale societies are female-based, or matrilineal. With few exceptions, such as orcas and pilot whales, males leave their mother's group at sexual maturity, and join other groups. Mating occurs when such groups meet at sea, so an individual's chances of mating are increased if they are part of such a group. Male sperm whales leave their mother's group at about 10 years of age, and join bachelor groups until they are about 27—when they are large enough to compete sexually. Female sperm whales remain with their mother's group for life; their calves are cared for by the entire "nursery school."

Are Whales Altruistic?

Toothed whales may risk their own lives to help or simply accompany a companion in distress. The theory is that altruistic, or selfless, behavior occurs between closely related individuals, because by helping one another they are improving the chances of their shared genes surviving. Altruistic behavior appears to be the basis of many mass strandings, where healthy individuals will strand with an ailing companion. Sperm whales were famous among old-time whalers for their habit of defending or accompanying a harpooned pod member. However, toothed whales are not always altruistic: in one incident, a pod of

ABOVE: A large pod of humpback whales in Alaska. Generally they are found in pods of two or three, forming larger groups for mating or feeding. When humpbacks were more numerous prior to whaling, larger groups may have been more common.

oceanic dolphins quickly abandoned one group member that had become entangled in a net. When released, it fled in their direction.

Status and Hierarchies

Dominance hierarchies, or "pecking orders," are clearly seen in captive cetaceans. In the wild, superior status may be expressed in the right of access to important resources such as food, or by segregation of animals in space. In some oceanic dolphins, schools form up to five layers, which reform after each surfacing—presumably the highest status animals are closest to the surface, where they expend less energy to breathe. Schools of toothed whales are often segregated according to age or sex.

ABOVE: An orca calf drapes itself over its mother in play. Whether male or female, this calf will remain with its mother's group for life, as orcas are one of the few species of whales in which males do not "leave home" on reaching adolescence.

RIGHT: A coordinated pod of dusky dolphins enjoys rough seas during a gale. Off Argentina, these dolphins are known to feed in small groups, and form into larger groups to rest and socialize. Off New Zealand, their group size is more constant, whether feeding or socializing.

Dolphin Society: Bottlenose Dolphins

The complexities of toothed whale societies are well illustrated by inshore bottlenose dolphins. This dolphin species has been more closely studied than any other. Their society is matrilineal, with adult females forming the permanent basis of a group. Males leave their mother's group on reaching puberty.

Alliances and Friendships

Bottlenose dolphin society is known as a "fission–fusion" society, with the composition of groups changing frequently as individuals come and go. There are clearly defined dominance hierarchies, with the largest males being the most dominant animals. The strongest and most enduring bonds, known as "alliances," appear to be among mature males. These alliances may exist between two or more males, who feed, travel and socialize with one another.

The key to the importance of such male alliances is that females mate only every four to five years. This means that sexually receptive females are rare in any population at a given time. Therefore, males must attempt to maximise their chances of mating with them. Male alliances chase females in order to subdue and herd them prior to mating. In Shark Bay

BELOW: Many bottlenose dolphins are heavily scarred from tooth rakes as much dolphin behavior is aggressive. Besides biting, other tactics include slapping with fins or flukes, pushing, shoving, clapping of the jaws, hitting, and squawking.

ABOVE: Bottlenose dolphins and silky sharks congregate to feed on schooling bonito. By forming alliances, or other social groupings, these dolphins enhance their chances of successful feeding and reduce the likelihood of shark attack.

in Western Australia, these chases are successful in an average of three occasions out of four. However, the actual mating has not yet been observed during these encounters. These chases may be rough affairs, with females often being pushed, hit, and bitten. Also in Shark Bay, relationships have been discovered among various male alliances: some cooperate to herd females, while others will actively compete to the point of fighting, and attempt to "steal" females from each other. Friendly alliances are maintained by frequent social contact.

Female associations appear to be less rigid. Some are "social butterflies," associating briefly with many other females, while some have longer, more stable relationships. Females have occasionally been seen hiding from male alliances that were harassing them, or have been sighted protecting other females from such harassment. Suckling of calves may last for up to four years. Sometimes mothers and daughters remain together for life.

Social dominance also extends to feeding. Certain dominant dolphins observed following fishing boats had first choice of discarded fish, while less dominant animals went without.

RIGHT: A solitary bottlenose dolphin echolocates for small fish buried in sand. Solitary dolphins are a perplexing anomaly in such a social species, and they have to feed and defend themselves without any assistance from other dolphins.

Conversely, bottlenose dolphins are well known for their cooperative feeding behavior, in which schooling fish are herded and contained while individuals take turns to feed. They may also hunt singly along rocky foreshores.

For such remarkably social animals, the bottlenose dolphins display one puzzling anomaly: the solitary dolphin. These are animals that have either been ostracized socially for some reason, or choose to live outside of their society. Major advantages of group life, such as cooperative feeding and defense against predators, are no longer available to them. In Monkey Mia, Western Australia, some solitary dolphins have a habit of wearing sponges over their beaks, possibly for protection. They spend most of their day foraging for fish, and their infants get little opportunity to play with other dolphins.

Sexual Behavior

Frequent physical contact reinforces bonds between individuals. Sexual mounting, such as between males, or between calves and adults, may occur outside actual mating. Calves prepare for adult life by copying many of the behaviors of the group, such as play fighting. Dolphins are often seen stroking or touching each other. Sexual behavior seems common and casual in bottlenose society; one researcher has described it as being "like a handshake."

Courtship and Mating

Left: An active mating group of bottlenose dolphins off the southern Australian coast. With this and many other species, courtship and mating are often vigorous and sometimes violent activities.

Whales and dolphins have evolved a variety of mating systems and strategies to reproduce. No cetaceans pair for life, as some humans or albatrosses do. Most species are promiscuous, with both males and females having more than one mate. Some species, such as pilot and sperm whales, are polygynous: the males mate with multiple partners. Such males, when mature, are often much larger than females, and the greater size of the older males may serve to deter competition without conflict from the smaller, younger males.

The first stage of courtship for both sexes is to locate a suitable mate. No one is sure how females signal that they are in estrus; possibly they use secretions in their urine. Before mating can commence, several males may compete to temporarily escort a female.

Baleen Whales

In humpback whales, males advertise their presence with song, and a female chooses her "principal escort." Other males attempt to displace him, in violent competition involving head-butting, fluke slapping, and jostling. No one knows on what criteria a female bases her choice. Such competition may be the female's way of ensuring that the strongest male fathers her calf. The challengers lose interest when they are unable to take his place. Less rough and more peaceable courtship behaviors, such as slow slapping of pectoral fins, help to synchronize the prospective mate's mood and behavior with that of her suitor.

Gray whales form mating groups consisting of a female and several males. These groups break up when the female has mated with most, if not all, of the males. Male southern right whales use a system called "sperm competition." They have by far the largest testes of any animal, with a combined weight of up to one ton, and produce copious amounts of sperm. Over several weeks, many males will copulate many times with each receptive female. Females will readily copulate

Left: Once chosen by a female, a humpback male must defend his position against challengers. This often results in a surging group of as many as seven males engaged in physical combat around the female, striking each other with their heads and flukes, all seeking to become her principal escort.

ABOVE: A young male spotted dolphin (lower) mates with an older female. Apart from being the means of reproduction, copulation may also be useful as a mechanism for maintaining social bonds between individuals.

with several males, often in quick succession. There is much activity, but no aggressive competition as with humpbacks, and some males even appear to assist each other by restricting the movements of females.

Toothed Whales

Apart from bottlenose dolphins, the breeding behavior of most other toothed whales remains a mystery. Male narwhals use their tusks to duel for access to females. In beaked whales, many males are heavily scarred by tooth marks, suggesting that they also engage in boisterous or even violent male-to-male contests, although these scars could be inflicted during courtship and mating.

Male sperm whales usually travel singly or occasionally in pairs among nursery schools, mating with all the available receptive females before moving on to other schools.

ABOVE: Southern right whales often mate near coastal cliffs where they can easily be observed. Mating whales may lie side by side on their backs at the surface. The males' mobile, probing eight-foot-long penises have been likened by one researcher to "fire hoses."

Whale Communication

Whales have exploited the sound-carrying properties of water by developing superior acoustic communication abilities. Their sounds range from the ultrasonic moans of blue whales to the high-frequency clicks of some dolphins. Although both ends of this spectrum are beyond the range of human hearing, many whale sounds are audible to us.

Baleen whales probably use their larynxes to produce sounds that are generally of lower frequencies than those of toothed whales. The low-frequency sounds of blue and fin whales may travel hundreds or even thousands of miles. This raises interesting questions about our concept of what constitutes a whale group, which may be defined as a number of animals in contact with each other. All whales use sound to varying degrees to communicate.

Above: Hector's dolphin from New Zealand uses only clicks to communicate. Unlike sperm whales, their high-frequency clicks are above the range of unaided human hearing. Certain types of clicks seem to be associated with feeding. Others occur when dolphins are excited or threatened.

Whistles, Clicks, and Codas

Most toothed whales produce two basic types of communicative sounds: whistles and clicks. Low-frequency harmonic sounds have also been described in bottlenose dolphins, while orcas use a fourth type, pulsed calls. Bottlenose dolphins and probably many other species use "signature whistles," unique to individual animals. Constant whistling in gregarious species may be an ongoing "roll call," by which animals signal their continued presence. While there is no evidence yet that any cetacean uses a formal language, bottlenose dolphins use complex vocalizations in a variety of contexts, and may be able to convey relatively complex meaning by sound, possibly including information about food or predators. Whistling often accompanies excitement, stress, and intense social interactions.

While clicks are used by all toothed whales for echolocation, they may also be used for communication. Along with porpoises, sperm whales are one of the few species known to use clicks exclusively. They seem to communicate using patterns of clicks known as "codas." Some of these codas may be individual signatures, while others appear to be shared by more than one animal. Their meaning remains unknown, except to the whales.

With orcas, several resident pods may join to form a community. Each pod has a unique dialect, similar to other pods in its community. It is quite different from the dialects of other pods with which they are not in contact. Nevertheless, all orcas make similar types of sounds, regardless of their geographic origins.

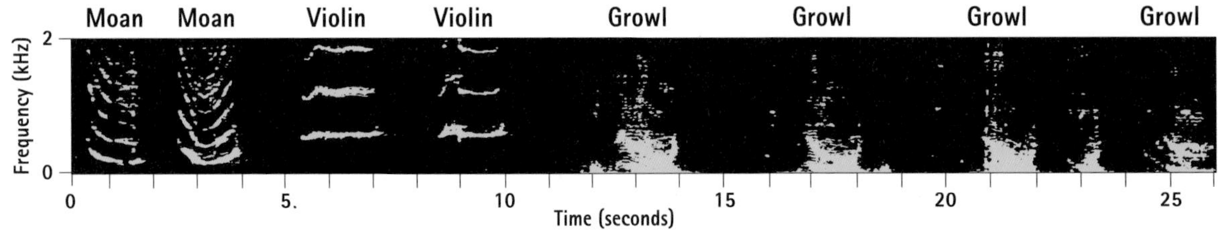

Left: Converting sound to marks on paper, this sonogram graphically represents a sequence of humpback whale songs. Researchers invent their own terms to describe sounds.

HUMPBACK SONGS

Humpback whalesong consists of fixed sequences of what have been described as "farmyard" sounds—moans, grunts, chirps, and whistles. They may last from five to15 minutes before being repeated many times, often for hours. Whalesong commonly occurs on breeding grounds and during migration, and very rarely on feeding grounds. Singing is almost invariably the preserve of males, and is thought to be used to court females. It is probably audible to other whales for many miles. Each migratory population has a unique song, sung by all its singers with slight individual variations. There may be similarities among the songs of different populations living in the same ocean basin, supporting other evidence that animals of different populations mingle in feeding areas. Songs of populations occupying different oceans or hemispheres, however, are commonly quite different from one another. Whalesongs are constantly evolving as minor modifications are made here and there. How and why these changes occur and are transmitted through a population remains a mystery.

WHALESONG

The extraordinary songs of humpback whales are unique in their elaborate complexity, although they can also use simpler sounds to communicate. Humpback songs show regional "dialects," and other species show similar variation. Blue whales have a very simple "song" consisting of as few as four drawn-out notes, the context of which is uncertain. Right whales are one of the more taciturn species, uttering occasional moans, belches, and grunts, and apparently relying more on physical contact than sound to communicate. Bowheads are more vocal, and scientists can count how many there are by the sounds these whales make while migrating.

NON-VOCAL COMMUNICATION

Much communication is non-vocal and whales use their bodies as instruments to convey a wide variety of meaning to each other. There is a spectrum of subtlety in non-vocal communication. At one end is the most spectacular behavior of all, the breach. Many species breach, from dolphins to blue whales. A fully grown whale breaching is an impressive visual signal, and the thump of its landing can be heard for some distance. On the other hand, cetaceans frequently communicate with the gentlest of touches, or the subtlest of gestures, such as a gentle tail flick.

BELOW: Orcas are a highly social species. They seem to use their calls to coordinate hunting behavior and to maintain contact with other members of their pod.

Aerials and Acrobatics

Considerable energy is required to breach, and one wonders at the meaning of a humpback whale breaching as many as 100 times consecutively, as has been observed. Several explanations have been proposed for breaching. It may be an overt warning to another whale or to a boat that has come too close, or it may signal the breacher's presence in rough conditions when vocalizations cannot be heard. It may be play or a sign of excitement, a distress signal from a calf separated from its mother, or even a way to dislodge parasites.

Many species use other "aerial" behaviors, such as "lobtailing" (slapping the tail flukes on the water) or "pec-slapping" (slapping pectoral fins on the water). These are both visual and audible signals that may convey a range of meaning. Lobtailing is sometimes a response to harassment, but at other times it is a leisurely activity possibly related to courtship. Pec-slapping is commonly seen in humpback courtship, when their very long flippers come down with a crack that can be heard for miles.

Aggressive Non-vocal Tactics

Many behaviors signal threat or challenge. When fighting, male humpback whales often inflate their throat pleats, possibly to appear larger. They sometimes blow streams of bubbles underwater to deter rivals. An explosive blow in the presence of a nearby whale or boat may signal irritation or a warning, something whale-watchers should be

ABOVE: Most whales prefer to land on their well-muscled backs than on their softer undersides, and here we see the belly of a humpback whale in full breach. Humpbacks often breach in a direction away from any nearby boats.

alert to. Dolphins often clap their jaws loudly; male bottlenose dolphins use this sound to threaten females in order to herd them.

Threatening gestures reach their extreme in jostling, biting, slapping with fins or flukes, or head butting. For many species, however, threats have become ritualized gestures, and actual violence is not used. A right whale, for example, may quietly orient its body to point its flukes (its main weapon) at an unwanted intruder. The message is clear—stay away—and it is usually respected. The omission of such gestures also has meaning, so if a right whale's posture remains unchanged as another whale approaches, the approaching whale may assume that it is welcome.

Gentle Non-vocal Gestures

Cetacean communication also includes the gentle touches and caresses associated with courtship. Mothers and calves have their own subtleties of communication. During the calf's early life they are in frequent physical contact, which probably reassures both mother and calf. Calves may communicate their displeasure at being refused a feed by throwing "temper tantrums." These may involve head butting and fluke slapping, and a mother sometimes physically restrains her calf in these situations, even clasping it with her pectoral fins. In the event of a possible threat, such as a boat, she may interpose her body between the threat and her calf in order to protect it from potential harm.

BELOW: A humpback whale lobtailing in response to being followed too closely by a boat. It had earlier signaled its annoyance by several sudden changes of direction, and its displays became more forceful as the unwanted attention continued.

ABOVE: Non-vocal communication may signal the presence of food. Dusky dolphins leap from the water when schools of fish are nearby. This may alert distant dolphins to join in, for the more dolphins herding the fish, the better the chance of a good feed for all.

Echolocation

Equivalent to radar or sonar, echolocation is the production of sound, the returning echoes of which give the animal an acoustic "picture" of some part of its environment. Echolocation clicks must have two basic properties. They must be loud enough for the echoes to return to the animal, and short enough so that the echo of one returns before the next one is sent out. The clicks are emitted in a "train." These may be widely spaced while scanning, but as the whale or dolphin "locks onto" and approaches a target, the interval between clicks may shorten until the train sounds like a buzzing creak. Higher frequencies may be used at shorter range, as these probably give better image resolution.

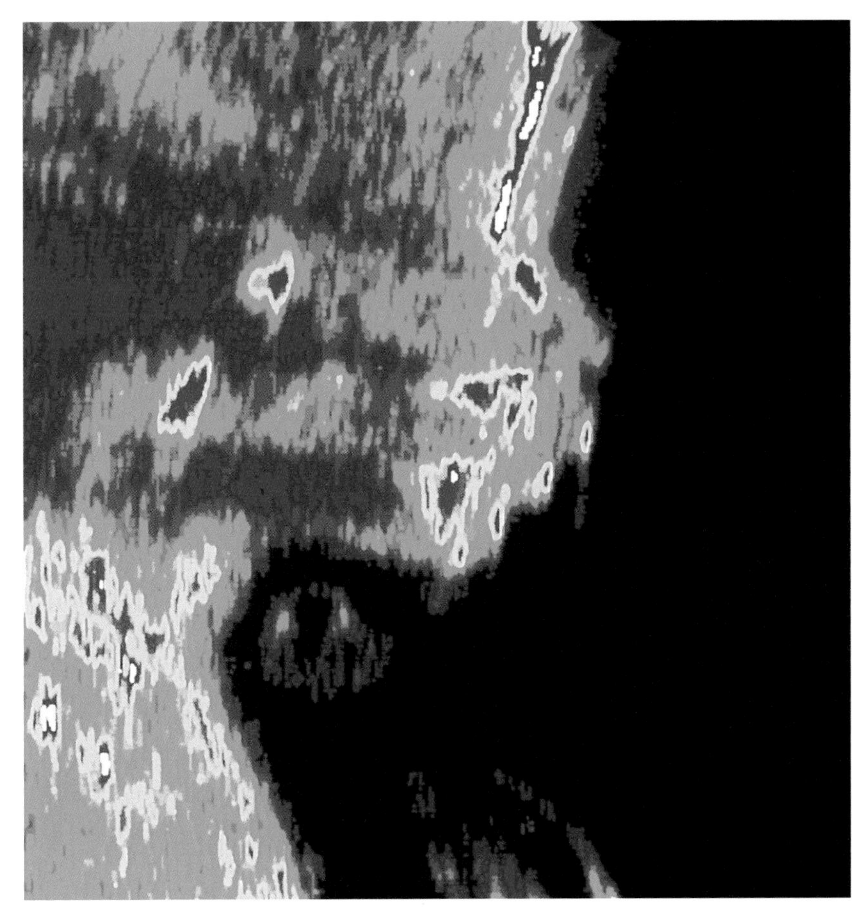

Processing Echolocation Signals

It is impossible to know how cetaceans process the information that echolocation gives them. The auditory centers in toothed whale brains are very well developed, indicating that complicated processing of sound occurs. As humans rely so heavily on the sense of sight, we find it hard to imagine "sound pictures." Yet it is thought that sound can convey more

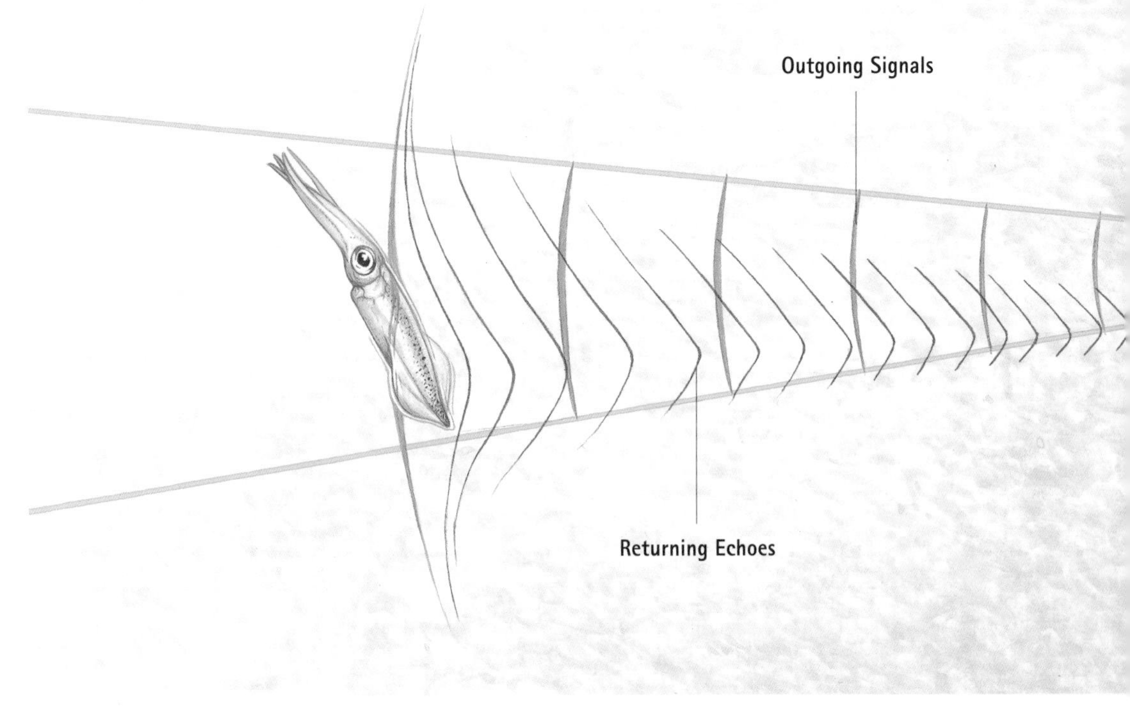

Echolocation
Echolocation clicks are produced in the upper nasal passages and then focused ahead into a narrow, directional beam. The front of the skull may act as a parabolic reflector, but focusing seems mainly to occur in the bulbous fat-filled melon, which can probably change shape to alter the beam's focus. The returning echoes are received through the lower jaw, part of which contains fat. It is speculated that the teeth of some species may act as an "acoustic window" for receiving sound.

LEFT: Medical ultrasound is a human technological analogy to echolocation, but it is probably ridiculously crude in comparison with the echolocation that dolphins use. Ultrasound relies on a visual image, but cetaceans "see" with their hearing.

complex information than light and, by echolocating, cetaceans may experience three-dimensional images of a richness possibly comparable to human sight.

RANGE AND LIMITATIONS

In bottlenose dolphins, echolocation seems to be effective as least as far as 2,500 feet (762 m), and possibly farther in this or other species. The significance of such a sense is clear—in darkness or in murky water, cetaceans are able to scrutinize objects on the sea floor and locate and track prey and predators. One drawback is that echolocation operates in a narrow beam directly ahead of the animal, but a wider target area can be covered by swinging the head from side to side. River dolphins do this lying on their sides in order to scan the full depth of shallow water.

Studies of captive dolphins show that they can use echolocation with remarkable ability to discriminate among several objects differing only subtly. These include metal balls made of similar material but of slightly different sizes. They can also differentiate between hollow and solid balls and balls with different surface textures. Dolphins can even distinguish between balls of similar size made from metals of different densities.

BELOW: Besides toothed whales, certain bats appear to be the only animals that have evolved the ability to echolocate.

The advantages of these abilities to the dolphins are tremendous. For example, they are able to distinguish between the shapes and textures of toxic and non-toxic fish. They also seem able to use echolocation to track fast-moving objects with ease.

Most toothed whales have very good sight and hearing, so there is no need for them to echolocate all the time. Much of their time is spent simply listening to the ambient sounds of the ocean. This may explain why many cetaceans drown in monofilament gillnets, which their echolocation is perfectly capable of detecting. Echolocation might be "switched on" only when interesting sounds have been heard, or when prey animals have been sighted by eye, or perhaps not until the whale has reached an area where prey is often found.

The acoustic behavior of sperm whales has been well studied. During feeding dives, they echolocate much of the time, with occasional intriguing silences. Their normal clicks may occur once a second or so, but every so often the rate will increase, faster and faster, until there is a "creak" like a squeaking hinge, then silence before the normal clicking resumes. The increased click rate may signal the approach of a squid, and the final buzzing creak could represent the last few feet of increasingly short-range echolocation before the squid is seized. From what is known of dolphin echolocation, a sperm whale is likely to be able to tell the distance, direction, size, shape, and the species of its prey, even at a considerable distance.

Echolocation may also play a part in interactions between cetaceans. Because echolocation can pass through the watery tissues of a cetacean's body, they may be able to get images of each other that give such specific

BELOW: There is speculation that various species can focus their echolocation into an intense beam that stuns their prey. Narwhals emit the most intense echolocation sounds recorded, leading researchers to wonder whether they may use this tactic.

ABOVE: Some species show specialized echolocation abilities that are adaptations to particular environments. Belugas, which navigate in ice-filled seas, are better able than bottlenose dolphins to discriminate target echoes from background "clutter," such as the echoes from numerous ice floes.

information as what they have been eating, and their physical or even emotional state. Dolphins may be able to detect the echoes of each others' echolocation, thus gaining "free" information about their surroundings.

Do Baleen Whales Echolocate?

One perplexing question is whether baleen whales use a form of echolocation. They lack the specialized anatomical adaptations, such as a melon, that enable toothed whales to detect small, fast-moving prey. But baleen whales undoubtedly have very good hearing.

Certainly rorquals, such as fin and minke whales, produce trains of pulsed sounds of frequencies that might be suitable for detecting large, slower aggregations of prey, such as krill swarms or fish schools, by using their auditory sense. On occasion, these sounds have been recorded as whales approached to investigate ships. There is still uncertainty about how baleen whales do locate swarms of prey.

ABOVE: Why have fast-moving squid not learned to avoid echolocating whales? One researcher has speculated that, as a means of countering the "stun beam," squid may have evolved "deafness" which leaves them oblivious to normal echolocation. Such adaptation and counter-adaptation is common in nature.

INTELLIGENCE

Cetaceans are usually described as "intelligent mammals." Yet there is a continuing debate about their intelligence between those who are convinced that whales are as intelligent as humans, and others who rank them somewhere down the scale with other mammals. An argument frequently used against whaling is that it is wrong to kill such smart creatures. Some people, however, think that animals which strand, or return year after year to areas where whalers await them, do not display great intelligence.

THE SIZE OF INTELLIGENCE

Intelligence is a notoriously difficult quality to measure, even in humans. Various definitions include the ability to reason, to invent, to learn from past experience, to solve problems, and to cope with new situations.

What evidence is there for high cetacean intelligence? Cetaceans have relatively large brains, with considerable development of the cerebral cortex. This is the region associated with higher functions such as learning and abstract thought. While this could suggest high intelligence, it is counter-argued that large brains are required simply to coordinate their large bodies' motor processes. Even then, the ratio of brain-to-body size in some cetaceans, such as large baleen whales, is not high.

There is speculation that the size of cetacean brains is related to sound processing. Because they need to process complex echolocation signals, toothed whales have the most complex brains. Sperm whales have the largest brains of all, but bottlenose dolphins have the highest brain-to-body size ratio, and they have been a major focus in studies on cetacean intelligence.

LANGUAGE AND LEARNING

So far, attempts to teach captive bottlenose dolphins to comprehend human language have not progressed beyond basics. They can be taught simple sentence structure, and appear to

BELOW: There have been attempts to teach dolphins language, both verbal and sign. Bottlenose dolphins appear to be able to grasp the rules of language, such as the concept of a sentence, as well as other abstract concepts such as "similar" and "different."

ABOVE: A bottlenose dolphin's brain weighs five times that of a chimpanzee, but this does not make them five times smarter. The brain is about 0.75 percent of bodyweight in both species. Humans have the highest brain-to-bodyweight ratio, at nearly 2 percent.

understand abstract concepts, like "sameness" or "difference," and the "rules" of their training while carrying out even quite complex commands.

These dolphins are capable of innovation, are superb mimics, and their auditory skills are remarkable. However, whether these or other cetaceans have "purpose" or "intent" in their actions is something that has not been proved scientifically. It is impossible to know their subjective experience, as we do not share a language with them, and because our own understanding of cetacean communication is rudimentary at best. One commentator concludes that dolphins appear able to communicate *what*, *where*, *who*, and possibly *when*, but so far there is no evidence that *why*, and *how* are relevant to them.

SKILLS AND AWARENESS

In the wild, there is abundant anecdotal—and scientific—evidence of cetaceans acting in apparently intelligent ways. One oft-cited example is that of sperm whales swimming upwind when pursued by whalers in sailing vessels. This suggests that they not only have an awareness of the consequences of being caught, but an understanding that sailing vessels could not sail directly to windward, something these whales learned by experience.

Dolphins are known to use tools—a skill regarded as indicative of higher intelligence—such as wearing a sponge as beak protection when foraging in sand, or using the poisonous spines of a dead fish to drive an eel from its lair. It is tempting to infer near-human intelligence from these abilities. However, many other animals use tools: the chimpanzees in the Mahale Mountains of Tanzania use twigs and sticks to probe in tree trunks for ants; and Egyptian vultures are known to break open the tough shells of ostrich eggs by using rocks held in their beaks.

Many researchers use their imagination and intuition in an attempt to understand cetacean intelligence; after all, we share a common mammalian heritage. But there the similarity ends, and we must be careful when using human senses and intellect to understand the mental processes that cetaceans use. They have adapted, through evolution, to a medium quite alien to us, and their intelligence may be very different from our own.

RIGHT: A false killer whale in an oceanarium is taught to perform complex tasks. Much of the research done on cetacean intelligence is carried out using such captive animals, simply because studying wild animals in open ocean is fraught with so many logistical difficulties.

WHALE STRANDINGS

ABOVE: A right whale that was washed ashore dead near Wellfleet Harbor, in Massachusetts. Strandings of live right whales are almost unknown, as coastal shallows are their usual habitat throughout much of the year.

Most cetaceans die somewhere at sea. The majority probably sink or their carcass is devoured by sharks, but a small proportion, usually solitary animals, are washed ashore by the wind and currents. Sometimes they are already well decomposed. Causes of death may include parasitic infection, shark attack, disease, net entanglement, collision with vessels, or toxic contamination, but often it is simply old age.

MASS STRANDINGS

Single, live, stranded animals are often old, sick, or suffering from injuries, and may be too weak to continue swimming. Being air-breathers, perhaps they find a few last hours alive on the beach preferable to drowning.

Although most live strandings are of small groups of animals, sometimes a herd of many hundreds of toothed whales or dolphins may appear close inshore and then seemingly deliberately beach themselves. Baleen whales usually strand singly or in very small groups. The once cherished view that whales are "committing suicide" is no longer accepted, and other explanations have been proposed.

A wide variety of species is known to strand, many of them deepwater animals such as pilot and false killer whales. They possibly follow prey into unfamiliar coastal waters. Species that spend much of their time in nearshore waters, such as humpback and right whales, rarely strand. Some small cetaceans strand to avoid predators such as orcas. Strandings may result from disruption to normal navigation. Parasites occurring in the brain or the ears may interfere with the whale's sensory abilities.

Physical topography seems a significant factor in strandings since they are often more concentrated near certain coastal features. In New Zealand, mass strandings are more

ABOVE: *A large group of long finned pilot whales stranded in Golden Bay, New Zealand. The flat-bottomed shallow water is likely to have been a significant factor in this particular stranding.*

common where a long, gently sloping beach lies near a protruding headland. The headland may divert whales toward the beach, where the shelving bottom returns no echolocation signals, creating the illusion of open water ahead. Sand bars may compound the confusion, channeling animals into the surf zone where they are driven ashore. Onshore winds and currents may also play a part.

Mass strandings demonstrate the strength of close social bonds in toothed whale groups. In some strandings a single animal may be distressed by injury or disease and strand itself. Initially its companions may mill about just offshore, but then often join it in shallow water, and refuse to leave it at their own peril. On a falling tide, animals become properly stranded. When individual animals are returned to the water, they will often re-strand immediately, possibly because their social bonds are stronger than their aversion to being out of the water. Occasionally, when an entire group is rescued, they may soon re-strand at the same beach, or at another one nearby. No one knows why.

GEOMAGNETIC NAVIGATION

A phenomenon that may yet explain many strandings is cetaceans' suspected geomagnetic navigational sense, possessed by other animals such as homing pigeons and sea turtles. In Britain and the east coast of the USA, strandings have been related to anomalies in the earth's magnetic field, and there is some other evidence that cetaceans use contours in the field for navigation. However, a New Zealand study found no relationship between strandings and magnetic anomalies, so the evidence is not yet conclusive.

RIGHT: *At low tide, this pod of 65 pilot whales is completely stranded. Under these circumstances, whales are totally helpless, and a large pod such as this creates enormous logistical difficulties for any people attempting a rescue.*

Rescuing Stranded Whales

LEFT: Volunteer helpers carry out first aid on stranded false killer whales. Their heads have been oriented away from the surf to protect their blowholes; their skin is kept wet, and they are being gently reassured.

There is no doubt that most strandings are due to natural causes, and it is likely that they have occurred for millions of years. Yet in recent decades, humans have increasingly devoted their efforts to returning stranded whales to the sea. Some see this as a kind of atonement for the way that humans have treated cetaceans in modern times.

With very large whales, rescue is usually impossible—they are simply far too heavy to move without causing them injury. The sight of a large stranded whale, or a herd stranding of smaller cetaceans—450 pilot whales in one New Zealand stranding—perhaps in pounding surf on a remote beach where access is difficult, can produce a feeling of overwhelming helplessness in those arriving at the scene to assist in their rescue.

Once stranded, whales are subject to extreme and abnormal stresses. They can be injured in surf or on rocks. No longer supported by water, they may be crushed or suffocated by their own weight. Sand can block their blowholes, or damage their eyes. Wind and sun dry and burn their sensitive skin, and they may be attacked by carnivores such as polar bears or predatory gulls. They may have become separated from their pod, in itself a highly stressful situation for toothed whales, which are very social animals.

Assisting at Strandings

Anyone coming upon stranded whales should immediately try to notify the relevant authorities: either the local wildlife officers, the police, or the local natural history museum. No attempt should be made to return animals to the sea without expert help—they may become injured, and they may immediately re-strand. A mass stranding, in particular, requires extremely specialized knowledge and equipment to deal with it.

On the other hand, there are certain first-aid measures that should be taken, if possible. Try to roll animals upright (don't use their fins as levers) to keep their blowholes clear of the sand, and orient them so that their heads point away from the breaking waves. Gently rinse sand away from the eyes and blowholes, but take care not to pour water down the open blowholes. If possible, keep the skin wet, either by splashing water on it, or by covering it with a wet cloth. Speak quietly and move slowly—stroking and talking to the whales calms and reassures them. Stranded whales are normally gentle with humans, but take care to keep clear of their flukes and teeth.

If possible, take note of the first animal ashore. In certain cases, a vet may decide on euthanasia for animals beyond hope of rescue, either by injection or shooting. As toothed whales often strand with sick or injured pod members, such action may prevent more whales coming ashore, drawn by the distress calls of those already stranded. While this can

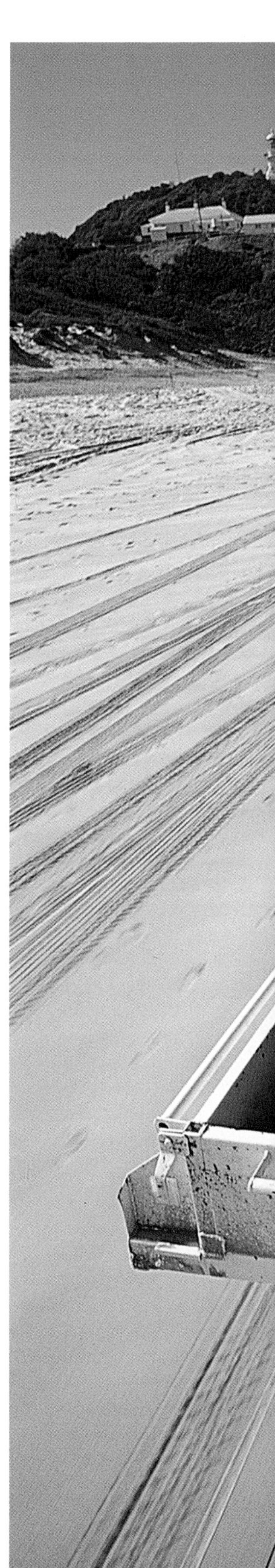

be traumatic for onlookers, the decision is a humane last measure for animals that are suffering and deemed unlikely to survive if returned to the water.

Rehabilitation and Rescue

For many years, single stranded animals have been taken to rehabilitation facilities to recover—many die in these places from the debilitating condition that caused their stranding. But in Australia and New Zealand in recent years, a procedure has been used that has sometimes proved spectacularly successful, even in mass strandings of species such as pilot and false killer whales.

It involves removing animals from the stranding site, using cranes, trucks, and trailers, and taking them to a holding site in sheltered waters nearby, where the surviving pod members are reunited. Then the entire group is led out to sea. This can occur only where there are suitable bays or estuaries in the area. Pontoons may be used to keep individual whales afloat until they regain enough strength to swim. Given the right conditions, larger whales, such as young humpbacks, can now be rescued by attaching specially made harnesses to them from a boat and towing them off very gently head-first.

Each stranding presents a new piece of information in the jigsaw puzzle of whales' lives. Living whales are measured and photographed, and dead ones examined both for standard biological data, and for possible clues to the stranding. Surviving whales are sometimes tagged with a harmless freeze brand, or with a radio or satellite transmitter, so that their movements can be monitored after their release. Strandings represent a golden opportunity to attach these devices, something that is very difficult to do with free-swimming whales.

LEFT: A whale is taken by trailer from the site of a herd stranding near Seal Rocks in eastern Australia, to a nearby sheltered estuary before it is released. In this rescue, 37 out of 49 whales were successfully returned to the sea.

Whales and People

Whales have always had a place in human consciousness, as creatures of myth and legend, as animals to be hunted and eaten, as fellow travelers on the ocean, and now as symbols of the environment. Human contact with them is often intense and moving. Sadly, human activities threaten their future in a changing world.

Whale Lore: Art, Myths, and Legends

Archeological evidence shows that humans have long been fascinated by whales and dolphins. Five thousand years before the classical Mediterranean civilizations celebrated dolphins in art and poetry, neolithic societies in Norway etched whales in rock.

Other vanished hunting peoples, such as the Dorset Culture of northern Canada, carved graceful representations of whales and seals in ivory and bone. Ancient societies that still survive today, such as the Inuit of Alaska and the Nootka of British Columbia, also have fine traditions of artwork, dance, and myths featuring cetaceans.

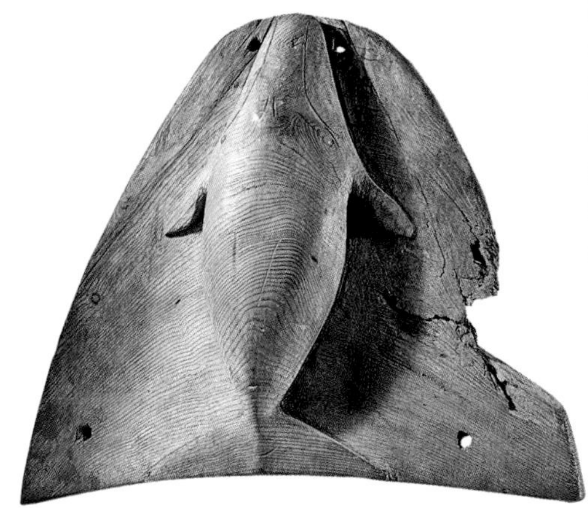

Left: The Inuit believed that game was not "taken" but allowed itself to be killed. This Inuit effigy of a bowhead whale would have been lashed to a boat. The Inuit went to great lengths to please the spirits of the animals they depended on for their survival.

Classical Art and Mythology

The ancient Greeks' understanding of cetaceans was based on actual experience. As far as we know, the philosopher Aristotle (384–322 BC)—a very reliable observer—was the first to claim that whales are mammals. His collected stories of dolphin natural history still ring true today.

The icon of the dolphin, which was regarded by the Greeks as a sympathetic, sacred animal, abounds in classical Greek mythology. The word "dolphin" derives from *delphys*, Greek for womb, and in one version of Greek mythology all creation emerged from the womb of a dolphin.

Other archetypal images include that of a youth riding a dolphin. The Roman Pliny the Elder (23–79 AD) tells the story of a boy who rode on the back of a friendly dolphin called Simo. In Greece, there was a similar story of the dolphin of Iassos, who fell in love with a beautiful boy and allowed him to ride on its back, even far out to sea. In both of these stories, the boy dies, and the dolphin then dies of grief. In a similar vein is the myth of the lost sailor who is saved by dolphins.

Fearsome Whales

Unlike the ancient Greeks, other cultures depicted whales as terrifying, tusked, scaled monsters. Because of their size and power, whales in many old stories, such as the biblical tale of Jonah and the whale, are often fearsome creatures. In a similar 19th-century tale, a swallowed whaleman was bleached white by the whale's gastric juices. There is a story that during Alexander the Great's campaign in India in 4 BC, his men became so alarmed by the mass blowing of whales around them that they dropped their oars in terror.

In the North Atlantic, whales were prominent in myths as well as true accounts. Red-headed whales were feared by Icelandic seamen. They believed they were born of a curse, and specialized in destroying ships and eating their crews. Others, such as fin whales, were regarded as friendly, and many believed that they drove herring inshore. Norwegian fishermen were angered when modern technology enabled these whales to be killed.

Above: Classical Greek art depicted dolphins realistically. One of the earliest known works of art portraying dolphins is this fresco in the Palace of Knossos in Crete. It is believed to be from the late Minoan Period, about 1450–1400 BC.

ABOVE: *According to Genesis, Jonah was punished for disobeying God's instructions to preach to the sinners of Ninevah. He was thrown overboard by sailors who blamed him for a terrible storm, and was swallowed by a whale that regurgitated him after three days.*

RIGHT: *An Aboriginal rock painting of a dolphin from Nanguluwur Gallery in Kakadu National Park, Australia. Although less than 500 years old, it predates European settlement. The barramundi-like tail indicates that the artist was more familiar with drawing fish.*

Every culture familiar with whales has some lore about them. Myths, tales, art, and poems about whales come to us from such diverse places as India, Africa, Korea, and Polynesia. Interestingly, a lack of folk tales about whales in Hawaii led researchers to conclude that the humpback whale now migrating there may have done so only during the past 200 years.

ABOVE: According to legend, St Brendan, an Irish monk who lived in the Middle Ages, landed on a whale so big that mariners were fooled into thinking the creature was an island. The error was not realized until the voyagers lit a fire on the whale to cook their dinner, whereupon it heaved and began to dive. Sinbad the Sailor had a similar experience.

A Pragmatic View Emerges

In Europe, as commercial whaling took hold in the 16th century, the mythology of whales as fantastic creatures began to disappear. It was replaced by a more pragmatic view of whales as commercial products. However, there was still a great appreciation of them by those who actually sought them on the oceans. This era can still be glimpsed in the whalers' songs and shanties, many of which have been preserved, and in scrimshaw, the delicate carvings made on whale teeth. Whaling expressions from this period, such as "thar she blows," are well known and are commonly used.

The adventurous life of the whaler has been the subject of numerous books, many of them factual accounts of 19th-century whaling, by whalers such as Frank Bullen and William Scoresby. In fiction, the best known of all whaling literature, of course, is *Moby Dick, or The White Whale* by Herman Melville. Melville spent several years whaling, and his book is full of accurate observations. However, it is famous not only for its natural history but for its symbolic and metaphysical undertones, which are still open to interpretation. The image of the "whale island" was echoed in another literary classic, Jules Verne's *Twenty Thousand Leagues Under the Sea*, in which Captain Nemo's submarine, the *Nautilus,* is mistaken for a gigantic whale.

LEFT: Keiko the Orca, star of the film Free Willy, *is now on view in an oceanarium in Newport, Oregon. Whales have also featured in Hollywood television series such as* Flipper *and in movies such as* Star Trek.

Modern Mythology

In the 20th century, cetaceans continue to feature large in poems such as "Whales Weep Not!" by D.H. Lawrence, in novels such as *The Deep Range* by Arthur C. Clarke, in songs, and in paintings and photography. More recently, numerous books and television documentaries have popularized scientific studies of whales, and international conservation efforts have dramatized their plight. For many, whales are spiritual symbols that have become synonymous with the welfare of the earth.

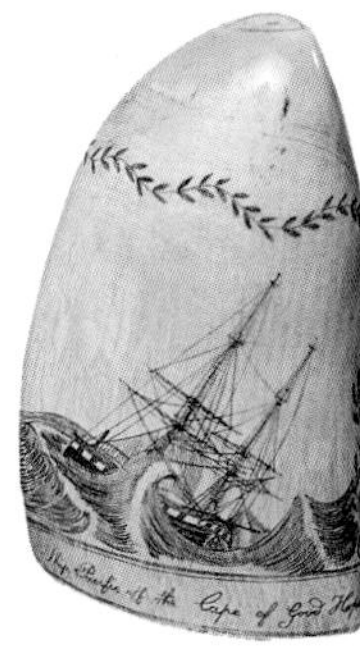

ABOVE: Commercial whaling produced its own culture, which can be seen in artwork such as scrimshaw—the engraved teeth of sperm whales, carved by the whalers in their spare time. Today, scrimshaw is valued as collectable folk art.

RIGHT: In medieval Europe, narwhal tusks were highly prized. They may have inspired the myth of the unicorn, which was often depicted in works of art, as in this 16th-century Flemish painting.

History of Whaling

ABOVE: *A kayak or umiak of walrus hide, a bone harpoon head on a wooden shaft, a line of skin or gut, and a float made of the inflated stomach of a seal were all that Inuit hunters needed to kill a whale. Today, they often combine their skill, knowledge, endurance, and courage with more modern weapons.*

Humans first utilized whales that had become stranded on the shore. Meat and blubber were hacked off for food, blubber was stripped away for fuel; sinews, bones, and baleen all had their uses. A stranded whale provided great bounty. For those observing whales or dolphins that ventured into bays, the next step may have been to drive them ashore, using canoes or similar craft. Echoes of such drive fisheries can be seen today in Japan and the Faeroe Islands, near Iceland. The final step was the transition to killing whales offshore. The simple technology required was employed by the Inuit and other northern peoples until very recently. Sometimes dugout canoes were used, as by the Makah people of the northwest Pacific who killed whales up to 20 miles (32 km) offshore. Indigenous whaling was also conducted by Vikings and their descendants in the North Atlantic. Throughout the history of indigenous whaling, people revered the great cetaceans even as they hunted them down.

Commercial Whaling

Commercial whaling originated with the Basques in the Bay of Biscay, northern Spain. By the 12th century, bay whaling for right whales, the practise of rowing out to kill whales nearby, had achieved economic importance. Whaling was no longer a subsistence activity. The Basques were great seaman and explorers, and by the 16th century, they had expanded their activities as far afield as Newfoundland. The British then discovered right and bowhead whales around Spitsbergen, Norway, and employed Basque whalers to hunt them.

In the early 1600s, Holland emerged as a whaling power. The Dutch developed the practise of killing whales at sea and cutting them up alongside their boats, pursuing them farther and farther north as bay-whaling fell off because of declining whale numbers. The whales were boiled down,"tried out," on deck, a procedure that sometimes resulted in a fire which damaged or destroyed the ship.

ABOVE: Whaling ships had to rely on the most basic navigational aids. Wooden pegs were used to plot the ship's course on transverse boards such as this to keep track of its position.

Colonists in New England started whaling early in the 18th century, when whale oil became increasingly important for street lighting and for use in textile manufacture. Baleen also grew in economic importance. By the late 18th century, England was *the* global maritime power, with the largest whaling fleet. The prime whaling grounds were then in Davis Strait, between Canada and Greenland, although at this time Samuel Enderby started the Southern Hemisphere fishery, which expanded into the Pacific Ocean in 1789. This opened up lucrative grounds around Australia, New Zealand, and in the North Pacific for right, humpback, and sperm whales. However, the industry experienced financial problems, including the introduction of cheaper coal gas for street lighting in London in 1809.

Whale Exploitation

The unbridled exploitation of right and bowhead whales inevitably took its toll, and by 1850 they were no longer commercially viable in the Atlantic and South Pacific. By this time, attention had shifted largely to sperm whales. (Sperm-whale oil burns brighter and with less odor than other whale oil, and spermaceti oil is one of the finest lubricating oils known.) While French, British, and Australian whalers were also at work, the New Englanders, known as the Yankee whalers, had been honing their whaling skills and now dominated the world scene. At their peak in 1876, there were 735 Yankee vessels, from ports such as New Bedford and Nantucket. They discovered and wiped out bowheads in the Bering Sea in the 1840s, severely reduced the numbers of gray whales off the Pacific coast of the USA, and killed countless thousands of sperm whales. Their downfall was the discovery of petroleum as a fuel in 1859, which soon rendered sperm oil valueless. Added to this was the declining numbers of whales.

Although we may imagine whalers' lives as adventurously romantic, they lived in brutal squalor, wearing filthy, stinking clothes, greasy from constant contact with dead whales and the soot of "trying" blubber. The legacy of disease, drunkenness, and social disintegration that they left on many of the remote islands where they landed made them a significant agent of change, particularly in the Pacific. In places such as Tonga, the West Indies, and the Azores, they also left behind unique open-boat whaling cultures.

BELOW: Towing their catch, whalers could haul for days at the oars of a whaleboat, only to have a dying whale drag their boat to the bottom. Frequently flogged and poorly fed, whalers were often ill and quarreled violently with each other.

ABOVE: A whaling vessel being repaired in the whaling port of New Bedford, Massachusetts. Whaling was a dangerous occupation, and many ships were lost in storms or ran aground on uncharted reefs. Whalers were often away for years on voyages.

Whale Products

Left: The "Spécialité Corset," advertised in 1911, was boned with real whalebone. The advertisement claims this "gives it lasting suppleness so different to the substitutes with which most of the present-day corsets are boned." Wearing one would aid "an erect and dignified carriage when walking."

Until recently, whales provided many products that were regarded as necessities in increasingly industrialized societies. Now the wheel has turned full circle, and advances in technology mean that, with the exception of whale meat, most of the products of whaling can be synthesized from other sources.

The Era of Whale Oil

Oil was the main commercial product throughout the era of commercial whaling. It lubricated the machinery of the Industrial Revolution, and fired the street lamps of London and New York. The availability of electricity ended its use for lighting, but new processes made it usable in the production of soap, margarine, and cooking fats.

A few other more recent uses of whale oil include preservatives, waxes, paints, varnishes, crayons, adhesives, cosmetics, pharmaceuticals, leather processing, candles, and inks—in fact almost any product that requires oil as part of its ingredients and manufacture.

Spermaceti oil, a superfine lubricating oil, has been used for missile inertial guidance systems, among other things. Whale oils have since been replaced by vegetable oils.

One of the most valuable whale products was also the rarest and strangest. Ambergris is the hard, waxy substance occasionally formed in the large intestines of sperm whales. Once worth its weight in gold, ambergris was used for fixing scents in perfume manufacture, and also had pharmaceutical uses. The largest lump ever found weighed nearly 1,000 lb (453.6 kg), and is reputed to have saved the company that killed this whale from financial disaster.

Baleen, Corsets, and Bones

Baleen, or "whalebone" as it was known commercially, was a very valuable product with many uses. Its flexibility and stiffness made it useful in watch springs, riding crops, umbrella ribs, ladies' corsets, hoops, brassieres, brushes, and shoehorns, just to mention a few. The long baleen of right and bowhead whales became more valuable than their oil content, but the commercial extinction of these species, coupled with the introduction of synthetic plastics, saw the demise of the baleen industry.

Teeth and bones also had their uses. Teeth, being ivory, were used for buttons and piano keys, as well as for the decorative scrimshaw for which they are best known.

During the era of industrial whaling, whale bones were ground into fertilizer, but in earlier days they were used as building materials, and the paired jawbones of baleen whales were often used as entrance arches. Inuits used bone of various species to make fishhooks and sewing needles. The skin of some whales was tanned for leather, and, in Scandinavia, the transparent gut was stretched taut over window frames as a window pane.

The Whalebone

ABOVE: *During the heydey of whaling in the late 19th century, whales were hailed as useful commercial resources, providing materials for an enormous variety of purposes, some of which are illustrated here.*

THE MECHANIZED AGE OF WHALING

LEFT: In the early days of Norwegian-style whaling, the whales were processed either at shore stations, or alongside factory ships in sheltered waters. This picture shows a whaling fleet anchored in Spitsbergen, north of Norway, in 1905.

BELOW: Photographed in Norway during the 1890s, Skipper Duncan Greys mans a version of Svend Foyn's harpoon cannon. The skipper of a whale chaser was usually the gunner, and would hurry from the bridge to the cannon once the quarry was within shooting range.

Hvalfangerskibet Dūncan Greys Skytter og Kanon

In 1864, a development occurred that was to change the face of whaling. Few right whales remained, so Norwegian sealer Svend Foyn pondered the abundance of rorquals. Except for the slow humpback, these whales were uncatchable with rowed whaleboats. He refined designs for a cannon-fired, barbed, explosive harpoon, mounted on the bow of a fast steam-powered ship, with a winch for retrieving the whale and a shock absorber to relieve strains to the line. This became known as a catcher vessel. By 1886, 19 companies were using Foyn's radically new technology in Norway, and similar stations were set up in Iceland and the Faeroes, catching mainly fin, sei and some blue whales. In 1895, a Norwegian station opened in Japan. "Norwegian whaling" was the model for the new century.

EMERGENCE OF THE FACTORY SHIP

Ironically, Norwegian companies were driven out of home waters by cod fishermen, and began whaling in the Shetlands, the Outer Hebrides, and, after the turn of the century, Spitsbergen. After factory ships began to appear, the whales were towed in by catchers to be flensed (stripped of their blubber) in the water alongside, then rendered to oil. By the start of World War I, rorquals were in decline in the North Atlantic. While large numbers of rorquals were known to exist in Antarctic waters, the distance from European ports delayed serious attempts to commence whaling there. However, the Norwegian Carl Anton

Larsen persuaded Argentinian business interests to back him in a whaling venture at South Georgia Island, and thus, in November 1904, began the greatest whale slaughter of them all.

Early seasons at South Georgia brought big catches of humpbacks, which fed around the rich waters of the island. Factory ships were used initially, but by 1911, there were seven shore stations on South Georgia, and others, mostly Norwegian operations, at King George Island and other islands near the Antarctic Peninsula. The British, who administered South Georgia as part of the Falkland Islands Dependency, attempted to regulate the whaling, protecting rare species such as right whales as well as mothers with calves. But just before World War I, there was an enormous increase in oil demand for the manufacture of soap and margarine. Whalers responded to the market, increasing their catches to alarming levels well into the 1920s.

Until 1925, whales were flensed either onshore, or alongside factory ships at anchor. In that year, stern ramps enabled processing to be carried out on deck, independent of land. After this, development of deep-sea Antarctic whaling was rapid, expanding west to the Ross Sea. In the 1930–31 season alone, 41 factory ships, operating 205 catchers, killed more than 37,000 whales, including about 30,000 blue whales. This season glutted the oil market, and many people feared that Antarctic whaling was out of control.

Self-management

Attempts at self-management by the industry during the 1930s were ineffectual. Japan and Germany entered the fray in the mid-1930s. A system of "blue whale units," which remained in force until 1972, was adopted; this equated the oil content of one blue whale with that of two fins, two-and-a-half humpbacks, or six seis. Because these quotas could more quickly be reached by killing larger whales, blue whales became very rare. Attention shifted to fin whales, until World War II brought some respite. After the war, even more nations than before took up whaling. In 1947, the International Convention for the Regulation of Whaling, administered by the International Whaling Commission (IWC), came into force. Although the Convention stipulated protective

BELOW: Using an implement that has remained basically unchanged for centuries, a Japanese whaler wields his flensing knife on the blubber of a fin whale at an Icelandic shore station.

ABOVE: *Alaskan Inuit cutting up a bowhead whale. Traditionally, every part of the whale is used, from the raw blubber ("muktuk") to the sinews. The entire community participates, and everyone receives a portion.*

measures, and many IWC scientists warned of disaster, enforcement was non-existent. Whaling operated by boom-and-bust economic principles, and in the 1950s and 1960s a ferocious assault led to population collapses of Antarctic blue, fin, sei and humpback whales. Sperm whales were also heavily exploited. Apart from the large "legal" fleets, ruthless "pirates" operated outside all international agreements.

In 1994, the world was shocked by disclosures that for many years Soviet whaling fleets had concealed as much as 90 percent of their catch. As well, they had hunted protected species, and mothers with calves, and had operated outside agreed areas and seasons. These revelations helped to explain the surprisingly low rates of post-whaling recovery in some species.

By the mid-1960s, all nations, except Japan and the USSR, had withdrawn from Antarctic whaling. In 1986, a "moratorium" on commercial whaling worldwide was adopted by the IWC. The Soviets withdrew from the Antarctic in 1987, leaving the Japanese to focus on minkes, the smallest of the rorquals and the only species that remained in large numbers. Up to this point, about 1.5 million whales had been killed in Antarctic waters, reducing many species to critically low levels and seriously disrupting the marine ecosystem.

Meanwhile, outside the Antarctic, whaling fleets operated in the Indian, Atlantic, and Pacific Oceans, and coastal whaling stations proliferated around the world, such as in New Zealand, Canada, Iceland, the Congo, South Africa, Peru, and Australia. These contributed to general declines in whale populations.

WHALING TODAY

Japan still sends a fleet to Antarctic waters each summer. This whaling is technically classified as scientific research, although the IWC rejects the necessity for it, and the meat is sold commercially. "Small-type coastal whaling" occurs in Japan, Norway, Greenland, and elsewhere, and drive fisheries involving pilot whales and dolphins are conducted in Japan and the Faeroe Islands, south of Iceland.

International trade in whale products is banned under the Convention on International Trade in Endangered Species (CITES), yet there is still a flourishing underground trade in whale meat. Thousands of dolphins are harpooned yearly in Japanese waters, and deliberate dolphin kills on an unknown scale occur in many parts of the world.

Many pro-whaling nations firmly intend to resume commercial whaling in areas such as the North Atlantic and the Antarctic. They argue that the abundance of minke whales will sustain such whaling, and that coastal communities have a right to harvest the oceans' resources. Opponents argue that commercial whaling has never been a controllable or sustainable activity, that whales are ecologically important and should be left alone. Many people oppose whaling on ethical grounds, because it denies whales their right to life; and for humanitarian reasons, because it inflicts inhumane levels of stress and pain that would not be permitted, for example, in commercial abattoirs. The IWC is struggling to agree on a theoretical framework to provide the best possible controls if commercial whaling resumes.

ABOVE: Canned whale meat was sold in the USA before international bans were placed on trade in whale products. Protected species have recently been discovered for sale in Japanese markets, and illegal shipments of meat are sometimes intercepted.

Subsistence Whaling

In some areas, such as Alaska and the Philippines, subsistence whaling has survived, sometimes with the use of simple technology such as kayaks or open boats. In others, such as eastern Siberia, so-called subsistence whaling is carried out by modern whale catchers. Genuine subsistence whaling has had little impact on populations, although there is widespread concern when critically endangered species, such as bowhead whales, are hunted. As human cultural diversity diminishes, more indigenous peoples, such as the Makah of the northwest Pacific, are asserting their claim to resume subsistence whaling as a traditional element of their culture.

RIGHT: A Soviet whale catcher in Antarctic waters tows its catch of minke whales to the factory ship. A catwalk connects the bridge to the cannon platform in the bow.

Whales in Captivity

The first time cetaceans were kept in captivity was in 1913 when harbor porpoises were put on display in a New York aquarium. Since then, many other toothed whales have been kept in captivity around the world, including bottlenose dolphins, pilot whales, orcas, belugas, common dolphins, humpback dolphins, spotted dolphins, Amazon and Chinese river dolphins, false killer whales, pygmy killer whales, and finless porpoises. Baleen whales, because of their size and feeding habits, have rarely been kept in captivity.

Captive cetaceans have been used for both commercial and military purposes. We are all familiar with dolphinariums, where trained whales and dolphins entertain paying audiences. Less familiar are the reputed uses of whales for, among other things, the recovery of missiles, the placement of mines, and even to use weapons to attack and kill enemy divers.

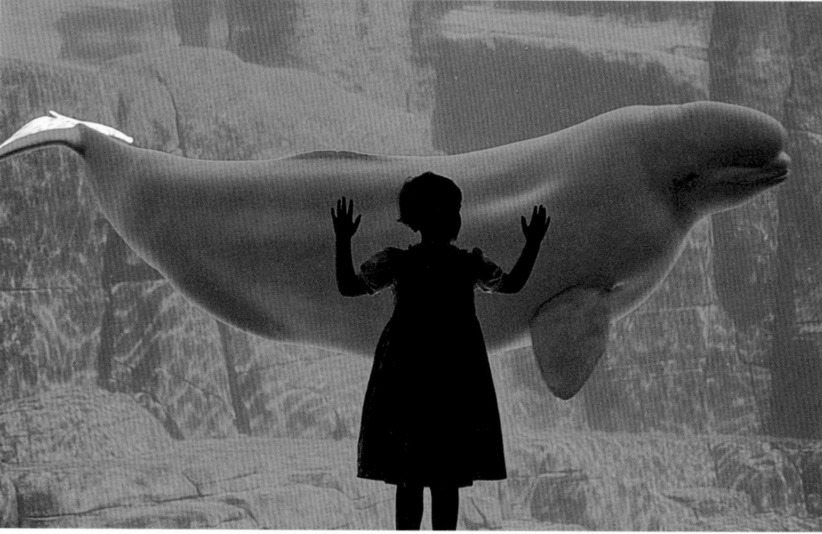

Above: A fascinated child watches a beluga through the glass wall of an aquarium in Vancouver, Canada. People opposed to keeping whales in captivity claim that conditions such as these are distressing for the whales.

The Case For Captivity

Opinion for and against the captivity of cetaceans is strongly polarized. Those in favor argue that it is vital for educational purposes, and that most people would never see a whale or dolphin in the wild. Exposure to captive animals, they claim, increases public awareness and understanding of cetaceans. They point to famous captives such as Namu, an orca that was kept in a Vancouver dolphinarium in the early 1960s. At a time when orcas were persecuted because they were widely perceived as dangerous killers, Namu's charm helped to create a sympathetic attitude toward this species.

The opportunity for research is a common argument in favor of captivity. Cetaceans in the wild are often difficult even to locate, let alone observe for extended periods; captive animals are at hand. The study of many captive species, particularly bottlenose dolphins, has yielded valuable insights into their breeding behavior and reproductive cycles; social behavior; sleep and dreaming patterns;

Left: A trained Pacific bottlenose dolphin is put through its paces at Sea Life Park in Hawaii.

intelligence; and methods of communicating, both with other dolphins and with humans.

Criticisms of public displays as mere circus acts have resulted in a trend to incorporate natural behavior into these exhibitions. And in answer to charges that many dolphins have been captured from the wild, there are figures showing that in the USA 40 percent of captive dolphins were, in fact, born in captivity. Dolphins in captivity form social groups, and they produce calves that know only captivity as a way of life.

Dolphins may also play a role in human therapy, by eliciting responses from people suffering from autism and other socially debilitating conditions.

THE CASE AGAINST CAPTIVITY

People who object to whales being kept in captivity claim that it is demeaning for the animals and point to the stress that unnatural confinement causes. They claim that pools, no matter how commodious, cannot begin to replicate the open ocean. A pool lacks the varied stimulation provided by the natural environment, while its concrete surface creates a confusing auditory world of echoes. There is also a constant risk of disease and infection from food or unclean water.

Opponents also point to artificial social structures, and consequent aberrant behaviors that develop in captivity. In the wild, groups are often fluid—an animal that deviates from a group's behavior patterns may join another group. But within the confines of a pool, it is impossible for them to change groups. Even normal sexual behavior may not be possible in captivity. For example, wild males of many species wander from group to group, seeking females to mate with. In a pool, they may mate only with females in the same group.

It is impossible to predict the long-term psychological and behavioral consequences of keeping whales in such constricting conditions. However, critics of this practice point to recent events, such as at least one incidence of an orca killing its trainer, as an indication that all is far from well.

BELOW: Captive cetaceans often develop close relationships with their trainers. This orca is learning to respond to its trainer's hand signals.

Whale Research

Because of their habits and the environment in which they live, whales and dolphins can be difficult to study. Most of them live away from coastlines in remote or inaccessible areas. Even those that do occur close to human settlements spend most of their time beneath the surface. Whales are often elusive, and except in the calmest weather, can be very difficult to observe. Some species are so rarely sighted that there is only a handful of reliable records for them.

The Impact of Whaling on Research

Modern whale research had its origins in the 19th century, with the study of animals that were stranded or had been killed by whalers. It was really the expansion of whaling in the 20th century, as a result of improved technology, that led to the growth of cetology as a science. Carcasses, which were measured, dissected, and examined, either at whaling shore stations or aboard factory ships, yielded much information about the anatomy, physiology, life history, reproductive biology, and diet of a wide range of species.

A technique that was widely employed in earlier whale research involved the use of "whale marks"—numbered stainless steel darts about a foot (0.33 m) long. These were fired into the whales by means of a shotgun. If, and when, a marked whale was later killed, the recovered dart enabled researchers to determine how far it had traveled. This process was the first step in piecing together a detailed understanding of whale migration.

After the collapse of whale populations in the 1960s, and the subsequent winding back of whaling activities, the practice of studying dead animals gave way to more benign research methods. These, however, require much patience as the focus is on studying whales without unduly disturbing them.

ABOVE: From an observation tower perched precariously above the Cunningham River estuary, off Somerset Island in the Canadian Northwestern Territories, scientists can observe the movements of beluga whales.

OBSERVATION AND RECORDING

The most elementary and widespread benign technique is simple observation. Long and painstaking observations, and the careful recording of data, have taught us a great deal about how whales relate to each other and to other species, as well as about their movements, and their feeding and breeding behavior. Observation can include the collection of fecal samples, or of plankton in the water, in order to see what whales have been eating.

One specialized form of observation is the sightings survey. Conducted from boats, aircraft, or land, these surveys are usually intended to investigate whales' distribution patterns and abundance, our knowledge of which is still scant. However, survey results are increasingly being related to state-of-the-art data on climate, oceanography, and prey distribution. The resulting picture of whale ecology will probably prove more valuable for long-term conservation and management of cetaceans than estimates of the numbers alone.

Most species of whales have natural markings and these often make it easy to identify individuals. Identifying marks can include pigment patterns, scars, damaged or missing extremities, or, in the case of right whales, callosity patterns. By using cameras to record these features—a process known technically as photo-identification—scientists have been able to track and record the movements of individual whales. Photo-identification has been useful in such widely separate studies as humpbacks in the North Atlantic, orcas in the northwest Pacific, and bottlenose dolphins at Monkey Mia in Western Australia.

ABOVE: Because the distinctive pigment patterns on the flukes and flanks of humpback whales remain stable for many years, researchers can use these to study the whales' migrations, the frequency with which they calve, and associations between individual whales.

LEFT: Scientists photograph a minke whale near Scott Base in Antarctica. Although these people do not study whales themselves, such "incidental" observation can be very useful to whale researchers.

LEFT: Researchers Tony Martin, Tom Smith, and Jack Orr (left to right) attach a transmitter to a beluga whale off Somerset Island in Canada. They tracked the whale by satellite for 86 days before the signal eventually faded more than 500 miles (800 km) away in Baffin Bay, off the coast of Greenland.

While most present-day research focuses on live whales, dead animals, such as stranded whales, or those found entangled in fishing nets, can add to the data gathered from other sources. Toxic contaminants, such as heavy metals, for example, accumulate in a whale's body organs, and dissecting a carcass is the only way to discover them.

Tissue Sampling

By means of an arrow with a special tip, small plugs of skin and blubber can be taken from free-swimming whales and used for analysis. Because many toxic pollutants are soluble in fat, and so are stored in cetacean blubber, analysis of blubber obtained in this way has added significantly to our knowledge of marine pollution. DNA from the skin, too, can provide genetic information such as the sex of a whale, the population it belongs to, and even the identity of its parents. Genetic sampling has shown that some populations, previously believed to be entirely homogenous, actually consist of two or more distinct genetic groups. Being smaller groups, they are more vulnerable to stresses, such as availability of prey, pollution, and disease.

Keeping Track of Whales

Tracking whales by satellite has enabled scientists to monitor movements, and the diving and feeding habits, of distant animals without having to take lengthy field trips. One of the problems with this technology is that it involves attaching transmitters to whales so that they remain in place without discomfort.

Another tool that may prove useful is the "whalecam," a video camera that is temporarily attached to a whale by a tether, which can show, for example, their feeding activity in much greater detail than was previously possible.

RIGHT: This directional hydrophone, suspended from a stationary boat, is being used to record and track the movements of sperm whales in the Indian Ocean near Sri Lanka.

LEFT: Research scientist and telemetry expert Bruce Mate satellite-tags a blue whale off California in the Santa Barbara Channel. Each time the whale surfaces, the transmitter sends a signal to a satellite, which records the time and precise location, as well as the depth and water temperature of each dive.

Acoustic Research

Because all whales use sound to communicate, acoustic monitoring—listening to whales in the deep—has become an important means of studying them. It has added significantly to the knowledge already gained from visual and other forms of observation. It has fewer limitations because whales can be heard much farther away than they can be seen and the passage of sound is not affected by conditions such as darkness and fog. An acoustic survey may, for example, indicate which species is in a particular area, the numbers of whales that are present, and, sometimes, exactly what they are doing.

Whale sounds are picked up by underwater microphones, known as hydrophones. These can be dangled from a stationary boat, towed by a moving one, or attached to sonobuoys and monitored by radio. Hydrophones can even be attached to the seafloor. US Navy submarine monitoring devices on the North Atlantic seafloor have been used to track the low-frequency calls of individual blue and fin whales over thousands of miles.

Contact Between Whales and People

There are many recorded incidents in which whales have initiated "friendly" contact with humans. Given our past treatment of them, why are they not afraid of us? Perhaps they are simply curious about alien creatures in their environment, or perhaps they enjoy the company. Some people speculate that they are trying to communicate with us.

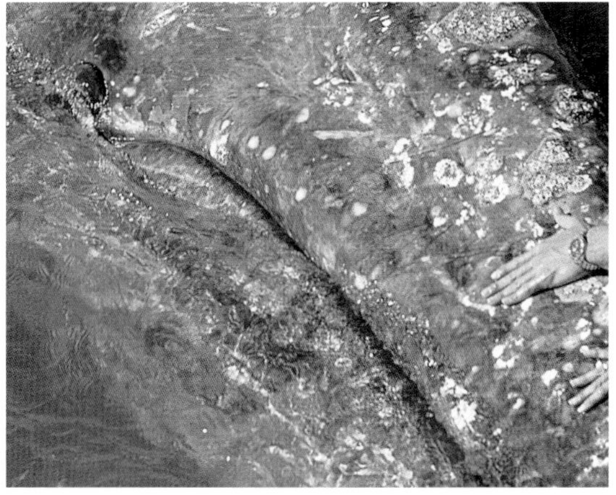

Left: Gray whales in Mexico have become so comfortable with the presence of tourist boats and the people aboard them that they regularly allow themselves to be patted and stroked.

Friendly Dolphins

Numerous stories suggest that there has always been a special affinity between dolphins and humans. As far back as AD 66, the Greek writer Plutarch wrote that dolphins had a gift for "unselfish friendship."

One of the first documented examples of spontaneous cetacean friendliness in modern times is that of a Risso's dolphin known as Pelorus Jack. For 24 years—until 1912—he escorted steamers past the mouth of Pelorus Sound in Cook Strait, New Zealand. In 1955, a female bottlenose dolphin known as Opo began approaching people on the beach in Hokianga Harbour in the far northeast of New Zealand's North Island. During the 1960s another bottlenose dolphin, dubbed Charlie, often approached divers near Elie Fife in Scotland, and in 1972, two more bottlenose dolphins, in different parts of the world, attracted wide attention. One, known as Nina, swam with humans at La Coruña in northern Spain, while for six years, Donald ranged along the west coast of Britain, befriending people from the Isle of Man to Cornwall. Donald played with boats, towed divers, and allowed people to ride on his back. According to reports, he would rescue people who were in distress, and on one occasion, guided a lost diver back to his boat. In some areas, such as Mauritania in Africa, there are authenticated

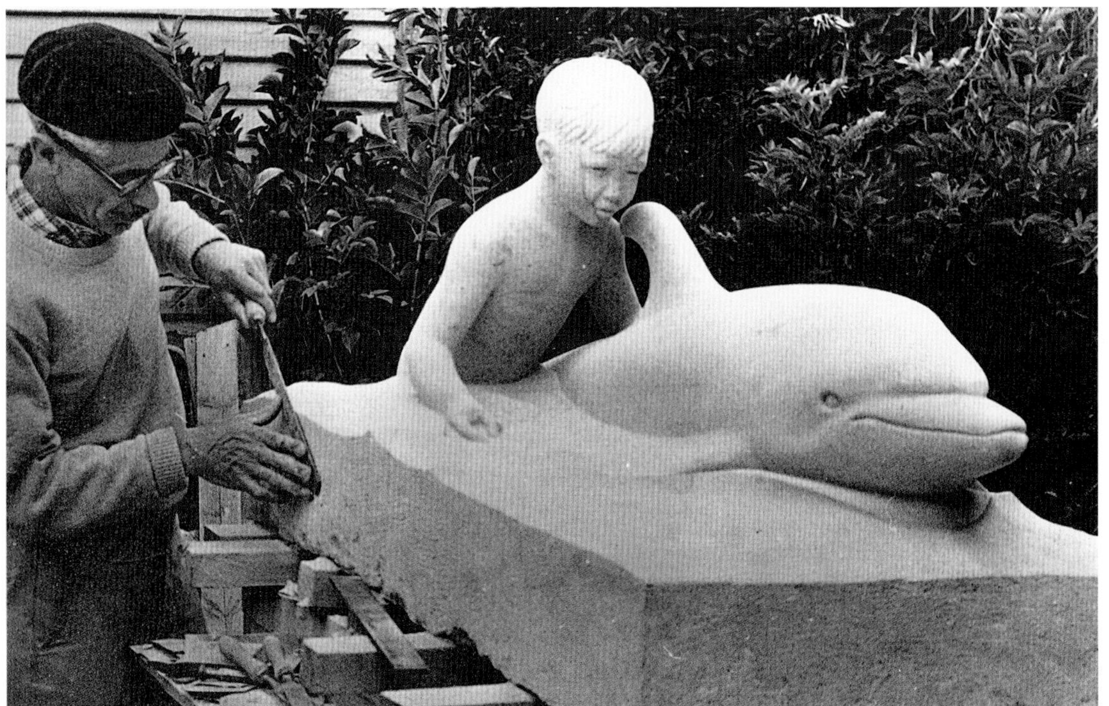

Left: Sculptor Russell Clark putting the finishing touches to the memorial to New Zealand's Opo in 1960. This friendly dolphin attracted such crowds that an Act of Parliament was passed to protect her. Ironically, the next day she was found dead, apparently killed with dynamite. She was buried with full Maori ritual.

ABOVE: The sheer numbers of tourists that flock daily to Monkey Mia, in Western Australia, means that human–dolphin interactions must be strictly controlled. The dolphins are accustomed to being hand-fed by the tourists and often "play up" to their admiring audiences.

cases of bottlenose dolphins cooperating with fishermen to herd fish.

There are numerous accounts of various dolphins that aided mariners who were in difficulties, or warned sailors of unseen hazards. The noted French yachtsman Bernard Moitessier told of how dolphins caused him to avoid running aground on Stewart Island, off the southern tip of New Zealand, in 1968, by making passes past his boat and then turning right, thus guiding him to safety.

Perhaps the best-known instance of contact between dolphins and people is the case of the bottlenose dolphins at Monkey Mia, in Shark Bay, Western Australia. Sometime in the early 1960s, dolphins began arriving at what was then a remote fishing settlement and befriending the inhabitants. Originally there were seven: five adult females and two male calves. Unlike Donald, Nina and Charlie, who would not accept dead fish, these dolphins learned to solicit fish from fishermen who were cleaning their catch. They also permitted people to stroke and pet them. The calves grew up accustomed to this contact, so successive generations of people-friendly dolphins have continued to frequent the area.

Other Whales

Larger whales also seem to seek and enjoy human contact. Minke whales are noted for their "ship-seeking" behavior, while others, including humpbacks, can appear fascinated by smaller craft and their human occupants, and may repeatedly circle and dive underneath the boat, or spyhop frequently. Whales are usually careful not to bump boats. They will often approach and interact with swimmers, even to the point of physical contact.

Whales are quite gentle and their awareness of where swimmers are in relation to their extremities is truly remarkable. One southern right whale cow, followed too closely by a swimmer, first felt cautiously behind with her flukes to ensure he was clear before delivering a sharp sideways warning flick of her tail.

CONSERVATION AND SURVIVAL

Since the beginning of the Industrial Revolution more than 200 years ago, humans have been modifying the natural environment in unprecedented ways. Environmental degradation, especially in recent decades, has created a succession of crises that have had a serious impact on cetaceans.

ABOVE: This striped dolphin was caught and drowned in a driftnet in the Mediterranean Sea. The bycatch of non-target species, such as dolphins, whales, and turtles, in driftnets and coastal gillnets is a serious problem, yet the use of these nets is increasing worldwide. In some areas nets are set specifically for the purpose of catching cetaceans.

HABITAT DEGRADATION AND POLLUTION

Habitat alteration is one phenomenon that has occurred both on land and in marine environments. Inshore habitats of cetaceans, as well as their prey, have been affected by, for example, the damming of rivers, the draining and filling of mangrove swamps, the destruction of seagrass beds, the development of coastal foreshores, the siltation of rivers resulting from deforestation, and discharges of industrial waste and sewage. Industrial development has also brought increased noise, a greater volume of traffic, and serious pollution to areas of the open ocean. Items of litter, such as fragments of fishing nets that can entangle whales and plastic bags that they mistake for squid and eat, are also potential hazards.

Chemical pollutants pose a major threat, and some of the most insidious of these are heavy metals, such as mercury, which concentrate in whales' brains and other vital organs, and organochlorines, such as DDT and PCBs. These substances, carried throughout the oceans by currents, become more concentrated as they pass up through the food web. Some stranded dolphins have been so heavily contaminated that authorities declared them to be "toxic waste."

Organochlorines are stored in blubber, from which a mother's milk is manufactured. As a result, many first-born calves die from a transfer of the toxic load accumulated by their mothers. PCBs, which can cause cancer, suppress immune systems, and cause reproductive failure, have been implicated in the decline of belugas in Canada's Saint Lawrence River.

During the past decade, hundreds of cetaceans, mostly dolphins, have died in "mass die-offs" linked to viral and algal outbreaks, possibly induced by pollution.

CLIMATE CHANGE

Climate change resulting from human activity may prove to be the most critical threat facing whales and dolphins. Rising sea temperatures would, for example, modify patterns of currents and upwelling. Again, they could cause polar seas to contract, thus reducing suitable habitat for whale prey, such as Antarctic krill, allowing incursions by warmer-water species. They may also affect the supply of phytoplankton and lead to the spread of toxic algal blooms. Increased ultraviolet radiation, from ozone depletion, could cause cancer in whales, as well as harming the plankton or other prey on which they feed.

ABOVE: This pile of beach-washed plastic, at the remote Falkland Islands in the far South Atlantic, highlights the extent to which such marine debris has become a serious global problem.

Threats, Direct and Indirect

As burgeoning human populations seek ever-increasing supplies of protein, overfishing of some species—for example, Antarctic krill—may seriously deplete the prey available for many whales and dolphins, and so indirectly lead to their decline. As well, huge numbers of whales die when they become caught up in coastal and river gillnets and deep-sea drift-nets—a phenomenon known as "bycatch." *Purse seine* nets, for example, which are set to catch tuna, have killed millions of dolphins in the eastern Pacific, and humpback whales frequently drown when they become entangled in cod nets off Newfoundland, Canada.

Increasing shipping traffic along coastlines is a source of danger often overlooked. An unknown number of vessels each year collide with whales. More significant, perhaps, are the noise pollution and general disturbance that passing ships cause; these may seriously disrupt whales' communication, navigational ability, and social patterns. Harassment of whales by whale-watching vessels and recreational boaters, and even sometimes researchers, although not necessarily intentional, is also unfortunately widespread.

Quite apart from die-offs, up to two million small cetaceans are killed, either deliberately or accidentally, throughout the world every year. When we consider that most baleen whale populations are still reduced as a result of previous widespread whaling activity—and blue whales show little sign of recovery—we can only conclude that the survival of many cetacean species is still far from assured.

RIGHT: To a whale, these plastic bags floating in the sea off Ambon, Indonesia, can resemble squid or other marine invertebrates. Whales have been found starved to death, their intestinal tracts blocked by plastic litter they swallowed by mistake.

ABOVE: *Greenpeace activists in an inflatable boat protest alongside the Japanese whaling factory ship "Nisshin Maru" in the Antarctic, while minke whales are butchered on board. Japan continues to whale unchecked within the internationally recognized Southern Ocean Whale Sanctuary.*

Conservation Organizations

In recent years, considerable publicity has been given to the plight of many cetacean species, and the threats to their survival. As people have become more aware of the issues involved, and familiar with the findings of scientists and other researchers, governments have come under increasing pressure to adopt more environmentally sensitive policies. But governments are often slow to respond, even to widespread public opinion; it has taken many years, for example, for warnings about global warming to be heeded at official levels.

Much of the initiative for change comes from animal welfare and conservation organizations, which act as pressure groups, and actively publicize environmental issues. In the USA, these groups range from the relatively conservative Humane Society, to the radical Sea Shepherd Society, and all points between. Organizations across this spectrum rely heavily on public support, both for their finances and the personnel that they require to undertake their campaigns.

The Importance of Public Involvement

There is little doubt that public pressure was instrumental in changing attitudes to whaling. Thanks largely to widespread concern, expressed in demonstrations and other forms of public representation, former whaling nations, such as the USA and Australia, now have a political mandate to promote whale conservation at the International Whaling Commission (IWC). But whaling is an issue that is politically "safe"—one that easily

ABOVE: It's Whale Day in Paris, and a child adds a spash of color to a mural celebrating whales. In non-whaling nations, public support for whales reaches across all ages and social groups.

involves human sympathies, and has relatively clear-cut solutions. People are less aware of the many other problems facing whales and of the ways in which these problems are consequences of our modern lifestyle. For example, each of us contributes to global warming through our energy use; we use products made from the toxic chemicals that pollute the oceans; and many of us eat driftnet-caught tuna. Pressure groups and governments cannot make us choose our lifestyle. We must look at ways in which we can reduce our individual impact, such as by reducing our energy consumption, by buying environmentally safe products, by opposing detrimental coastal developments, or by disposing of our wastes appropriately. We can all take responsibility for global problems.

WHALE SANCTUARIES

Whale sanctuaries are zones where commercial whaling is prohibited, and the whales receive special protection. In 1979, the IWC, with the agreement of all nations bordering the Indian Ocean, declared this great body of water to be a whale sanctuary. In 1991, the Republic of Ireland became the first nation to act independently by declaring its waters to be a whale sanctuary. In May 1994, the IWC adopted the huge Southern Ocean Whale Sanctuary, which covers all Antarctic waters and offers at least nominal protection to the world's largest whale populations.

Japan, one of the few nations that still undertakes whaling, strongly opposed the declaration of this sanctuary, maintaining that culling of minke whales in commercial quantities does not threaten their survival. Other smaller sanctuaries, which have recently been adopted in Hawaii, Australia, and New Zealand, provide further evidence of the effectiveness of concerted public pressure.

RIGHT: Swiss school children present a petition of 70,000 signatures calling for an Antarctic whale sanctuary. In May 1994, their call and that of millions of others, was answered with the adoption of the Southern Ocean Whale Sanctuary.

WHALE-WATCHING

Whale-watching has become a global industry, but it can be enjoyed by any individual who has an elementary knowledge of whales and knows where to look. One way to observe whales is to go on one of the whale-watching cruises, near places such as Monterey or Cape Cod in the United States, and entrust yourself to the experts on board. Alternatively, you could find a good vantage spot on land. Indeed, some of the best whale-watching can be done from the shore.

SHORE-BASED WHALE-WATCHING

Successful whale-watching requires patience, a good pair of binoculars, and an awareness of the prevailing weather conditions. You also need to know what species of whales are likely to occur in a particular area. To some extent this is predictable, because the migratory patterns of many species are well documented. Gray whales and humpbacks, for example, are known to migrate seasonally along coastlines, and to congregate in breeding and feeding areas. These include Maui, in the Hawaiian Islands, the fiords of Alaska in the United States, and Baja California, in Mexico.

The best vantage points are usually the highest. Find a spot that offers good views along the coastline as well as of the open ocean. Whales can often be seen well out to sea, and can even be visible underwater if they are close inshore.

Early morning and late afternoon are the best viewing times. Not only do whales seem more active then, but the low, slanting light highlights their blows and splashings. Very calm, glary conditions in the middle of the day make sightings difficult. Overcast days, on the other hand, are good for viewing, because they rest the eyes and blows show up well against a gray sea and sky. Spotting is almost impossible when winds are strong—to the excited

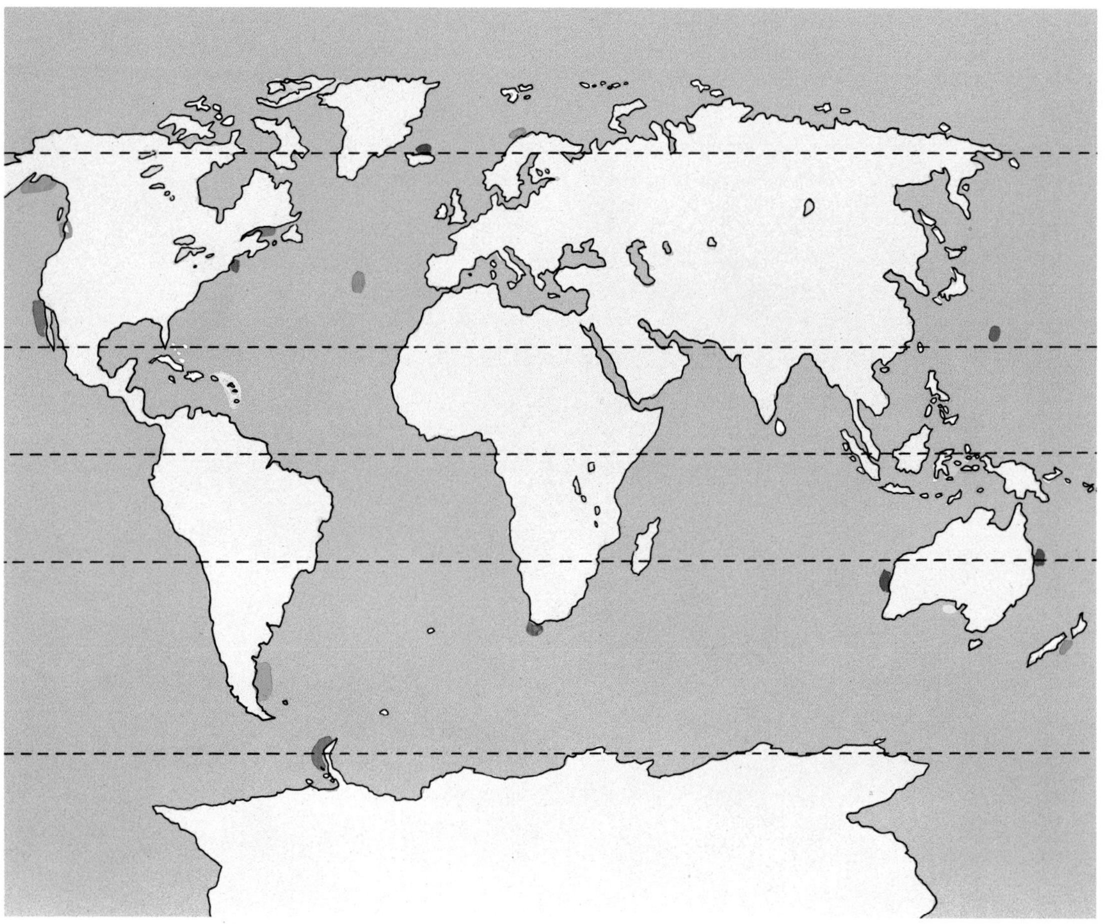

WORLD WHALE-WATCHING SITES
This map shows several of the world's best-known whale-watching locations. In some places, the best watching is from the land; in others you will need a boat in order to approach whales well offshore. There are thousands of other sites around the world that offer memorable encounters with whales.

Map Key
- Gulf of Alaska
- Vancouver Island, Canada
- California, USA
- Quebec, Canada
- Bar Harbor, Maine, USA
- Caribbean
- Patagonia, Argentina
- Azores
- Husavik, Iceland
- Andoya Islands, Norway
- Hermanus, South Africa
- Bonin Islands, Japan
- Monkey Mia, Australia
- Hervey Bay, Australia
- Kaikoura, New Zealand
- Antarctic Peninsula
- Nullarbor, Australia

ABOVE: Armed with binoculars, and perched on a high cliff at the head of the Great Australian Bight in southern Australia, a group of whale-watchers observes a southern right whale.

imagination, the white cap of every wave can look like a whale. Unless the whales are close, you will need binoculars in order to identify species and observe details of their appearance and behavior. Serious whale-watching is time consuming; it may take a whale an hour or more to pass a particular spot, and during this interval there will probably be a number of excellent photographic opportunities. Remember that, between breathing sequences, whales may dive for 10 minutes or more. Because they are unlikely to surface in the same place, you may lose sight of them for considerable periods of time.

WHALE-WATCHING TECHNIQUES

When you begin a whale-watching session, scan around in a slow, methodical way, using binoculars if necessary. Focus on the direction from which migrating whales are likely to come. Look for anything out of the ordinary: a movement, a dark shape, a splash of white, or the cotton-wool puff of a blow. Your first sighting might be of a full breach, or merely a dorsal fin barely protruding above the surface.

LEFT: The patience of these whale-watchers has been rewarded by a good sighting of orcas passing close inshore along the coast of Washington State.

When you sight a whale, use a field guide to identify its species. Make notes of your observations, especially anything out of the ordinary, such as the sighting of an unexpected species. Try to discuss what you see with local wildlife officers. Ask if there are any whale research programs nearby; you may even be accepted as a volunteer whale-spotter.

Whale-Watching from Boats

Commercial whale-watching, which began as recently as 1975 off New England in the USA, is now well established throughout the world. In many former whaling communities and nations, it has proved to be a lucrative alternative to whaling—a benign form of whale exploitation that gives thousands of people an opportunity to experience living whales in their natural environment. Its introduction in Japan's Bonin Islands, for example, may be a sign that attitudes toward whaling in that country are starting to change.

Most operators are responsible, and display a genuine concern for the animals' welfare. Many cruises have qualified naturalists on board to provide background information and interpret whale behavior. But in this highly competitive industry, there are some who are insensitive to whales' needs. It is not unusual for boats to pursue whales that are trying to avoid them—even though this practice is illegal. It may be that those operating the boats simply do not recognize a whale's avoidance behavior, such as frequent changes of direction, an increased breathing rate, or more spectacular displays, such as breaching. The fact that whales remain in areas where they are subjected to regular harassment does not mean

Whale-Watching Limits

In many countries, there are strict guidelines designed to ensure that whales are not unduly disturbed by whale-watching activities. In the United States, marine mammals are protected under the Marine Mammal Protection Act of 1972. This law prohibits harassing, capturing, or killing of any marine mammals, and prescribes penalties of up to $25,000, or imprisonment. Local rules governing whale-watching vary considerably from one region to another. Alaska's set limits are the most stringent in the United States. They are:
For boats: Minimum approach distance is 300 feet (91.4 m); approach or leave whales at "no-wake" speed from the side or behind (never from ahead) with no sudden changes in speed or direction; if a whale approaches, put the engine in neutral and allow it to pass; never follow whales, or herd, drive, or separate them, particularly mothers and calves; only one vessel at a time at the minimum approach distance; there is a time limit of 30 minutes per vessel at the minimum distances; swimmers should not approach within 150 feet (45.7 m).
For aircraft: the minimum permitted height is 1,500 feet (457 m).

Below: Sea kayakers observe orcas at close quarters in Orca Sound, British Columbia, Canada. Whale-watchers in small craft often find themselves being approached by whales. There is usually nothing to fear if the whales are shown respect.

ABOVE: *A tourist boat takes visitors to the Kaikoura coast of New Zealand to watch sperm whales. For most people, their first experience of whales occurs on commercial whale-watching boats, and responsible operators often provide truly memorable encounters.*

that they are undisturbed by such behavior; there may be no alternative habitat available. When treated with respect, whales will often approach boats out of curiosity, providing some close and very rewarding encounters.

Whale-Watching from Small Boats

If you have your own boat, study the local whale-watching limits carefully; they are as much for your protection as for the whales' welfare. Whales are usually incredibly gentle when they approach small boats, but if your actions seem to threaten them, or if you position yourself in an inappropriate place, such as in the middle of an actively feeding or mating group, or between a mother and her calf, you may provoke aggressive behavior. As soon as you sight whales nearby, you should slow down, then stop and watch. The whales may well come to investigate you.

Simply being near whales on the water is a memorable experience, which can easily be recorded in photographs or on videotape. If you wish to extend your observations by listening in to their calls and songs, you could use a hydrophone kit, available from many scientific equipment suppliers. A hydrophone will allow you to "tune in" to this fascinating aspect of whale behavior, even when the whales are not visible or are at a distance.

INDEX

Figures in *italics* indicate photographs and illustrations.

CONTRIBUTORS AND PICTURE CREDITS

CONTRIBUTORS

PETER GILL is an independent researcher, photographer, lecturer, and writer, Peter has been involved in studying whales since 1983. Most of his work has been concerned with humpback and right whales. Peter spent two years working for Greenpeace as marine mammals researcher. He has undertaken extensive yacht-based research, observing whales at close hand, and he has had the extraordinary experience of observing a group of 25 blue whales.

LINDA GIBSON has been involved with whales and whale strandings for 15 years as part of her job in the Mammals section of the Australian Museum. She has attended numerous strandings of whales, and participated in a ten-year research project on observing—and recording the songs of—the humpback whales that regularly migrate up and down the eastern coast of Australia. She is a recognized authority on cetaceans, and gives lectures to the public and special-interest groups, as well as writing articles for the media.

PHOTOGRAPHIC CREDITS

AKG = AKG Photo, London
APL = Australian Picture Library
Auscape = Auscape International
BCL = Bruce Coleman Limited
Bridgeman = The Bridgeman Art Library
FLPA = Frank Lane Picture Agency
Hedgehog = Hedgehog House
Minden = Minden Pictures
MMI = Marine Mammal Images
OSF = Oxford Scientific Films
PE = Planet Earth Pictures
PM = Picture Media
TIB = The Image Bank
TPL = The Photo Library, Sydney
TSA = Tom Stack and Associates
t = top, b = bottom, l = left, r = right, c = center, i = inset, b/g = background

Front Jacket Francoise Gohier/Auscape **Back Jacket** t Doug Perrine/Hawaii Whale Research Foundation NMFS permit no. 882/Auscape; i Flip Nicklin/Minden **1** Colin Monteath/Hedgehog **2** Chuck Davis/TPL **3** Mike Osmond/Pacific Whale Foundation/Auscape **6–7** Tui De Roy/Auscape; i Doug Allan/OSF **8**tl Geospace/SPL/TPL **8–9**tr Jean-Marc La Roque/Auscape **9**bl Kevin Schafer/Hedgehog **12**tl TPL; br Rolle/Gamma Liaison/PM **14**r Steve Burnell **15**tl Randy Morse/TSA; tr James D Watt/PE; b Jeff Foott/Auscape **16** KC Balcomb-Earthviews/FLPA **17**t Jean-Paul Ferrero/Auscape; b Tui De Roy/Auscape **18**tl Jean-Paul Ferrero/Auscape **19**br Jean-Paul Ferrero/Auscape **20**t Tui De Roy/OSF; cr Doug Allan/OSF **21** Peter Gill/Albatross Associates **22**t Flip Nicklin/Minden; b Kim Westerkov/Hedgehog **23**t Doug Perrine/PE; b Thomas Henningsen/MMI **24–25** Kim Westerkov/TPL; i Paul Ensor/Hedgehog **26** Jeff Foott/TSA **27**t Steve Burnell; cr Barbara Todd/Hedgehog; b Tui De Roy/Hedgehog **28**t Jean-Paul Ferrero/Auscape **29**t Doug Allan/OSF **30–31**t Duncan Murrell/OSF **31**br Flip Nicklin/Minden **32**t Pieter Folkens/PE; b Galen Rowell **33**t D Parer and E Parer-Cook/Auscape; b Flip Nicklin/Minden **34**t Scott Sinclair/Earthviews/FLPA; b Francois Gohier/Ardea London Ltd **35** Stuart Westmorland/TPL **36–37** Francois Gohier/Auscape; i Flip Nicklin/Minden **38**t TPL; b Godfrey Merlen/OSF **39** Flip Nicklin/Minden **41**t Barbara Todd/Hedgehog; b D Parer and E Parer-Cook/Auscape **42–43**t Francois Gohier/Auscape **43**b Marineland/FLPA **44**t Flip Nicklin/Minden; b Flip Nicklin/Minden **45** Astrida Mednis **46** Doug Perrine/PE **47** Kelvin Aitken/Ocean Earth Images **48–49**c Mark Deeble and Victoria Stone/OSF **49**t Nigel Hicks/Picture Media; b Flip Nicklin/Minden **50–51** Michio Hoshino/Minden; i James Watt/PE **80–81** Flip Nicklin/Minden; i Francois Gohier/Ardea London Ltd **82** Flip Nicklin/Minden **83**tr Paul Ensor/Hedgehog; cl Flip Nicklin/Minden **84** Howard Hall/OSF **85**t Flip Nicklin/Minden **86**t Hulton-Getty/TPL; b Flip Nicklin/Minden **88**t D Parer and E Parer-Cook/Auscape; b Steve Burnell **89**t JM LaRoque/Auscape **90**l Jean-Paul Ferrero/Auscape **91**Kelley Balcomb-Barton/MMI **92**tr Michael Nolan/MMI; bl Tui De Roy/Hedgehog **93** Flip Nicklin/Minden **96** Peter Gill/Albatross Associates **98**t Francois Gohier/Auscape **99**b Jean-Paul Ferrero/Auscape **100**t Brian Chmielecki/MMI; b Francois Gohier/Ardea London Ltd **101** Steve Burnell **102–103** Francois Gohier/Auscape; i Steve Burnell **104**t Doug Perrine/Auscape; b Steve Burnell **105** Flip Nicklin/Minden **106** Michio Hoshino/Minden **107**t Mike Nolan/Innerspace Visions; b D Parer and E Parer-Cook/Auscape **108** Francois Gohier/Auscape **109**t Klapfer/Innerspace Visions; b Doug Perrine/Innerspace Visions **110**t Steve Burnell **110**b Jean-Paul Ferrero/Auscape **111**t Doug Perrine/Auscape; b Doug Allan/OSF **112**t Flip Nicklin/Minden **113**t Flip Nicklin/Minden; b Flip Nicklin/Minden **114** Erwin and Peggy Bauer/Auscape **115**l Peter Gill/Albatross Associates; r Dennis Buurman/Hedgehog **116**t GCA-CNRI/SPL/TPL **117**t ZEFA/APL **118** Flip Nicklin/Minden **119**t Tony Martin/OSF; b Gary Bell/APL **120** Frans Lanting/Minden **121**tl Yann Arthus-Bertrand/Auscape; b Ford Kristo/PE **122**t Rose/Gamma Liaison/PM; **123**t Barbara Todd/Hedgehog; b Tui De Roy/OSF **124**t Jean-Paul Ferrero/Auscape **124–125**c Jean-Paul Ferrero/Auscape **126–127** D Parer and E Parer-Cook/Auscape; i British Library, London/Bridgeman **128**t Field Museum of Natural History, Chicago/Werner Forman Archive; b R. Sheridan, Art and Architecture Collection **129**t British Library, London/Bridgeman b Jean-Paul Ferrero/Auscape **130**t Granger Collection; b Paul Vandevelder/Gamma Liaison/PM **131**tl National Maritime Museum, London/Bridgeman; r Fitzwilliam Museum, University of Cambridge/Bridgeman **132** Galen Rowell/Mountain Light **133**tl Stromness Museum/Werner Forman Archive; bl Private Collection/Bridgeman; br North Wind Picture Archives **134**l Hulton-Getty/TPL **135** Private Collection/Bridgeman **136**t Hulton-Getty/TPL; b Mary Evans Picture Library **137** Yves Lanceau/Auscape **138**t Galen Rowell/TPL **139**t ACS-G Bakker/MMI; b Mitsuaki Iwago/Minden **140**t Grant V Faint/TIB; b Mark Newman/Auscape **141** Flip Nicklin/Minden **142–143**t M Peck and D Fernandez/Hedgehog **143**tr Francois Gohier/Auscape; b Chris Rudge/Hedgehog **144**t Flip Nicklin/Minden; b Flip Nicklin/Minden **145** Flip Nicklin/Minden **146**t International Photographic Library; b New Zealand Herald **147** Gilles Martin/PM **148**t Peter Rowlands/PE; b Mark Spencer/Auscape **149**t Colin Monteath/Auscape; b Mark Spencer/Auscape **150** Greenpeace/CUL/APL **151**t Rouillois/Greenpeace; b Adair/Greenpeace **153**t Richard Smyth/Auscape; b Steve Satushek/TIB **154**b Joel Rogers/TPL **155** Barbara Todd/Hedgehog.

ILLUSTRATION CREDITS

Illustrations by Ray Grinaway except the following:
Martin Camm: 28–29, 30, 85, 116–117, 82–83
Chris Forsey: 97, 152
Robert Hynes: 99
David Kirshner: 10–11, 18–19, 40
Frank Knight: 86–87, 13, 52–79

CAPTIONS

1 Tourists in an inflatable boat observe a humpback whale off the Antarctic Peninsula.
2 Bottlenose dolphins off Santa Catalina Island, California.
3 A pair of humpback whales heads toward the surface.
6–7 A blue whale in its winter feeding grounds in the Sea of Cortez, Baja California, raises its tail prior to diving.
Inset: Eye of a southern right whale.
24–25 An adolescent humpback whale cruises just beneath the ocean surface.
Inset: Baleen of a minke whale.
36–37 A group of Atlantic spotted dolphins.
Inset: The recurved teeth of an orca.
50–51 A humpback whale blowing at the surface.
Inset: A humpback landing after a breach.
80–81 Narwhals in an ice break in Canada's Northwestern Territories of Canada.
Inset: Barnacles on a gray whale.
102–103 A pair of bottlenose dolphins leap clear of the water.
Inset: A group of southern right whales.
126–127 A pair of orcas bowride alongside a fishing boat in British Columbia, Canada.
Inset: Detail from "Jonah and the Whale," in a 17th-century atlas.

ACKNOWLEDGMENTS

The publishers wish to thank the following people for their assistance in the production of this book: Edan Corkill, Robert Coupe, Lynn Cole, Greg Hassall, Kylie Mulquin, and Shona Ritchie.
Index prepared by Garry Cousins.